Being Higher Self

2016 Frederick Dodson

Table of Contents

1 Higher Self Consciousness
2 Upgrade Your Identity
3 Realms of Bliss and Ecstasy
4 Enlightened Consciousness
5 Transcend the Ego and Be Free
6 Infinite Awareness
7 Life Is a Spiritual Journey
8 Advanced Meditation and Non-Duality
9 Hyper-lucid Dreaming
10 Deeper Relaxation

1

Higher Self Consciousness

Receiving Answers from Higher Self

1. Write Down Your Question

Ask any question you like, but phrase your question in a positive frame. For example "How can I be happy?" is a more positive frame than "Why am I sad?". Write your question at the very center of an empty sheet of paper.

2. Circle Your Question

To activate subconscious focus, take a pen and circle your question over and over and over again until there is a thick circumference around the question at the center of your sheet of paper.

3. Answer it yourself from higher Perspectives

Ask yourself "How might a higher version of me answer this?" or "How might my confident-self answer this?" or "How would love see this?". Then answer the question yourself, to the best of your ability, common sense or intuition. Write down the answer, no matter what it is.

3. Lie down and practice circular breathing through the top of your head

Circular Breathing is soft breathing without a pause between in and out breathe. Imagine breathing in through the top of your head and breathing out through your nose. Continue for a few minutes or until you are fully relaxed and feel no effort.

4. Imagine Higher Self and ask the Question again. Then let go.

Imagine a higher version of you, a higher being or source, a mentor, coach or soul guide. Wait until you have a clear impression. Then ask that higher being the question again. The answer may come instantly or in a dream or in signs throughout the next day. Let go of the question for now.

© Reality Creation LLC

How to Discover Your Real Passion

A useful technique of discovering your real passion and perhaps even your life purpose is to imagine that you already have everything you've ever wanted. Then, from this new state and position you ask yourself: "What would I like to do?" Whatever answers you get from this "mountaintop position" indicate your true heart's desires. Answering the "What would you like to do?" question from a normal, daily-life struggle position will often not provide the real answers but merely survival-based secondary programs.

An example: In your Imagination you transport yourself to a really beautiful or luxurious place and relax there, imagine living there. Once you have settled in, you have someone enter your space, perhaps a servant, and ask you: "Madam/Sir, what would you like to do today?" Whatever answers you have to that question should be written down after you awaken from your Meditation Session. The state of deep relaxation, coupled with guided imagery, accesses your subconscious. The imagining of "already having it all" accesses your higher self. To then ask: "What would you like to do today?" supposes that, even though you already have everything, there is something that is simply true to who you really are, regardless of how much you have or own. To aid in this practice, I have created a 5-minute Audio titled "Discovering Your Real Passion." It can be downloaded in "Member Downloads" on my website, realitycreation.org

Broken Trust vs. Total Confidence

Manifesting your dreams does not work if there is a lack of trust in life and in oneself. Doubt and lack of confidence come from looking at how the external world behaves. **The naive little child is fully trusting and equipped with exuberant confidence**. Then, over time, the child sees how friends, parents, and teachers lie and break promises. As a person grows older s/he sees how partners, the media, CEOs, and politicians lie and break promises. If there was an especially big break of trust, some will subconsciously attract more people who abuse and break their trust. A life of suspicion, paranoia, and lack of confidence are the result. Why? Because **the subconscious mind**

records all of these events and draws conclusions. "So everyone is lying all the time, therefore nothing and nobody can be trusted." Even if your conscious mind decides: "I will now start trusting!" the much more powerful subconscious mind will override your new decision and simply continue not trusting. Because *Reality Creation* is really a matter of trust, belief, and faith. Let's now examine how to build those qualities.

Obviously the external world does not offer an abundance of causes for trust and confidence. If you rely on a politician, CEO, or spouse to save the day, your reliance is misplaced. The confidence you are looking for can only be found internally. Your confidence can be built if you are able to trust yourself. You can teach your subconscious that the things you say are true, that you will do what you say, and that your actions are in alignment with that. So, it is *integrity* that builds trust. It is *integrity* that makes you a more powerful reality creator. If you say to me, "I will complete this project tomorrow by 6 pm," and then you really do that, you have taught your subconscious that your word can be relied upon. The subconscious then thinks, "OK...this is something stable I can trust." As you build your trust with integrity, the subconscious will also support you when it comes to bigger things: "I will make this dream come true by the end of the year!" Building this confidence over the years, makes you a powerful reality-creator. Then when you think or say something, it comes true over time. Many incidents of broken trust usually make very weak reality creators. Allow your word to be reliable, stop lying and pretending, and honor the agreements you have entered into. If you become someone others can trust, you begin attracting and noticing people, places, and organizations you can trust.

The more true to your word you are, the stronger your word gets. This is not really as easy as it sounds, but it works very well. One of the keys is not to make any promises you aren't 100% sure you can keep. So this involves saying "No" more often than is common in society. "Yes" is only said when it is really meant and can really be kept. Even if it's sometimes unpleasant to reject someone's request, I'll say, "No," if I am not sure and confident that I can fulfill the request. Another key is to stay true to time. So, if you say you will meet someone at 3 pm, be there at 3 pm. It is in small details such as these that your subconscious learns whether your word can be trusted. This is something you ask of yourself, not necessarily of others (unless you are their coach or mentor). Expecting others to be 100% true to their word will only make you frustrated. I see and hear people break their word every day, and they are not even conscious of it. One says, "I'll write that email to you later this evening," and he doesn't. Or another assures, "I'll transfer the money on Monday," and she doesn't. People will say, "I absolutely enjoyed that movie!" and not mean it. They'll say, "I will do exercise every morning for the next 4 weeks," but won't. But this is not so much your problem, it's theirs. By being untrue, inauthentic, and without integrity, people weaken themselves; they take the wind right out of their sails. Liars don't need my punishment, they have punished themselves enough already. If you tell a lie, the subconscious registers: "Ah…so his words do not necessarily have anything to do with reality."

Train your subconscious that what you say comes true. You make a command, and it happens. You say a word, and it comes true. If you have a goal that you would love to manifest as reality, bring it out of the vague realm of mere thought by defining the specifics of that dream, then defining by when it should come true, and finally defining actions you will take toward it. And then stay true and loyal to it. **When you have high confidence** and believe with the wholeness of your body, subconscious, mind, and soul, **you magnetically attract** what matches it.

Going a little deeper, into the phenomenon of psychological projection: If you see liars everywhere in the external world, putting too much attention there, it shows that you are suppressing "the liar within". That's how I secretly know that people who are continually telling me about the "evils" of other people, the "evils" of various Neighbors, Colleagues, Customers, Ex-Spouses, Enemies, Governments, Organizations, Corporations, and Religions ...are not to be trusted! I *never* do Business with people who see evil everywhere. It's one of the more obvious alarm-bells. I am not saying that these evils don't exist. However: **"It takes one to know one,"** and someone who has his attention focused on lies too often, is suppressing his own non-integrity, instead of owning it. Whatever is present but suppressed in oneself is projected onto the external world. Therefore, only a liar notices liars everywhere. And so he blames all those liars and evil people, without even seeing his own untrue ways and weaknesses. If, on the other hand someone sees grace, beauty, and truth all over the place, it's because s/he is that way. S/he tells me about all those great Neighbors, Colleagues, Customers, Spouses, Organizations, etc., and I know s/he is projecting his/her own Greatness.

You see the world as you are. If you think the world is boring, you are. If you think the world is falling apart, chances are high that your own life is falling apart. If you think that God is a punishing and aggressive Being; you are. You may not see it or be aware of it, but being punishing and aggressive is stored in your own subconscious, and you've projected it onto what you think "God" is. If you think that God is a loving and caring Being; you are. You may not see it or be aware of it, but being loving and caring is stored in your subconscious. If you think that the Universe is full of life and fantastically interesting and amazing places, it's because you have such places within. It means you are a fantastically interesting and amazing person.

Why the Mind Censors the Spontaneity of the Soul

For maximum happiness it is advisable to "follow

your bliss;" to follow your heart and soul. Doing so sometimes involves unexpected actions and word considered "completely inappropriate" in regular society. So half of the time, I allow my mind to override my soul's inclination, to censor my words and actions.

For example, because I teach intuition, people often ask me, "So what do you feel intuitively about me, Fred? What can you say about me?" And sometimes I just blurt out the truth – spontaneously. "Well, you are absolutely frustrated with your boyfriend and are instead highly interested in the guy sitting over there," I recently said to someone in front of a group of people. I just blurted out what I had intuitively picked up. And even though it was spot-on true and received hilariously by the group, it was taken as "completely inappropriate" by the person who had asked the question. Not only was my answer completely inappropriate, but her following her true heart's desire was also viewed as completely inappropriate in the professional setting we were in. Seeing the commotion I had caused through telling the truth, I reminded myself to censor soul-self a little, allowing a mind-override.

You see, even though people constantly request truth, request soul-information, and request-reality, when you **really** deliver it to them they realize they would rather not have it. They would prefer things to be safe. So we use the mind-override to respect other people's limitations and reality-frames. There is nothing wrong with the mind-override and nothing wrong with suppressing the soul. The problem arises when we do that too often. Then our true heart's desire gets buried beneath the mind's need to "fit in", need for approval, and need for conformity and safety. As long as you *know* what your soul is saying and feeling, as long as you *know* you are currently overriding it, it is alright because you are in charge; you are the boss. You have mind instead of mind having you. But done too frequently you may lose sight of that gentle and happy voice of intuition, guiding you towards truth and bliss. It is good to balance heart and mind, to sometimes follow your heart, sometimes follow your mind. You follow the mind to fit into earth-society, conduct Business, to look respectable and "legitimate", but you follow your soul to be happy and joyous.

World-Self and Higher Self

The 3 Heads of the World-Self (Ego)

Snake

The snake energy is a cold-blooded, viscious energy that is primarily concerned with heartless attack and domination. This head runs rampant in our society where many have no interest whatsoever in anything but their small little self and bare survival. The snake energy is void of compassion or understanding. Everything that it encounters it's trying to calculate an advantage for itself. "What can I get out of it?". It secretly hates humanity. The snake-energy of the world-self can be transcended through Relaxation and Compassion.

Chicken

The chicken is the restless energy, pecking around here and there, never focused, always moving, pecking even if there is nothing to peck. This head runs rampant in our society where the attention of the average human shifts from one thing to the next, reading hundreds of news items but not going more deeply into any one subject, following this, that and that but not learning anything, trying this, this and that but not mastering anything. The chicken-energy of the world-self can be transcended through slowing down, focussing attention and meditation.

Pig

The pig is a heavy energy that is primarily into indulging in food and sex. And after its desires are fulfilled it is stuffed and complacent. This head runs rampant in our society where there is hardly interest in spiritual matters but in the quick fulfillment of supposed "needs". The main point of having dinner with others is then not to join the person and exchange information and energy, but to eat. The main point of sex is then not to join the person and exchange love and energy, but to gratify an addiction. The pig-energy of the world-self can be transcended through self-control, poise and compassion.

The 3 Aspects of Higher-Self (Spirit)

Observe

Typical qualities of the observer-mode of Higher-Self: Calm, little attachment, heightened awareness, heightened interest, non-judgmental attitudes, peacefulness, humour, birds-eye-view, better choices, playfulness, joy, intuition.

Create

In its creative mode Higher Self likes to do, make, produce, contribute, develop, generate, create, build beauty, art, music, architecture and all other things in the universe. It is happiest when growing, learning and improving.

Love

In its compassionate mode, Higher Self likes to spread care for people, warmth and respect toward all beings, regard for life and its places and objects, appreciation of big and little things, gratitude for gifts already received, forgiveness of self and others and full attention to the present. Its compassion includes forgiveness of the world-self.

Copyright Reality Creation LLC

Silence the Inner Critic

If you're a human being with a mind, then there is this inner drill sergeant you sometimes use to put yourself down, beat yourself up, criticize yourself, and tell yourself what you "should", "could" and "must" do. It is commonly believed that self-doubt and self-criticism will motivate you to take action, to stop procrastinating, and to get going, but I have found that this is not true long-term. Too much self-criticism takes away energy, it does not provide it.

"I'm not good enough."
"I'm a loser."
"I will never get going."
"I make the same mistakes over and over."
"I am boring."

Such thoughts make it so. The moment you believe in and act upon these thoughts, you get that attitude, that sluggishness, and that tiredness. When working with habitual procrastinators (people who put off important tasks), the inner critic is especially loud. As I've said before, we all have an inner parent and an inner child. The inner child is timid and shy, easily overwhelmed and hurt, and constantly looking to "feel loved" and "feel good". As you become a spiritually mature adult, it is also important to outgrow the inner child, but this section focuses on the inner parent. The inner parent is the one who always hoists new expectations upon you, is never satisfied, and is always critical. A little bit of this is good, but too much is a nuisance. I met a man who had such a strict inner critic that he went jogging until he injured his muscles. It's not the first time he had an injury from overdoing it. He now sees how ineffective it is to overdo things because now he will be out and injured for weeks. Had he treated himself more gently and moved upward more slowly, there would be no injury and he could still be jogging. He criticized himself every day for not doing all the tasks he put on his to-do list. His inner critic had caused him to put way too many items on the list. "You better get going, or else!" Once I told him that "less is more", to slow down, and to put less items on his list, it was easy to fulfill all of his intentions for the day. And that's what makes a success: Only making action-intentions that you know you can and will do. Then, when you do them, your subconscious learns that your intentions come true. Thus, confidence is built over time.

One way to handle the inner critic is by seeing it as a frustrated drill sergeant who is shouting at you. Seeing it this way unmasks it. This might be followed by patting the sergeant on the back and telling him to relax just a little. All that pent up frustration is hiding fear of mediocrity and fear of running out of time. But all this tension is not really helping because most people, in this day and age, are no longer driven and motivated by threat and fear. Trying to motivate them in such a way is no longer as effective because we are living in different times and in a different consciousness. Many coachees that I have had who had really, really strict and rigid parenting, become just the opposite extreme as adults: Lazy. They are being lazy as a rebellious response to the drill sergeant; lazy as a response to being indoctrinated and forced to act, rather than acting from their own free choice.

Another way to handle the inner critic is by calling up the "Inner Council". This is done by making a circle of a few chairs, sitting on one, and imagining the various inner voices sitting on the other chairs. On one there is…

…the inner critic, parent, or drill officer,

…on another the inner child,

…on another the inner dreamer,

…and on another the successful version of you.

(For example: You can remove or add others you deem appropriate). Then, you simply have an imaginary conversation with each member of your inner council or observe how they have conversation among themselves. Imagination here is used as a tool to access the Subconscious. Your job is to have a calming effect on the inner parent and inner child so that they don't bother you in daily life.

Yet another way to handle the inner critic is to send yourself love and approval, respect and attention, acknowledgment and confidence. Of course you could follow the inner critic's advice and do more for your self-improvement. That sometimes gets the inner critic to shut up. That's when the inner critic is useful. **You cannot make your days longer, but you can make your days better.** But if the inner critic is a chronic choleric, then he will stay the inner critic no matter how much you do and achieve, and he will never allow you to just relax. He will drive you to overstretch and hurt yourself. It's also vital to know that "doing" is not the only or even main ingredient of success. Reflection is. **Taking some time each day for quality thinking and reflection is the most underestimated success tool there is.**

It's also helpful to know that you have the most energy in the mornings and many have the most creativity at night. And another important point, especially for procrastinators, is that sometimes getting into the flow of new tasks requires a little nudge, a little breaking through resistance. Too many people I work with say, "Well, first I have to feel right, then I can work." Their emotional state is dominating their lives. But if you get into action regardless of your state, your state soon changes for the better. This is a lesson I repeat so often because it is such a common mistake. That's not to say you should work when you are terrified, exhausted, grieving, or completely frustrated. Those are best times to relax. But if you always shy away from acting because you "don't feel like it," you won't get that much done at the end of the day.

Regarding the inner critic, it is paramount to know that guilt-tripping you for not acting is a huge waste of energy. If you failed to do something, failed at a project, or overate, it is important not to guilt-trip yourself. Because all that guilt is saying is: "I might do it again. I may have not learned the lesson." So **the moment you allow yourself to wallow in guilt over not having done something, you are setting yourself up for failing again.**

"Failing" is not the failure...not trying, that's the failure. The inner critic says that shooting the ball beside the goal and missing the goal that is the "failure". But the real failure is not even shooting out of fear you might miss. To be a success, you need to shoot the ball at the goal hundreds of times – which includes missing hundreds of times. So, you can see how missing the goal is NOT the problem.

Not shooting, not practicing, not trying, and not acting is.

Focus on the Best in Your Field

Whenever you are feeling small, a nice technique to quickly remedy your state is to "focus on the masters". The masters I am talking about are whoever is the best or excellent in your field or line of work. Throughout my twenties, every time I felt small as a life-coach, I simply thought of my favorite life-coaches. **Simply remembering your favorites instantly shifts your state.** There is probably no quicker state-changer than that. If I needed confidence, I recalled someone confident.

If I needed compassion, I recalled someone compassionate. If I needed energy, I recalled someone energetic. So in your field of work, who are the masters? If you are a cook, who are the best cooks? If you are a dentist, who are the best dentists? "Who is your favorite actor?", "Who is the best teacher in your field?", and "Who is a master in what you do?" are frequent questions I ask students. While the question is answered, their eyes light up and their body postures improve. That is because **we begin energetically vibrating by the thoughts we hold in mind.** This is why people hang up pictures of their idols. Of course, it's not empowering to *worship* those idols or to mistake the pictures with the real person. That's what happens in dictatorships where posters of "the leader" are hanging everywhere. But if you look at a picture of the master in the right spirit, look at him as **an aspect of you** (an aspect of the whole is also an aspect of you), parts of you will begin vibrating like that person.

So it makes sense to be choosy about what you give your eyes to look at and your ears to hear. I teach to rigorously filter out anything that is below a certain standard. **Reality Creating is a process of reality-filtering.** That means saying "no" to a whole lot more things than the average person and saying "yes" to that which is above standard.

Use Your Unique Fingerprint
There are two physical parts of you that are completely unique: Your Irises and your Fingerprints. That's why law enforcement uses them for identification. In my view, they are the most

spiritual parts of your body, representing your soul. The eyes are used to **see and perceive** the world. The fingers are used to **make, do, and create**. Those are the two modes of reality creation: Perceiving and then Making or Doing, based on the data collected through perception.

These two modes are like breathing in and out. Perceiving is the breathing in, creating is the breathing out. What you perceive through your irises is unique, what you create through your fingers is unique. Almost all creating at one point involves your fingers. Whether you paint a picture, make a house, build a rocket, write a book, or craft a design, it all happens through your unique fingers. I'd go out on a limb (excuse the pun) to say that if your fingers aren't involved somewhere along the way, you are not creating anything. In colloquial slang they say, "He doesn't want to get his fingers dirty," meaning, he doesn't want to do anything. In our computer-driven world, finger-work has become more creative than ever before as *all* of our media is produced through them.

Not even "identical twins" have identical irises or fingerprints (There are some people who claim that people who have identical irises with someone else, are the reincarnation of that person. But I have yet to see any tangible evidence of this). Fingers and eyes are, of course, the mere physical representation of something much deeper: The uniqueness of the soul.

You have traits that are the same as everyone else, and you have traits that are different than anyone else. If you know how the ways in which everyone is the same, it's easier to know the ways in which they are different. I have worked in at least 25 different countries around the world and in each of these countries the way people's ego-mind operates is pretty much the same. It is even the same across all social classes. But the way the more creative soul expresses itself, is quite unique in each place. The more countries and cultures you get to know, the more clearly you can see in what we are all alike and in what we are different.

What is your unique imprint on earth? Many live their entire lives believing there is no such thing, and they have nothing special to give. But if you think that you were sent to earth to do nothing but eat, sleep, and procreate, you are missing the point. Others have this excuse: "If I am nice to my spouse, that's enough life purpose right there. I am not going to make myself crazy thinking I have some special purpose in life. I am content with being an insignificant nobody. If I am just loving, that's enough." While it is good to be calm and contented with one's life, without delusions of grandeur, while it is good to accept one's life as-is, and while it is great to "just be" and "just be loving", it doesn't quite touch the highest idea you are here for. That attitude is like having a super-advanced computer, but never using its functions. Body-mind-spirit is capable of much, much more than just existing. We tend to do that with everything: I own this smartphone but probably don't even use 10% of the super-advanced tricks it is capable of. It's just more comfortable to keep on using it just as a telephone, chat, and email device. Likewise, we probably don't even use 1% of what the mind-body-spirit are capable of because it is more comfortable to stay in the rut of what we are used to. You can experience more of yourself by leaving your comfort zone, by meeting new people, by traveling to new places, by trying new projects, and by learning new skills. Every new challenge requires some of your dormant abilities to be activated. The more you activate those **sleeping talents**, the more you access the abilities of your soul...which are truly unique. The analogy doesn't quite work here: You start using the unused parts of your smartphone, then the hidden parts, and then you begin accessing the unique parts. Of course the smartphone doesn't have a soul, it has the same parts as everyone else's. But if it did have a soul, it would become activated once the limits of its normal abilities were reached. Hence, through some challenge, you might discover your ability to lead, to speak like a poet or write with crazy passion, your ability to envision something, to invent something, to solve a problem in your neighborhood or community, or something we don't even know about yet at this time. It is then that you have expanded the universe which you are an aspect of.

Another way I often put this: If you learn an instrument, you first play the songs of former masters. But as you become very skilled at playing, you start making your own unique songs. Being able to play the songs of the masters is not the highest stage of mastery, even if your playing is near perfect. Becoming the **creator** of unique-songs yourself, that's the highest stage. The same applies to running a Business: In the beginning you base it on already existing success models. But as you become better, you create your own direction. I'd also say that if everyone were to do the job he or she is best at, and **only** do that, everything would become so much more flowing, and the evolution of consciousness would accelerate at lightning speed.

Good Is Better Than Perfect

What are the flaws you are trying to hide from others? And isn't it tiring to try to be something other than who you are?

If there are things you don't know and understand, that's alright.

If you make mistakes, that's alright.

If you feel sexually inadequate, that's alright.

If there is something you don't like about your body, that's alright.

If you are balding, that's alright. If you are overweight, that's alright.

If your hair is graying, that's alright.

If you are forgetful, that's alright. If you are tired, that's alright.

If you are depressed, that's alright.

If you are not wearing the right clothes, that's alright.

If you are getting older, that's alright.

If you get angry at someone, that's alright.

If you have private preferences that others would consider strange, that's alright.

Putting layers of resistance on your fallible human nature does nothing to prevent them. Compassion heals, resistance emphasizes. There are certain flaws and weaknesses that are simply part of being human and alive. Trying to hide them or distract from them is not only a waste of energy, but actually draws attention to them. Trying to be perfect at all times creates an inflexible and uptight personality that never allows any deviation from your mask. Perfectionism in work creates unneeded tension and pressure to live up to expectations that are never fulfilled.

That's why I say, "Good is better than perfect." There is nothing wrong with striving to improve. I improve something about myself or my life every day. But I'm content with improvement and do not expect perfection neither in myself nor in others. When you release the pressure and self-criticism you don't become less, you become more.

Self-confidence does not mean you have to cover-up your flaws. Self-confidence means being comfortable with who you really are. The insecure think they need to hide the fact that there is something they don't know or understand, need to hide when they are in pain, need to hide that they have bodily functions and needs, need to hide if they forget something or have some shortcoming. Paradoxically, the more you try to cover-up your shortcomings, the more these shortcomings are amplified and noticed by others, whereas when you make no big deal of them, their importance minimizes and the perceived "flaw" is less likely to be repeated. Self-forgiveness actually neutralizes the tendency to repeat a mistake, whereas guilt and shame extend the mistake on a timeline. Guilt and shame assume that you are inherently flawed, and that you will keep repeating the same mistake. Guilt doesn't say, "I failed this time," it says, "I am a failure." Saying, "I failed," could be a one-time-thing, but saying, "I am a failure," creates a completely unnecessary permanent state. Moreover, your own sense of guilt does nothing to correct the error or perceived error, nor does it compensate the person who was faulted. For example, if you lend me money and I fail to give it back at the time I promised to...**my guilt will do nothing to compensate you.** Only returning the money will compensate you. Rather than wallowing in shame and guilt, I'd rather work on returning the money.

An Exercise That Will Really Enhance Your Whole Life

1. List all imperfections you are trying to hide. View yourself with kindness while writing.
2. Note when and where you might practice openly showing, confessing to, or being OK with these weaknesses.
3. Once you have spent a few days or weeks being comfortable with your weaknesses, write down what qualities,

traits, or behaviors you would like to have instead.

- Note when and where you might practice deliberately showing or feeling these qualities.

Subconscious Identities and Secret Pay-Offs

Is there some behavior or issue you have tried to let go of and it keeps coming back? Is there something you consciously decided to change, but then went back to your old ways after some time?

Well of course there is.

We all have a subconscious. The conscious mind says one thing, but often the subconscious has other plans. So your conscious-self says, "I am losing weight!" but your subconscious-self says, "I continue to dig in to chocolate as if there were no tomorrow!" Or you consciously decide: "I will finally sell this house," but every time you meet realtors or prospects you get tired and inattentive, or miss appointments as if you are subconsciously sabotaging the house-sale. Or, you consciously intend: "I am self-confident when I meet new people!" but then your voice goes all Mickey Mouse when you stand in front of them.

Having applied The Enlightenment Technique you know there are many different "versions" of you within, each with different agendas. When a subconscious-identity acts differently than your conscious identity, it has reasons to do so; it has secret pay-offs. Secret pay-offs are **positive intentions of subconscious identities**. So the guy trying to sell the house had a subconscious identity that was saying, "I have invested so much love and energy into this house. I don't want to sell it." His conscious-self is saying, "I want to sell it." A subconscious part of him is saying the opposite. The secret pay-off of the chocolate-addict is that she feels empty inside, and the eating binges help her feel calm and safe. The secret pay-off of the lacking-self-confidence-identity is not to impose too much on other people!

Sometimes, when you make a conscious decision for something better or visualize a new reality, things will go well for awhile, then suddenly you hit some kind of roadblock, and it feels like you do not want the thing anymore. These are usually subconscious identities that have entirely different goals than your current conscious mind. They come from an earlier time and they had a different set of intentions. So despite your best intentions to change, the old reality keeps coming back!

Here is a session to fix this:

1. Close your eyes and assume that a part of you really *wants* the negative reality/behavior. Get in touch with that version-of-you.

2. Ask this part of you what the pay-off or *positive intent* is of creating that reality/behavior. What are the benefits?

3. Ask this part of you what it would feel like to get its way, and fully manifest what it wants.

4. Ask: "Now that you have what you want, what else do you want?" Whatever answer it gives, allow it to experience that too. If you like, continue with this for a few questions, until the ideal state is reached.

5. Now in this state, put your attention back to the original reality. Because the state has been reached internally, the external thing will no longer be needed. You could ask: **"Now that you feel what you want, could we let go of this issue?"**

Using the example from above:

1. I want to sell my house, but there is a part of me that keeps sabotaging it. So, I will assume that this part of me wants to keep the house, and I get in touch with that part of me.

2. The positive intent of this part of me is: "I invested so much love into this house, I want to keep it."

3. The feeling is one of achievement and comfort. So I give that identity what it wants: comfort and achievement (by visualizing it).

4. So I ask: "Now that you feel comfort and achievement, could we let go of holding on to the house?" In a state of completeness, it doesn't really matter whether the house is sold or kept, both are fine. And so your intention to sell the house is no longer sabotaged by that subconscious aspect of you.

The magic key is to know that any negative experience you have is actually desired by another version of you. I know that can sound far-out, but it's an extremely effective approach toward problems. "If something within you wouldn't want it, you wouldn't be experiencing it." By assuming that it is wanted, you re-connect to the part of you that attracted it in the first place. These may be very old parts of you, abandoned parts, forgotten parts, lonely parts, etc. By assuming you created it, you also move from a victim-position to a creator-position.

I understand that it's hard to conceive that there is something within you that actively wants negativity. So let me elaborate: When something bad is wanted, it's because the alternative seems even worse. So the subconscious aspect is not actually "wanting something bad", but rather wanting something better than the worse thing. There is always a positive intent there. For example I smoked for more than 15 years although I consciously new that it was "bad for me". A subconscious aspect however, thought it was relaxing, and soothing, and good for concentration. This subconscious self also knew that it was "not good", but the alternative would have been worse: A feeling of tension and concentration weakness. So the solution could only be to provide this aspect of me what it wanted: A feeling of relaxation and concentration. Once I was able to provide this to that part of me mentally, the interest in smoking receded.

Every external reality you think you need is actually an internal feeling that you could create easily without the external thing. And once the internal feeling is established, the external thing becomes more easily available.

Having, Doing, and Being

On a low to mid-level of consciousness, life revolves around "having". You then define yourself over your material possessions and trying to get various external objects and people for self-validation and well-being. When you meet a person at this consciousness level s/he will tell you boring tales about what s/he "has". "I have this kind of car, that kind of house, and I want to get that kind of girlfriend," etc.

At a somewhat higher level of consciousness, life revolves around "doing" instead of "having". You define yourself over your job, profession, and the things you "do". At this level, if nothing is being "done" you begin feeling uncomfortable because you rely on doing-ness for self-validation and well-being. When you meet a person on this level s/he will not tell you about what s/he has but about what s/he has been doing, is doing, and will do. Such as: "I am working on this project at the moment," "I participated in a Marathon," "I like to play the guitar," and "I will go sailing this year."

At an even higher level of consciousness life revolves around "being" instead of "doing" or "having". You define yourself over your inner state, who you are, and make well-being and energy your priority, regardless of what you "have" or "do". You rely on a proper state and physical as well as mental and spiritual condition first. When you meet a person on this consciousness-level s/he will tend to speak more in terms of being present, being loving, states, energies, atmospheres, experiences, observations, and roles rather than what s/he "has" or what s/he's been "doing".

A natural progression up the scale of consciousness is therefore to first take care of your "Havingness" so that you indeed do have the things you need for survival and to feel at ease. Once that milestone is accomplished, you let go of being too interested in what you have and become more interesting in your "Doingness".

Focus on "Doingness" of course leads to easier material success than the focus on "Havingness" because it's one energy-level higher. Once you are really good at Doingness and have a highly developed "action-muscle", you naturally ascend, and then your "Beingness" becomes your predominant focus. Focus on "Beingness" of course leads to better performance than the focus on "Doingness" because it's one energy-level higher.

The path of the world-mind is: "First I have to have X, then I can do X and then I can be X." The path of the soul/spirit is: "First I shall Be X, and from that the right Doing and Having will naturally arise."

Some examples of the thought-process of "Havingness" people:

"I want to **have** a big house at the lake. Then I can **go** out and find the right partner. Then I can experience **love**."

"I want to **have** a partner. Then I can **do** my job in a more focused way to make money. Then I can **relax**."

Some examples of the thought-process of "Doingness" people:

"I want to **work** hard. Then I can **have** money. Then I can **relax**."

"I want to **make** my Business website. Then I can **have** customers. Then I can be **well-known**."

Some examples of the thought-process of "Beingness" people:

"First I will become **relaxed** and **present**. And from this state I will decide what to **do** and **have**."

"First I will be **loving**. And from this state I will decide what to **do** and **have**."

Ascending to a place where your Being takes first priority means leaving the world of enslavement where your self-validation and well-being are dependent on all sorts of external objects, possessions, people, and actions.
When your sense of self is only dependent on your mental and physical state, it gives control back into your hands. You cannot control others. You cannot control the world. But you can control who you are being. It is at this point that authentic reality creation begins.

And if you're really honest…what good are the most fantastic and wonderful possessions or activities if you are not in a good state to enjoy them?

More Techniques to Contact Higher Self

This section provides the practical tools to contact "Higher Self". What is Higher-Self? It is the more expanded, broader-perspective, innermost version of yourself that is not incarnate. It is your soul; the part of you not dependent on mind and body. There are two ways of going about this: You can either communicate with higher-self as if it were a separate higher being, or you can become more higher-self by soul-congruent behavior.

Beyond Limits

Write down instances you went beyond your normal limits in doing or achieving something you had not done or achieved before.

After completing your list, contemplate:

What initiated these ventures into the unknown or to a higher level than before?

How did you feel after the experience?

Where in your life could you go beyond your normal limits again?

Letter to Yourself

Imagine you are 50 years older and wiser than you are now. Write a letter to yourself from the Future, with words of appreciation, advice, and inspiration, seeing your whole life from a bird's-eye-view. Put the letter in an envelope and send it to yourself. When you receive it, open it and read it.

Deeper Intuition

For this exercise you need a journal, diary or notepad. Your life is indeed a letter your Higher Self is writing to you. Your soul is communicating to you every day, but you do not often notice. It communicates in the form of signs, omens, "coincidences", name- and number-synchronicities, meetings between people, and hunches. Without getting paranoid about it and projecting too much meaning into these signs, spend a week of your life specifically looking out for and listening to communication from a higher source. Every time you think a higher source has communicated with you, **write it down**. Something might just fall in your lap, you might see something in a movie or newspaper, you might have a dream at night, someone might say something strange, someone you haven't talked to in a long time might call you... Whatever it is you feel is from a "Higher Source", just take note of it. Because you are now paying attention you start noticing more of this. There is a difference between the mundane and repetitive messages the Ego-Self/Mind creates and messages "from above". Enhance your understanding of life.

Being Higher Self

This is a technique I have used in a few of my coaching-sessions to help people receive new insight. The key to this technique is to raise your frequency and take on increasingly higher and higher viewpoints. In order to communicate with your soul, your soul will have to "lower frequency", and you will have to "raise frequency" so you can meet in the middle. You can understand the following technique as a "symbolic" means of contacting Higher Self, but it is a true and real communication channel. Higher Self does not always communicate as straightforward as people expect. Sometimes communication happens through "coincidences" that happen throughout the day, sometimes through hunches and intuition, and sometimes through dreams.

Preparation

Write down the following viewpoints/positions on pieces of paper or cards:

Female Mentor in 500 years	ME IN 500 YEARS	Male Mentor in 500 years
	ME IN 30 YEARS	
	ME IN 5 YEARS	
	NOW	

Now lay out the cards on the floor throughout the room, but approximately in the order you see them above. The cards should be a few steps far away from each other so you have to walk to them in order to occupy their position.

Read and memorize how the Technique works before applying it.

Begin by standing on the "Now" card, facing North (or in the direction of the Future "Me in 5 years").

Before you do anything, become fully aware of the present moment. Become aware of what you see, hear, feel, the objects around you, and your body. Once you feel fully present (and that may take anything from a few seconds to several minutes) look in the direction of the card "Me in 5 years".

With your imagination, imagine a 5 year older version of yourself standing there. Take your time to visualize that older version of yourself (who is either facing you or not), and get to feel his/her presence. It can take a minute or even a few to really get a sense of that version of yourself. Don't rush things; slow down. Once you have a clear image or feeling of that person, walk over there, stand on that card, take on his/her position and viewpoint. Be that person right now, as best you can.

Continue to feel and imagine yourself as that person; look out of the eyes of that person. Once you have rested into this new viewpoint, look at the next card which says "Me in 30 Years". With the help of your Imagination, get a clear image or sense of the version of yourself that is 30 years older. Then walk over and take his/her position. Really feel what it feels like to be that person, as best you can.

Give yourself a minute or a few (or longer) to settle into this viewpoint. And from this new viewpoint, look at the next position "Me in 500 years". Take whatever image of yourself in 500 years comes intuitively. It might be another body, it might be a light-body (soul), or anything else.

Stand there and get a sense of what is there before you walk there and take over that position. Once you are ready, take in the position by walking over and standing on that card.

Feel the exhilaration that goes along with shifting viewpoints.

Once you have settled into this version of yourself and enjoyed its higher vibration (you should be feeling differently than you felt at the previous position of "Me in 30 years"), look to your left and imagine a female mentor of yours or, what you would symbolize as a higher life form, standing there beside you. Behold that sight for a while.

Then, look to your right and imagine a male mentor of yours and behold that sight. If you have any questions to either of the two, ask them mentally or verbally. Hear, sense, or imagine answers.

Finally, take in the position of the female mentor by moving to that card and feeling what if would feel like to be her. And then take in the position, viewpoint, and identity of the male mentor and feel what it would feel like to be him. Even though you projected these beings as your "mentors", they are actually representations of your Higher Self.

Next, imagine you are integrating and taking all of the energy and insight from those positions with you, and go back to "Me in 500 years". And imagine you are integrating and taking all of the energy and insight from all positions with you and go back to

"Me in 30 years".

Actually see or feel yourself at these positions again, and take everything with you to "Me in 5 years". Then, integrate everything into the NOW so that while you go back to that card you allow yourself to feel that improved version of yourself even as you stand in the now. All viewpoints you just had are actually within you and can be accessed any time.

If you write a diary or journal, now is the time to take notes on your impressions and memories. The everyday-mind-self can be forgetful of special insights. A sense of elation, goosebumps, and wonderment are normal throughout this exercise. You are using the power of Imagination to access information from the soul-plane. And that is the actual purpose of Imagination. The recording device called "mind" cannot access soul-plane information. It can only access what it has recorded on earth. But Imagination can access it if used without distortion. (Imagination distorted by fear, for example, does not lead to insights from Higher Self but to delusion.)

This technique can be repeated any time you feel you have lost your soul-connection or any time you want to regain perspective.

Soul Retrieval

Another technique to re-access the agenda of your soul is as follows.

Ask yourself:

1. When was the last time I genuinely smiled?
2. When was the last time I genuinely laughed?
3. When was the last time I sang?
4. When was the last time I danced?
5. When was the last time told stories?

Living by Intuition

Intuition is a quality of the soul/higher-self aspect of you. If you're in good spiritual shape, you can live by intuition all the time. You then "just pick up" what stuff means, how stuff works, what is going on, and what the right track is. Many people, for example, do not need to visit a workshop to learn how operating a personal computer works. They do not need to read a manual in order to surf the Internet.

They intuitively understand how it works and learn as they go along. If on the other hand you are caught up in worry, you'd be concerned about learning stuff as you go along and shy away from it. If you don't dare click on some button out of fear that it could wreck your computer, there is a lot of fear in you. The fear causes compulsive thinking and lack of *just doing*.

When you live by intuition you learn languages without requiring translation. You spend time in the country and just pick up what words mean intuitively and by association. Not much thinking required.

When you live by intuition you don't need a time-planner. You naturally do the right things at the right time in the right way.

When you live by intuition you know how to raise your children and make them smile...without the need for piles of instructional literature and consultancy.

When you live by intuition you don't have to try to be something or someone. You are naturally and effortlessly who you are.

When you live by intuition...you experience life without filters, you experience life as it was meant to be: Very enjoyable!

The Path of Higher Self

A lesson of my book "Parallel Universes of Self" is that every here-now contains millions of **Options** to choose from. Options of what to look at, listen to, think, say, or do. Being aware of the sheer endless amount of options can be quite refreshing. The accumulated options you choose over the years shape your reality. Choosing good options transports you to a reality in which the options become even better. Life is a choice. Your life is the result of all the choices you have made. The choices you make are conscious or subconscious. Sure, there are a few contexts that may be there without you having chosen them, but the way you deal with these things is still your choice. You may have been born with a certain physical dispositions for example, but whether you make them your advantage or disadvantage is your choice. But seen from a pre-incarnate perspective, even such dispositions may have been chosen by you before you entered this life.

Every here-now contains several options of what to focus on or what to do. Some "shine" more than others. That means they are more interesting, more integrous, more joyful, more "the right thing to do", and/or more loving. These are six options or reality-bubbles, and one of them shines the brightest, so that's the best one to choose:

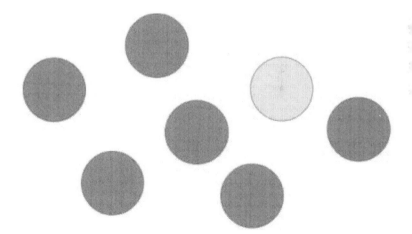

Why is it the best one to choose? Because it contains the most energy and because it leads you on to the "path of the soul", the "path of the heart", or the "path of the higher-self". Too many people lead their lives not choosing one of the options that shine because of what they have been taught they "should do" or "must do". When I was younger I was told I "should" go to a university, but I chose not to.

In retrospect, I am glad I didn't because that might have only put me on the 9-to-5 treadmill so many others are on. But just because the option of going to a university did not shine for me doesn't mean it won't shine for you. You mustn't listen to what I say or what anyone else says but to what your heart says. If you are too easily influenced from outside, you will not find your own path; you will find another's path. I have found that the path of the heart is often completely different than what the world, the media, academia, parents, friends, gurus, teachers, and experts recommend you do. And while all these sources are welcome advice, they should not replace what you know to be right-for-you.

Another lame excuse I often hear for not **choosing the light** is: "I don't know which option to choose because several of them shine!" That's like sitting in a restaurant, hungry, and saying, "I won't choose anything to eat because there are too many good meals." If more than one option shines brightly, then simply choose *one* of them. Any one of them will do.

For example, there are usually a dozen of jobs you would be good at and a dozen partners that would be a good match for you, *not only one*. **Your soul cares more about WHO you are BEING than specifically what job, partner, or life you choose (as long as it's a job, partner, or life that shines)**.

If you don't choose any, you don't start down your path. And if you are saying, "None of the options shine," that's also an excuse. There is always an option that is slightly more interesting, relieving, empowering, loving, or joyful than others.

Once you choose the shining option and go in that direction, you will start seeing other options from the new vantage point. **Options that you did not see before you started on that path**.

That would look something like this:

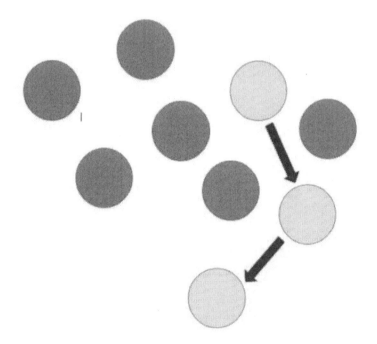

Once you go in one direction and experience whatever reality has shined forth, new sets of options will open themselves up to you. Options that were not available or even known before. That's why it's so important to "make the first step" in your preferred direction, why it's so important to choose and decide, and to get going in whatever it is you like.

Once you have fully experienced a reality (the previously chosen option), it is time to move on to the next thing that shines. A place where so many of us get stuck is that we stay with a previous reality-bubble even though we have "experienced it to its end". That means it no longer shines but because "it used to shine" we think we have to stay with it instead of looking at the new set of options and continuing to move.

Related to this error is the mistake of thinking that just because a previous reality-bubble no longer shines that it was "pointless" to move in that direction. It wasn't pointless, nothing is. It brought you to where you are now. But from here forward, it may be time for something new.

For example, a long time ago I owned a language school. That option shone for me for 7 years. But once it stopped shining and became dull, I let go of it and moved on to the next thing that shone: Reality Creation Coaching.

Even though at the time, my expertise, ability, and financial security lay in the language school, I gave it all up because there was no more happiness there. I knew the path to higher self. I knew that where something no longer shines it will soon stop supporting me financially and even adversely affect my health. Back then people warned me that I was giving up something that I was good at and that I "should" and "must" stay with it, but such was not my path.

You see, if you can succeed at one job, you can succeed at any job. Success is a consequence of focus and confidence, not of a particular job.

As you follow this "pearl-necklace of energy" as I call it, you more and more end up at who-you-really-are:

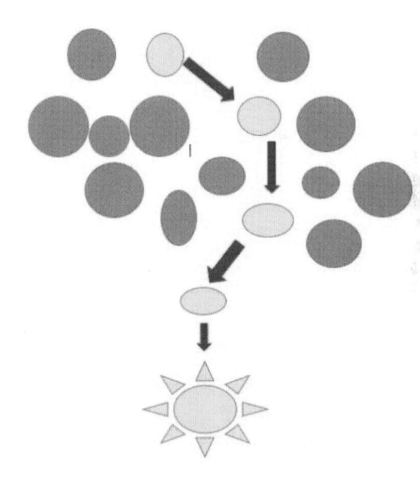

The longer you live, the more the puzzle pieces on the way to higher-self match and form a bigger picture in which it all makes sense. Even the difficult experiences fit into the bigger picture. All of this applies on a small scale and on a grand scale.

An example for small-scale is: This morning I had several options: To stay at home and work or to go out kayaking in the ocean were two of those options. And there were millions of other options, but none of them shone: I could have flicked on the TV, gone for a walk, read a book, struck up a conversation with the neighbor, or done laundry. The list really is endless... I could punch my neighbor in the face, meditate all day, spray graffiti on the fence, start a new project, or Skype with friends... I finally chose to go kayaking. That's what felt the most aligned to my primary intention of spending my summer in physical motion. Then, once that reality had been fully experienced and was "complete", I looked at which options felt the best in the new here-now and went from there.

This is how I spend a day, a week, a month, a year, and a life. So, was I "neglecting my work" by going kayaking? No. Once kayaking was fully experienced, the urge to work returned – then work shone the brightest, so it was chosen. If you go against what shines and choose a non-shining option, the first thing that comes up is an intuitive feeling that "something is off". You do not feel quite yourself. If you ignore this hunch and keep moving in the wrong direction, you will gradually start feeling worse. If you continue to ignore the warning, bad things start happening. This is why mis-emotions are useful; they help you stay on path.

There are only two modes of operation: Following your soul, or having excuses why you don't. The mind is good at creating excuses. Just like it can create endless options, it can also create an unlimited amount of excuses:

"Yeah, but I have a 9-5 job, so I have obligations, so none of this applies to me,"

"Yeah, but I have children, so I have obligations, so none of this applies to me."

But it does apply, even within limited contexts. Any context you live in has limitations. In my reality-domain I do not have the option to declare war on another country or go overseas to negotiate a peace deal for Israelis and Palestinians. (I would have those options if I targeted new reality-domains. And I still have the option to send prayer-vibrations in the direction of Israelis and Palestinians.) But within my limited reality-domain I still have trillions of options.

Likewise, if you are bound by a 9-5 job or a family, you still have trillions of options. You can create a fun job or family and you can create a mediocre one. There are so many different ways your day could go, no matter how many obligations you have.

So within those bubbles there are still many bubbles that shine and such that don't shine. And if the job bubble or family bubble no longer shines, and there is no more love there at all…well, then it's time to move on. "But I can't just leave them! It would break my heart!" you might exclaim. To which I would respond, "Well, then there is still some love there…it's still shining, there is still potential and still something you can experience there. So you best operate from within that bubble." "But I can't just leave my job, it's my only way to survive financially!"

you might exclaim. To which I would respond, "If you think a job (or anything else in physical reality) is the source of money, you haven't read my material attentively."

Choose what shines the most. If you don't know what shines, look at what feels good to you or interests you without it being harmful yourself or others (for example punching your neighbor in the nose might "feel good" to you, but it's harmful.) Then do it. Experience it fully. Once the energy is out of it, take stock **again** and look at the options you have now. And what shines the brightest in the new here-now…go there. Continue until **you** are the one that shines brightly and have found the path that is created by your own footsteps.

Life Is a Game of Chess

An attentive student recently asked me why I depict chessboards on my book covers, audio-materials, and website. In 15 years of me using the chess-pattern, he was the first person to ask me about it.

It's because chess is like a message or a code among metaphysical initiates to indicate a certain understanding of reality. The chess game, chess board, and chess pieces are somewhat reflective of the nature of reality on earth. The white-black checkered floor acknowledges the dualistic nature of the world. And the chess-pieces are reflective of the various consciousness levels. The King is the Absolute and stable aspect of self, the Queen is the multi-dimensional and flexible aspect. The bishop, knight, and rook are single-function aspects of self that cannot move in multiple-dimensions but rather either only diagonally, in a straight line, or in a skip...

In my 2006 book "Parallel Universes of Self", the cover of which shows a chess board, I presented various "Levels of Identity". I will now proceed to show how these seven identity-levels correspond to the pieces of a chessboard.

Levels of Identity

 Source, Creator
Ultimate, Infinite

 Higher Self, Soul
Singular Viewpoint
"I"

 Core Self, Singular
Viewpoint "I am"

 Identity, Personality, Role
"I am this, I am that"

 Secondary Roles, Desire
& Resistance Identities
"I hate being this, I like
being that"

 Projected Identities ("I am smart,
he is dumb", Approval Identities

 Subconscious, Borrowed and
Stereotypical Identities

a

At every moment you are either expanding or contracting. If you are contracting, you are operating in misalignment to the Universe, which is forever expanding. If you are expanding, you are in alignment with the Universe. The "Levels of Identity" Scale shows the path from Expanded-Self to Contracted-Self. On a mid-level understanding one could also say "from positive to negative" or "good to bad", but a high-level understanding sees these stations merely as *expanded or contracted*.

Contraction does have a purpose and that purpose is to pin-point focus to a more limited reality in order to extract particular experiences. If you have a buffet with a bunch of foods and choose only apples while disregarding all other foods, you limit yourself, but you also have the opportunity to taste the apple more fully and exclusively. In this sense, contraction/limitation is not categorically "bad" or "negative". And as difficult as this may be to accept, your soul **chose** many of the experiences you consider "negative" for exactly this reason…to taste certain aspects of reality, and to deliberately limit awareness and being.

Everything you are experiencing, you *wanted* to experience on some level. Realizing this puts you straight back to a non-role, non-chess-piece perspective above the game board. As pure consciousness or awareness (which is not infinite source but much closer to it than identities), you can see the whole chessboard and overview the whole game. The more you "Incarnate" into various roles and contract your energy, the less you perceive and experience.

If you examine chess from the perspective of it being an encoded sample of "how to play life", you will notice numerous interesting things. One of them is that the Kings never leave the board and cannot be "killed". Even at checkmate the opponent's King remains on the board (it is not proper rule to kick off the opponents King after winning. At checkmate, all remaining figures stay as they are and the game is complete.) This is because the "Higher Self" or the "Soul", which the King represents, cannot be killed. It is one of the most essential aspects of you.

The female Queen-aspect of self is more flexible than the Absolute King-Aspect. It is multi-dimensional and can go in all directions but at greater distance and speed than the King. It is more creative and in some respects has more ability on the physical-plane than the King, who is a little too far removed from physical reality to have those possibilities. Hence, the King only moves forward, backward, right, and left one step at a time, while the Queen can move in the same directions but many steps at a time.

Below those two "true selves" are various degrees of limitation. One might create: "I am a doctor." This automatically limits and focuses awareness on one aspect of the whole. If you are a doctor, then you are most likely not a lawyer or football player. As explained in the "Parallel Universes" book, **your identity also filters the reality you experience**. If you are the role "doctor" you will less likely experience the reality of illness because it is your job to stay healthy and help the ill.

If you start developing desire and resistance regarding your Identity, you fragment and split into more contracted selves. On Monday morning you despise being a doctor. When things get too hectic you wish you weren't a doctor. Sometimes you wish you were a better doctor. When you get recognition or help someone heal, you love being a doctor. You would however be a better doctor if you just stuck with the identity: "I am a doctor," or "I am a good doctor," period…with no add-ons. If your identity is based on resistance, then your whole life might be some kind of subconscious rebellion against your parents. Based on desire, your whole life might become some kind of subconscious attempt to copy your parents. A self-chosen identity is neither an imitation of parents nor a rebellion against parents.

However, if the desire to be a good doctor gets out of hand, you will start grasping for superiority and projecting inferiority on others. So if you see bad and incompetent doctors everywhere, and rarely find yourself praising or acknowledging other doctors, then you are creating projections. "I am a good doctor, he is a bad doctor," oftentimes such projections are subconscious and not seen by oneself. If you desire external approval and recognition too strongly, you will go into an "approval identity" that only does a good job in order to be perceived as a good doctor. Your motivation for being a good doctor does not come from above, it then comes from believing you are a bad doctor, trying to hide it, and making a "good impression" as long as patients are around. In other words:

If you keep having to affirm how good you are, and requiring confirmation that you are good, and keep having to convince others of your goodness, and react with anger when people criticize your work, then you don't really believe you are that good.

At an even more contracted state of being, your identity is based on and borrowed from stereotypes you saw in movies or in others. It is obvious to most people that the person is wearing a mask and not really being him or herself. For example, in my youth, in order to hang out with a group of schoolyard bullies, I imitated a "tough guy" image, but it quickly wore off and was seen through because essentially I was not that kind of person at the time. I was a soft and poetic person and playing "tough guy" looked ridiculous to any external observer. Now, after a whole life of experience, I am certainly tougher…but not as a stereotypical mask I wear out of fear of others, but as a genuine part of my personality. Personality is that which is accumulated throughout a lifetime. Most of it is discarded once the body dies, but some of its more interesting aspects are "taken with you to the other side". The "Queen" aspect of self most represents the soul that incarnates and discarnates, explores the Dimensions, and travels here and there. It is the colorful aspect of you, seen when your "true colors are shining through". It is the individualized version of your divine-self that takes on various good-parts of various incarnations. The heavy and contracted parts are usually discarded because with so much baggage you can't really travel anywhere (this is why I most frequently teach the Art of Releasing and Letting Go). And if you die with too much baggage, that baggage will keep you stuck to earth, and you will have to reincarnate here or even worse, become an *earth-bound discarnate entity* (ghost) in order to process all the baggage.

Contraction or Expansion is your choice every day. Contracted Emotion generates tightness in the chest and therefore fear. Expanded Emotion generates love...giving yourself and others time, space, and attention...expansiveness! **In many ancient languages, the word for "Heaven" is closely related to the word "Expansion".**

A good handle on life can be gained by being able to contract and expand at will. So in order to write this book, I have to contract somewhat and put myself into the mind of readers and also focus attention on detail. Once I finish writing, I can go back to expansive mode. Too much contraction would not allow me to write in a positive manner. Too much expansion would not allow me to write in a coherent manner because I would be too high for it to matter.

So know when and how to contract and know when and how to expand. Let's say a friend of yours is in a dire state of need and you say, "Heeey, take it easy man...everything is soooo mellow and expaaaansive," you are on an inappropriate level of consciousness or mood to address his need. If your boss says, "I don't appreciate you coming late to work every day," and you again say, "Take it eeeeeasy man," it is again too expansive an approach. But if you contract too much, you would start obsessing about coming in on time or helping your friend in need while ignoring any of your own needs. So the realm in which to operate for normal daily life is to be a little contracted and a little expansive. Then, when things start going downhill, you simply open up a little more, and expand a little more. And when you start flying away, you contract a little. Unless you are seeking total enlightenment, in which case you expand indefinitely.

You Are a Name, Not a Number

At a recent visit to the tax offices I did my best to feel light, but that's not easy when one's entire existence is defined in numbers. As I entered the area I had to draw a number to wait my turn. When my number appeared I entered a numbered room and was asked not for my name but my tax I.D. number. They did not look me up by name but by my number! The rest of the encounter also revolved around my life in terms of numbers – my income, my expenses, the numeric names of the forms I was supposed to fill out, my passport-number, etc. Not once in the entire meeting was my name spoken. Had those folks learned anything about customer-friendliness they would have known that it's quite reassuring for people to be addressed with their personal and unique names. I ended the meeting by asking the person what his name was and used it when saying goodbye. His eyes lit up.

People are, by nature, skeptical and wary of generalized, impersonal treatment. They are skeptical of marketers and advertisers who take generic "surveys", skeptical of census-takers, skeptical of number-assignments for factory-workers, etc. This is because seeing a human as a number, as one of many, as a mere cog in the wheel, a face in the crowd, and as an insignificant part of the collective is subtly dehumanizing.

Once you can convince someone that they are not unique, not of divine origin, and have no meaning, you can make them slaves. Whenever slavery has reared its ugly head in Human History, you notice that the slaves and slave labor were either stripped of their individual clothing or given identical uniforms, often with numbers on them. Slaves were to have no individual belongings that made them discernible from anyone else. In fact, in the old days slaves were often not allowed to use their birth names and were instead given either no name or a new "slave name" to further humiliate them and strip them of their own previous identity as free people.

The perils of decreasing people's individuality are not fully grasped in our society. The only people who seem to have a very vivid idea of its dangers are science-fiction authors. In almost all dystopian sci-fi movies you will notice that often either the people or the countries are no longer called by their name. Countries might then be called "District 1, District 2, and District 3" etc. and people will be known by some case-file or citizen number.

As a soul, you are unique, radiant, royal, and equipped with the freedom to think, choose, and act. A life-lesson you can take away from this book is that anything that treats individuals like a number, as in generalized mass-schooling, mass-media, mass-solutions, mass-belief-systems, mass-industry, and mass-society tends to move in a direction contrary to the soul and who you really are, and everything that treats you like an individual tends to move in the direction of spiritual reality.

So if you are a Business owner, you can improve your popularity by discarding the "one-size-fits-all" philosophy and treating each of your customers individually and with Custom-Made solutions. If you are a school principal, you can best serve the children by making smaller classrooms (which is sometimes easier said than done if a school is underfunded). If you work in Marketing you will not succeed long-term by sending generic letters to unspecified and non-targeted people as if everyone were the same (unless you are targeting a particularly docile crowd). If you are a Casanova, it is most important that you remember the actual names of those whose hearts you wish to conquer. Mistaking their names is a deal-breaker that reveals to them that you see them as exchangeable objects rather than humans. If you are a government, why not allow people to choose from a list of items they would most like to pay their taxes for rather than leaving them without choice? And if you are an individual, why not find your own unique style, way of doing things, and way of saying things? Don't just imitate, create.

Have you ever wondered why the concrete blocks of public and social housing in various cities around the world looks so generic and dull? Why you have parts of town with dozens or even hundreds of rows of buildings that look exactly alike? It is generally believed that it's because cheap housing does not allow for more style, color and creativity, but that is not at all true. It is entirely possible to build cheap housing with an individual or beautiful note. Some research into this will reveal that, at least in western countries, public housing is *deliberately made unappealing* so that people do not choose to live there all their lives (and thereby become a fiscal burden on the Government). However, it would be much, much smarter to make public housing look a little more beautiful and individual because that in turn would boost the inhabitants' personal energy-state and consequently, they'd be less of a "burden" on the Government.

The only manner in which we are all "the same" is in the highest and lowest sense. In the highest spiritual sense of having the same *Essence,* and in the lowest sense of our Egos/Minds being very similar to one another. On the one hand humans are unique as rocks, each one easily discernible from another. On the other hand they are all like bricks, easily exchangeable. The metaphysical secret being imparted here is that the earthly-aspect of you; the world-self (ego/mind) is not at all unique (but thinks it is), and the soul/spirit aspect of you is completely unique. Seen from a non-spirit perspective, you are just another face in the crowd. Seen from a spirit perspective, you are different from anyone else, your energy-field being a unique and beautiful signature that has evolved through countless eons, lifetimes, and universes.

If you listen to people's mind-stories only, you will notice that people from all over the world and of all ages, creeds, nationalities, and social classes are remarkably similar. They all tell similar stories and hold similar limitations. But if you look a little deeper and on a case-by-case basis, you will also notice that each human is unlike anyone you have ever met, a whole Universe unto themselves and that being with them will teach you new ways of experiencing the world. So to realize you are no more unique than a speck of sand on a beach prevents superiority-complexes. And to realize you are as unique as a star in the sky prevents inferiority-complexes.

To become aware of how you are similar to everyone else and different to everyone else helps you find out which part of you is your soul-self. Have you ever listened to yourself in conversation and thought: "Oh my, I sound just as boring as everyone else,"? That's the world-self speaking. And have you ever heard yourself saying things in such a way as nobody else has ever spoken? That's the higher-self speaking. So use this little mind-tool to find out more about who you really are and express your true colors. And reject being treated like a number.

The Akashic Library Trumps the Internet

The Akashic records are a place where all Information of Infinity is stored and sorted as in a Library and can be accessed by cosmic researchers and angelic librarians. I have detailed the place in my book "Lives of the Soul". Oh I'm sorry…should I have said, *"In my opinion* the Akashic Records are a place where all information of Infinity is stored and sorted…"? But I didn't. If you want any chance of accessing these hyper-dimensional halls of wisdom, you have to accept their reality as hard facts, not take them as opinion.

To me, the Internet is a physical-world copy of the "Akashic Records". You can access all the information you look for on the Internet…at least all the information that is known (plus at least 60%

falsehood *in my opinion*). The Akashic Halls are a supra-dimensional place (not two-dimensional like the Internet, and without all the Falsehood). To me, on the very rare occasions I have visited them, they appear as a Library, a library in which "moving books" are pulled out showing 3-D like movies of various lives and topics. There is a book on YOU there somewhere. If I had the rank of librarian, I could probably even access it and look up some stuff on your various lives. To say that the atmosphere there is really, really enormously wonderful would be a gross understatement. Having the records of all-that-is so neatly categorized and accessible is a very peculiar feeling.

We are going to talk about how to access the library. Obviously this is a skill for advanced practitioners only and of very little interest to the general public. The easiest access is on the non-physical plane, because it is a non-physical or hyper-physical place. The two main ways humans access the non-physical is through lucid dreaming and astral travel. If you know one of those, then all you really have to do is: a) Know the Akashic Library exists, and b) Target it while out-of-body or lucid dreaming. The amount of data you are able to access once there does depend on your level-of-consciousness. At one level, you can walk around the library, at another you can read your own "Book of Lives" with a lot of blanked out pages, at another you can read the whole thing, at another you can read others' Lives, etc. Of course, most of you do not habitually travel out of body, so then accessing the Halls may be more challenging. But there are methods of access even for dense citizens. For example: You pose a deliberate question to "the Universe", then you let go of it. By posing the question you stretch the rubber band, by letting go of it, the answer can lash down to this plane.

Another method to access Akashic data will be described here. The physical methods do not involve actually travelling there and partaking in its splendors, but you can sift out data if and when it is really required for your growth as a soul. The method is to write down the questions you have. Then to meditate yourself into the highest state you can get to at the moment. And to then open your eyes and write down the answers from a higher perspective. This requires you to imagine being a Higher Self, being a Soul, being an Angel, or being whatever you imagine a higher being to be. YOU do not have the answers, but another perspective does. So, in your Meditation you first imagine that higher being. Then you merge with that higher being and temporarily become it. And then, from that perspective, you write down the spontaneous answers that "just come to mind", without filtering or censoring. Do not use language first, use what you feel first. The feeling that comes into your body is the answer. This answer must first be translated into language; translated into the physical. So if a language-based answer comes up first, disregard it and go for the feeling first. Then, see how that translates into an answer you can write down. Put differently: Don't write down any answer unless you are in a state where you feel things you have not felt before starting to meditate. Higher sources send their answers as packs-of-energy and these are felt as feelings.

That's it…that's how many more things are knowable and accessible. That's how I write my articles too by the way: Without listening to earthly advice, without looking it up in earthly books, without using language first, but rather by simply being open while placing my attention on a certain topic. After I have written an article, I may later look it up elsewhere or see what others have to say on it, but I rely on intuition first and external advice only second. This has served me and many others very well.

How Would Love See It?

The third question of "The Enlightenment Technique" is: "How would love see it?" How would love see a problem you are facing? How would love approach a task? How would love decide? How would love behave? How would love rekindle a relationship? How would love deal with bodily pains? How would love…

The question serves to **instantly reframe any situation to a higher level**, to improve your state within a few seconds of asking the question. I have applied this question for the last 20 years in many different variations in my Coaching work. A guy had difficulty approaching women, so I asked him who his role model regarding women is. He said it's "Hank Moody" of a TV-Series called "Californication". So I asked in regards to women, flirting, approaching, talking, acting, and living, "How would Hank Moody see it?" "How would Hank Moody talk to women? How would he dress?" And so forth. Naturally his demeanor, body language, vibe, emotional state, looks, and voice changed the moment he recalled "Hank Moody".

In a recent Skype Coaching with a woman who is afraid of angry people and acts too submissively when others get angry, I asked her what her favorite movie is. "The Last Samurai," she said. So I asked, "How would a Samurai handle angry people?" "How would Tom Cruise deal with angry people?" Etc. I told her, "The next time someone is angry at you, simply remember the Samurai. **Just by remembering the Samurai you will be more calm and steady.**" As she repeats this **new reaction** to people's anger, and conditions herself to be different than before, she will gradually stop attracting angry people.

Movies and Movie-Heroes serve us to show "ways of Being", "ways of talking", and "ways of behaving". Like children, we need to be shown possibilities before we can believe in them or make them possible. The subconscious will not create any reality it is not familiar with. Where there is no frame of reference, there is no reality creation. By presenting examples of WHAT YOU COULD BE and examples that you can admire you gradually become that way.

I use this technique in countless variations all the time because I know that: "If you change your self-image and identity, your reality changes." And often it's enough to merely remember who you would like to be, but some people take it further by changing their hairstyle and clothing to more closely emulate a new self and corresponding reality.

I created the two Training-Audios of The Enlightenment Technique because they are the basis of the most important thing there is…finding out who you are ("Know Thyself"), being who you are, and being able to change who you are.

Beyond identity-shifting and role-shifting is the true and infinite self. This is merely the loving observer. All else are roles. Even the "personality" you think you are is ultimately a role. Any role attracts certain realities. Anything that is not Love and Bliss is a role and is not the "true self". So questions such as: "How would the Samurai see it?" define a new role and reality, whereas the question: "How would love see it?" defines no reality; it instead takes you back to source.

There are different depths you can take this question to…all the way to spiritual Enlightenment if you like.

Waking up from the Coma with a New Identity

Our Identity...who we think we are...is less fixed than we believe. Another piece of evidence in this regard is that some people's identities are completely altered after they wake up from a Coma.

An example is Ben McMahon from Melbourne, Australia. After a car accident, he went into a Coma. Upon awakening, he had lost all his memory but could unexpectedly speak *fluent* Mandarin Chinese, although he only knew the very basics prior to the accident. He was unable to speak his native English language for three days. To this day he has retained his fluency in Mandarin without having put effort into its study.

Cases like these are common enough to be reported several times a year. This article for example, reports similar miraculous language ability:

A teenager went into a coma and awoke speaking another language. The case of Sandra Ralic, 13, has doctors baffled. She spoke Croatian before the sudden coma and fluent German after. Her parents say she had only just started studying German at her school in Knin, southern Croatia. Local hospital chief Dujomir Marasovic said: "We are still trying to find out what caused the coma and why she has apparently forgotten how to speak Croatian."

Another example in this article:

As further evidence that the average human mind possesses incredible latent abilities, a Czech speedway driver who was recently knocked unconscious in a crash was reported to have come out of his coma with a previously unknown ability to speak perfect and fluent English. 18-year-old Matej Kus was unconscious for about 45 minutes after the accident, but when he woke up he conversed fluidly in English with paramedics. Perhaps even more oddly, he spoke in a clear English accent.

One possible explanation is that things that had been learned subconsciously and peripherally became activated and conscious through the comatose state. There is evidence that the subconscious **records** **everything** one experiences, and the conscious mind only retrieves data as needed. But this explanation does not account for cases in which people know a language they have never had contact with. I have personally experienced that.

Radical changes after Comas, accidents, and operations are not limited to language skills. They encompass one's entire personality. A few examples I have found:

Playboy-starlet Kerri Parker became a prude introvert after an operation for brain tumor. Three year old Layla Towsy fell into a Coma. After waking up she fluently sang the song "Mamma Mia" by Abba. She did not recognize her mother. After waking up from a stroke, the Walisan rugby player and banker Chris Birch ended the relationship with his girlfriend, his hobbies and his job as a banker and became a gay hairdresser.

Following a treatment with deep brain stimulation, a 60-year old Dutchman woke up and was suddenly a huge fan of Johnny Cash, someone who had never interested him previously.

One of the self-improvement techniques I have been teaching over the last 10 years is that of shifting into a "parallel universe version of yourself", where you are a different person with different skills, and attract different things into your life. Unlike these stories, you don't need an accident or coma for that to happen. You go down into a state of deep relaxation I call "zero point". From there you have direct access to your subconscious and higher-self, and can more easily make modifications. How good you get at this is just a matter of practice. Then, once you are content with who you are, you stop making modifications and get on with your life…until such a day you are ready for another shift.

Things that have happened to people in Comas sometimes go even further than just an identity change.

One of my favorite books of the last two years was this one:

In his book "Proof of Heaven", neurosurgeon Eben Alexander describes how a complicated operation caused a near-death experience that unexpectedly sent him to higher realms of consciousness. Upon returning, he was a changed man. His entire hard-scientific outlook was gone and replaced by a spiritual view of things.

If you think the Coma incidents are fascinating, there are things happening that are even more inexplicable. The following story caught my attention the other day (excerpts quoted):

A 3-year-old boy in the Golan Heights region near the border of Syria and Israel said he was murdered with an axe in his previous life. He showed village elders where the murderer buried his body, and sure enough they found a man's skeleton there. He also showed the elders where the murder weapon was found, and upon digging, they did indeed found an axe there.

In his book, "Children Who Have Lived Before: Reincarnation Today," German therapist Trutz Hardo tells this boy's story, along with other stories of children who seem to remember their past lives with verified accuracy. The boy's story was witnessed by Dr. Eli Lasch, who is best known for developing the medical system in Gaza as part of an Israeli government operation in the 1960s. Dr. Lasch, who died in 2009, had recounted these astounding events to Hardo.

This is almost the *opposite case* of those quoted above. Here is someone who *retains his identity and memory* even after death!

What all this points to is that we are heading towards a humanity in which the options are limitless. Once we figure out "how stuff works" we'll be able to "download" languages and other skills within seconds. But isn't it more fulfilling to have to go through some challenge and effort in order to acquire something? Sure. But by the time we are able to learn languages without effort, we'll have *other challenges* to get worked up about. The purpose of effort is to make the thing you focus effort on, effortless.

We'll be able to retain our identity after death and return. Retain our identity after death and not return (I don't believe Reincarnation is a default, as commonly taught, I believe it's an option you can choose if you have unfinished Business.), We'll be able to choose new identities and perhaps even be able to live several different lives and bodies on Earth, which will bring up a whole new set of challenges. Any variation you can possibly imagine will come to be (But until such days come to pass, I think it's best to work with what's "closer to home" – basic self-improvement.

2
Upgrade your Identity

Dressing as Who You Want to Become

Clothing can help you grow into a new version of yourself and has a subtle impact on others' perception.

I once knew a yogi who dressed very well, even on occasions where he knew he would sit in the dirt, walk into the filthy Ganges River, or walk in the dusty streets of Mumbai for extended periods of time. And yet, he would make a point of dressing up fresh and new every time, sometimes twice a day. I asked him why. "You are going to get dirty, why not just dress in something simple?" His response astounded me, "Just because I am surrounded by dirt, I don't forget who I am."

The way you dress reveals your intentions. It reveals how you intend to behave, who you intend to be, and in which direction you intend to be moving. With the exception of special occasions, it is not advisable to let external surroundings dictate how you dress, and it is not recommendable to dress randomly the majority of the time with no thought about how you are dressing. If you find yourself in dire circumstances, then by all means, dress as if you are moving upwards.

The mere ritual of dressing well will set you up for a different attitude for the day. The power of clothing goes far beyond your own attitude. It directly effects the realities of others too. If you are a massage-therapist and yet you dress all in white, you will be perceived as some sort of doctor. If you are a school teacher and you dress just like the teenagers, you will be perceived as a friend rather than an authority. That could come along with a whole number of advantages and disadvantages. If you wear clothes that display expensive brand names in bright colors and huge letters, most people will assume you're clueless.

Even you do most of your work from at home in front of a computer, it makes sense to get dressed rather than sitting there in a dirty t-shirt and underwear. It makes a difference in the way you work and the way you are perceived – even if nobody can actually "see" you with their eyes.

If you intend to become a success then dress that way. If you live in a *very* bad part of town, you will notice how this may be a challenge and how people may start viewing you with suspicion. Why is that? Because subconsciously they realize you have the courage to create a new reality for yourself and will soon no longer be part of their reality. Your sudden change of style is not in sync with that part of town. And by dressing for success you are no longer in sync with that part of town either.

For a moment, think about the person you want to become. How are they dressed? Take whatever your imagination gives you and try to imitate that in the here-now-today, dressing not as you are but as you want to become.

The Secrets in a Face

Just by looking at someone's face you can tell a number of things. You can tell whether you would like him/her or not, what his/her dominant character-traits are, what his/her general and current state of health is, his/her intelligence and even whether s/he has a sense of humor. What is less known is that you can also **read his/her conduct in life** – whether s/he has been good to people or not.

The older someone gets, the easier it is to read. Every line in their face tells a story. Looks are not a coincidence. If you *do* ugly, you *become* ugly. And if you *are* loving, you *become* beautiful and it shows in your face.

This is actually good news because it means **you can change your looks from within**. If someone was coldly self-absorbed for ten years, no amount of makeup will hide the traces of that. If someone was full of love and care for someone for ten years, the shining eyes and tender facial features will reveal that. When you are younger it is easier to hide your inner being. But the older you grow, the more obvious it becomes who we have been.

The purpose of using makeup excessively is to mask who you have been. The cosmetic industry would go broke if everyone knew the secrets of natural beauty-from-within. No product labeled with "beauty" can provide real attractiveness and radiance for you. Of course, the "beauty" referred to here is not necessarily what glossy fashion magazines define as such, but rather the natural spiritual emanation that is awaiting expression in every human being.

Your face is not set in stone, it can change very rapidly. **Good thoughts, words, and deeds will gradually change your facial features, the tone of your skin, even your face's shape**. You are an energy-being and a natural shape-shifter. Your face also changes many times a day depending on social role, environment, and mood. You wear a much different face when you want to make an impression on someone than when you are idly hanging around. Your face is determined by your inner state, but vice-versa, changing your facial expressions is also a good way to change your inner state. To feel different, act different. To act different, feel different. It goes both ways. There is another reason it is good to sometimes consciously change your facial expression: An expressive face makes it easier for people to relate to you. Unchanging faces come across as aloof and inaccessible. I mention this because many wear an unchanging or frowning face as a matter of habit, without noticing.

Obviously I do not agree that "you can't judge a person by outside appearance" because in fact, the **outside is a reflection of the inside**. I am not saying one should be judgmental in the sense of putting people down for who they are and how they look. I am not saying one should judge people by superficial things such as which handbag-brand they have or the size of their nose. No human is without some perceived "flaw". But I do know from experience that you can tell in an instant whether you will be a good match to someone or not. You can generally tell whether someone is an honest person to work with. You can generally tell whether someone could cause potential trouble. You can read a lot of that in faces. And as you combine facial reading with other factors such as voice, general appearance, body language, and a person's intentions, one can safely conclude that every person is a completely open book.

You Look like Who You Like

Have you ever noticed how couples who have been together for a long time tend to start looking alike? Well, you are not fantasizing, it's true! A scientific study carried about by the psychologist Robert Zajnoc and his colleagues, and published in the paper "Convergence in the Physical Appearance of Spouses" (1987) details a long-term experiment that shows participants pictures of men and women in their first year of marriage and the same couples after 25 years of marriage.

The 110 participants of the experiment were asked to figure out which of the couples are married to each other. Judging by facial features alone it was possible for most of the participants to correctly judge which of the faces were couples. The conclusions of the experiment and further extensive research was that couple's facial features usually began to resemble each other the longer they are together. The researchers suggest that this is because of **empathy**. When you empathize with someone you subconsciously begin mimicking and copying their behavior and facial expressions.

I agree with this but would like to suggest that there is a little more going on. Because psychologists don't usually learn or use spiritual terms such as "the law of attraction" and "energy transference" their means of communicating what is really going on is limited. But I have been teaching for 20 years that: *"You become what you give your attention to."* What you put attention to for extended amounts of time, you become an energetic, vibratory match to.

Of course this also reveals that the secret of beauty cannot be found in cosmetics with its multi-billion-dollar hype. You cannot purchase beauty. But if you give your attention to what is beautiful, you will become more beautiful. And you can make it much stronger if your attention is imbued with empathy or appreciation for whatever it is you keep looking at.

Being George Clooney

Now let's shine light on how and why we become like the people we admire.

Who would you like to be similar to? Who do you admire? What do you admire about him/her?

Children become similar to their parents because these are their prime examples of how one can be.

When I learn foreign languages, I pick out people who are especially typical of the mentality of their respective cultures and imitate them. By imitating their sound and manner, **I learn languages much more quickly** than someone who would be learning from a textbook.

I have applied the method of "modeling" many times. I seek out whoever is best in the field I would like to master and imitate them until I develop and find my own unique style. I have looked toward certain famous actors in terms of style of walking, dressing, and speaking. I have looked to successful coaches to be a successful life coach. I have looked to the great masters of reality – people such as Jesus, Rumi, and Buddha to learn about life. I will focus mental attention to that person and observe how they behave and act. Some of their style I will role-play myself.

Modeling is actually the word I prefer to "imitating", which, for some people has a negative connotation that takes away from the uniqueness of the individual. They will tell me, "I want to be myself; I don't want to imitate others." "Of course," I respond, "You are unique. And yet, your identity is also more flexible and expandable than you assume." Modeling is not about losing your uniqueness; it is about expanding your identity. Your core-identity remains intact. The superficial day-to-day identity which just lamely "goes through the motions of daily life" is not the real YOU anyway.

One of the easiest ways to apply the method of modeling is in how you dress, walk, talk, and behave. There are many other factors but those are the easiest to change. When I was in my twenties and my finances started looking bad, I started dressing "straight and proper" again and my moneys went back up. Why? Because how you dress indicates who you are becoming. By assuming a new role, I changed the reality I attracted.

If you would like to feel different you must first act differently. **If you walk down the street in haste, you will feel pressured. If you stride smoothly and confidently, you will start feeling confident.** If you extend help to a friend, you will start feeling a closer connection to him/her. If you then experiment with new roles and ways of being, your state gradually begins changing.

Something highly interesting happened to me recently. I watched a movie starring George Clooney. I liked the way he dressed in the movie, so I purchased something similar to wear and decided to walk around town "playing George Clooney" wearing nice clothes for a few hours. I tried the smile of his movie-character and also the mannerisms. On the day of writing this article (2009), I found myself conducting a seminar on a boat at Lake Como. When the boat driver pointed out that we are now passing George Clooney's house, it hit me like lightning – zap! I suddenly remembered that I had rehearsed Clooney's role and that, that was probably the reason I was now spending time in his environment. Real life is stranger than fiction.

Be It Before You Do It

Being trumps Doing. Most of us have it the other way around, emphasizing action over state. Have you ever seen someone struggling like crazy, but another person, who did not struggle, reaping the rewards? No doubt action and work are important factors, but they don't produce the wanted results if they are not imbued but aligned Being-ness. When you are with another person, have you ever noticed that being present and attentive with the other person has more of an impact than the particular activity you are doing with him/her? Have you noticed that when you are in an improved state, your doing/actions are more graceful and reap better rewards? When someone asks me, "What should I do to attract a partner?" I ask back, "Who could you BE that is attractive to that partner?" You can't get someone to love you but you can BE a person that is lovable.

Your actions are then a consequence of your being-ness. They'll ask, "What do I have to do to get this job?" And I ask back, "Who would you have to BE to get it?" While doing is certainly not unimportant, Being should be the first item on the list. If you tell me, "I have to do this program, then I can get a certificate, then I can BE a facilitator," you are doing it the wrong way around. The being-ness of being a facilitator must be inherent within you and from that the "doing the program" will more easily come. I was and defined myself as a writer many years before I even wrote the first book. Writing is what I liked, what I enjoyed, what I was, regardless of whether it got me any external rewards or not. Even if nobody acknowledged me as a writer, I wrote, and wrote, and wrote...because of who I AM.

The next time you go out with people and someone asks, "What should we DO tonight?" Ask back, "What should we BE tonight?" That's much more fun because it places one's state over external factors and locations. And from this new BEING, you might be surprised what pleasant activities can arise.

Communicating with Your Future Self

This is another way to playfully shift your inner viewpoint. Get comfortable somewhere.

1. As best you can, imagine a future version of yourself; you're Future-Self. Take on the perspective of your Future-Self as if you are slipping into that person's body. See the world from his/her eyes. How do you see your Present-Self from that viewpoint? Is there anything you have to say?

2. Remain in the Viewpoint of your Future-Self and look at a Past-Self; a younger version of yourself. How do you see that Past-Self? Is there anything you have to communicate to that younger self? Extend kind and forgiving energy in the direction of your past.

3. Remaining in the Viewpoint of your Future-Self, look at another version of yourself who is even further in the Future…a second Future-Self. See what that looks and feels like. Do you have anything to say to him/her? Does s/he have anything to say to you? Look, Feel, Hear.

Complete the Meditation-Experience and if you like, write down any insights you may have had.

Charisma Coaching

Simply put, you will vastly improve your Charisma with the information here.

The dictionary defines Charisma as "a compelling attractiveness or charm that can inspire devotion in others".

Sound good? So let's get right to it.

1. Presence
When you are sitting or standing in a room with a group of people, you either have Presence or you don't. If you do, then people's attention naturally gravitates in your direction. If you don't, then you are just one of the gray mass sitting in the room. You can develop this magnetic aura by **becoming present** yourself. Becoming present means to be "fully here and now" with the people, with the room, mindful of the people's moods, mindful of the room's interior, mindful of your own body, and mindful of the various relationships between the people. As a rule of the thumb: "Interested people are

interesting." The more mindful you are of the subtle nuances of everything happening in the room, the more you "control" the room psycho-physically so to speak. I have coached numerous public speakers, and this was always the main breakthrough point – developing presence. Presence presupposes that you are not preoccupied with other places, other people, other times, mind-stuff and so on.

Presence will improve your communication in every manner. Are you checking your phone? You're not present. Are you trying to peddle your own concerns instead of listening to what people are saying? You are only half-present. Are you telling people how great you are? You are not present. Are you interrupting others because you are eager to defend your viewpoint? You are not present. Now if interrupting others comes from-presence, that's a little different, but that's not the way most people interrupt. Presence is calm and poised, an observing witness in a sea of chaotic thought that is normally present at gatherings. Is your walk deliberate? You are present. Are you commenting on someone's new hairstyle? You are present. Do you consider before you speak? You are present.

2. Tone and Voice

Proper breathing improves the tone and voice of your speech, making it more adjustable. As you become more present, you will be able to match your voice and the tone of your voice to that of the people you are speaking to (and you will also be using vocabulary that best suits them).

The more comfortable and confident you feel in a group, in front of a group, or with other single persons, the more your voice will improve and have impact. This is a matter of relaxing your tensions deliberately.

3. Appearance

Do you actually take the time in the morning to look good? If you have come into the habit of "just wearing anything" this can take away from your charisma. On the other hand, if people notice you are mindful with your clothes they automatically assume you are mindful with other things as well. Dress for success, especially when you go to important meetings. Take the time to improve your facial and physical looks as well. Women are better at this than men it would seem. As a man you could at least trim the hairs out of your nose and ears, for example. Purify and clean yourself. You will thus have an easier time feeling better and that in turn will affect your energy-aura.

4. Listen to or Read Motivational Material
If you listen to a lot of motivational speakers or read their works (or even read my Blog!), it will gradually influence your own thinking and speaking.

Your speech will become more inspirational, directed, precise, and motivating. As you motivate and inspire others, your charisma increases.

5. Be Physical
Become a physical being who practices a physical discipline. Do not live your life in your head. Do you like sports, workout, yoga, bike riding, nature, water, air? As you become more attuned to physical reality, your connection to it (and thus to others) will improve. As you are pleased with the shape of your body, your Charisma increases.

6. Be Skilled and Knowledgeable
Learn. Acquaint yourself and become familiar with a broad number of subjects and things to communicate. Don't bore people by talking about the weather. Can you recite Shakespeare? Can you

speak Japanese? Can you taste the nuances of Italian Wine? Do you know which music groups are en vogue with teenagers? Are you familiar with the latest Internet inventions? The point is, do not alienate yourself from what is happening, so that you can **relate** to the people you meet. Also, be expert at a few things. It subtly shows in your energy-field and body posture.

7. Be Joyful
Being joyless and never laughing is just a habit. You can break that habit by making a deliberate effort to laugh and smile more. You can hang up a memorizing-card somewhere that reminds you to smile or laugh more often, to talk to strangers more often, and to open up more often.

Each of these steps in and off themselves will increase your Charisma – guaranteed.

Assembling a New Identity

With work on self-image and identity I have personally witnessed thousands of rapid transformations and make-overs. These are among the most interesting of the last years:

- An unemployed guy who became the boss of a well-running health-food delivery service.
- A lifelong office-cubicle number-cruncher who rose up to department-leader within two months.
- A bored rich kid who became a happy backpacker and adventurer and now films travel documentaries.
- A sad assembly line worker who is now an art curator for the most expensive art.
- A struggling pro soccer player of the 4th League, who made it to the first league at the late age of 27.
- A broke investor who went on to sell patents worth Millions.
- A girl who, from car accident injuries, was supposed to be in a wheelchair for life, but can now walk.

Of course, not everyone needs or wants change on such grand scales. But all of these cases really didn't require that much. The big breakthrough realization for these people was that you attract into your life and reality not what you want, but **who you are**. With that in mind, it makes sense to look at "how to assemble an Identity". This assumes you are not so strongly identified with your current

Identity to think: "That's just who I am." When you assemble a new YOU, you role-play it until you are convinced of it. Then you attract brand new energies, people, events, and anything else that corresponds with your self-chosen self.

The more into detail you go with your new-self, the better. This comic snippet explains why:

The more detailed and "one of a kind" a new identity, the more unique and distinct it is and the more likely to attract something different than randomness.

Some professional identities (such as lawyers, doctors, astronauts, & athletes) require a formal education and training to be more easily acknowledged as real by the world. But even here, without deliberately assembling a distinct persona, you'll remain a mediocre lawyer, doctor, astronaut, or athlete.

You'd be surprised to learn that most professional identities are 50% self-created. Professional identities in the arts and business are almost 80%-100% self-created. Identities referring to a person's character and character can be 100% self-created.

Here are some building-parts of a new Identity:

The best way to get started with assembling a new self is to create a comparison chart: You would list the speech patterns, dress style, skills, typical locations, beliefs, owned objects, goals, and actions of your old-self and then do the same for your new self. Not all aspects of the old self have to be dropped, of course. For example, you may still have the same circle of friends. But by comparison you learn what to gradually let go of, and what to emphasize.

The second step would be to apply the Identity Shifting exercise…repeatedly over a few weeks. And the third step would be to implement the changes step by step, without overwhelming or alienating yourself or others. Of course, you needn't be too careful about other's responses. For example, in 2014 I created a new identity for myself called: "I am now an Atlantis Researcher ". Doing so was a deliberate experiment in Identity-Shifting.

To support my new identity I started writing a book on the subject, crafting a website on it, and even planning trips to some places for research. In the "owned objects" department I purchased a rough and worn looking "adventurer's backpack" to remind me of my new role as a researcher who went on adventures out into exotic places in search of lost civilizations. The public reactions to my new identity were not all favorable. Many people unsubscribed from my Newsletter because of it. One publisher in Russia withdrew their book-contract with me.

I am telling you this so you know and understand that any creation of a new reality may cause a little bit of turbulence with people who expect you to stay fixed to your old one. It's similar to what actors experience when they play a role that is different than what the audience is used to. People tend to project certain expectations as to "who you are" and if you are any different, they'll have to re-configure their minds…apparently that's stressful to some! For the very same reasons it's not a good idea to live with your parents as an adult. Your parents do not see you as an adult, they project the "little boy/girl" image onto you and whenever you behave like an adult, some conflict may arise.

In any case, if you stay true to your new identity, without caving in at the slightest external disapproval, you will succeed with it. You'd be surprised to learn that you can succeed with almost anything you **stay true to**. It is in your reaction to external pressure that your new identity is built. So when the publisher withdrew their book contract with me citing "philosophical differences" due to my Atlantis-book, I was actually *happy* because it showed me that my new Identity was working. Had I reacted sadly or caved in and removed that work, I'd have resorted back to my old Identity in order to conform to external expectations. So the **external**

pressure was used to *support* my new reality rather than put it into doubt. Does that give you a sense of how this reality creation stuff works?

Of course, if I were to change my Identity every few weeks, I could not generate any momentum and consistency. And then it would be understandable that others feel alienated. Identity-Shifting is therefore something that is done every few years or even decades, not every few weeks.

While shifting is a cause of joy, identity-consistency is a cause of success. It takes some time and focus to establish a new self. But it is exciting and fun when such a change starts bearing fruit and catapulting you to entirely new and fresh ideas, energies, and situations.

"I" Is the Most Used Word in the World

Who are you? Are you your body, your thoughts, your story, your name, your title, your emotions, your age, your past, your memories, or your job? Or are you something more mysterious than that?

The word "I" is the most used word in the world. But who is this "I" that we keep referring to? Here is an experiment: Can you go one week without using the word "I"? Or even just one day? You may use the word "You" frequently. Could you also move from *seeking* acknowledgement to *giving* it? There are several awareness-expanding experiences to make with this technique, but I am not going to tell you what they are. Find out for yourself.

The Spirit Beneath Your Mask

When unobserved, people have a different facial expression. Their mood changes in social situations. As explained in my book "Levels of Energy", most people wear "social masks". These are faces they put on to appear more sane, friendly, or comfortable while socializing with others. We act out higher energy-levels out of respect to others but also to look good to the public.

Sometimes the shift is incredible. In one of my recent workshops I spotted a student who thought he was alone and his face wore a stone-cold grimace of frustration and pain. As soon as he returned to the seminar room with the other attendees, his face brightened up and he appeared jovial and happy. Of course, if you are intuitive or can read lines in a face, you would have known that he is not.

With spiritual maturity you seek to have less of a difference between actual energy-state and social-mask. You are less concerned about how others see you or whether they approve of your mood or not. Not wearing masks saves energy. Taking in a much higher state than your native state actually costs plenty of energy, which is why partaking in social gatherings will make you tired. If on the other hand you wear no masks, social gatherings will energize you. The way to feel energized from meeting others is by not trying to be anyone different than what you are.

Recently a book-fan, who was also a life coach, asked to meet me in person for some coffee and a chat. I wrote back to him saying, "Sure we can meet, but not as fan-author. Let's meet from coach-to-coach." The identity with which we met changed the entire context, mood, and conversation. Had we met as "fan meets author" the atmosphere may have been a little more formal or tense, whereas "coach-to-coach" created a more relaxed mood.

Sometimes a more formal setting may be appropriate, but you should know that WHO you walk around as, determines your experience.

Beneath all the social masks you wear, there is spirit – a unique, wonderful, fascinating, and radiant being. "I'm good," "I'm bad," "I'm a doctor," "I'm a teacher," are just definitions that act like filters covering up the true self. In a near-definitionless state you are the most humorous, loving, and radiant because no energy is wasted trying to cover something up or display something. In this state, the things that come out of your mouth and the actions you take may actually be surprising, or they may be entirely mundane. In any case, it's easier and more fun to live without pretense.

Parent Self, Child Self and True Self

What follows, is to help you discover more of your True Self and to determine whether your thoughts, words and actions are "really you" or something else.

In my work I characterize the Ego-Self (World-Self as opposed to Soul-Self) into two basic Categories:

Parent Self

Child Self

The "Parent-Self" is the part of you that keeps criticizing you, putting you down, and putting you under undue pressure and expectations. It is the inner censor that squelches dreams, punishes joy, and is doubtful of success.

The "Child-Self" is the part of you that rebels against the world, rules, authority, and the Parent-Self. It is the self that seeks approval, seeks pleasure, seeks money, seeks sweets, and seeks instant gratification but has difficulty actually getting any of these things.

The authoritarian Parent-Self and the anti-authoritarian Child-Self are two sides of the same coin. But they have nothing to do with the True Self. The True Self is pure, Radiant love, Joy, and Awareness.

Look inside for and notice the Parent-Self. Notice the part of yourself that puts you down all the time, saying things like, "You are wasting your time. You better work harder. You are a failure," Note the difference: Higher-Self says, "I failed," when you failed and parent-self says, "You ARE a failure." Big difference. While observing that part of your mind, send it some love. Send it some attention. Breathe with it. Send it some calm. And then ask yourself, "Could I just let go of this part of myself?" You may have to repeat this over the months until the Parent-Self disappears completely.

Look inside yourself and notice the Child-Self. Notice the part of yourself that is needy and negative all the time. "Before I can be happy I need this, this, and that." "Do they like me? When will they call me? What does she think of me?" "My neighbors are stupid." "Life is unfair." "The powers that be are to blame." The Parent-Self says, "I am a failure" the Child-Self says, "They are a failure." While observing that part of your mind, send it some love. Send it some attention. Breathe with it. Send it some calm. "Could I just let go of this part of myself?" You may have to repeat this over the months until the Child-Self disappears completely.

The parts of you sending yourself (and others) love and asking, "Could I let go of this?" is the True Self.

It is light, unburdened, full of goodwill and humor, and it cannot be exhausted.

Counterfeit Identity vs. Spiritual Identity

Another way of putting this is that there are three ways a human defines his identity while growing up:

1. By copying his parents

2. By rebelling against his parents

3. By self-creation

Running the programs 1 and 2 is not being entirely free but insecure. Most difficulties in your life are connected to these sub-identities. Simply determine which of your behaviors are copied from your parents (there are more than you suspect), which are a subconscious or conscious rebellion against your parents (there are more than you suspect), and which are self-created (there are less than you suspect).

Be brutally honest in listing this. For example, your entire career, love-life, health situation, or political outlook may be based on running a 1 or 2 program.

If you find out that that is so, that does not mean you have to quit your career or relationship. It just means you realize that you are running a program that is based on much deeper motivations, some of which are negative. You can then make the conscious decision to either abort the program or to continue it. But it will then be consciously decided and not running on default.

That career, relationship, view of the world, or whatever it was that was based on a 1 or 2 program will then feel different and yield more success and joy. Creation in-opposition-to or as-a-copy-of never works as well as creation-out-of-the-blue. Something that is created that is not based on anything previous (at least not entirely) but comes as an "inspiration from above" has the power to make a real impact.

So just who do you think you are? You can approach this by making a list of "I am _____" statements, followed by an indication whether it's a

1, 2, or 3 program. Those "I am" statements can regard your health, your love life, your spiritual views, your political views, your career, your financial state, your well-being, your circle of friends, and any trait you think you have.

Once you have determined the program-1 items, try to remember an instance from your childhood where you saw the same thing in your parents. Really try to look into this, it will surprise you. For example, I am very orderly. When I was younger I was very unorderly. If I recall my childhood, my mother was demanding orderliness in our household. I recall many such instances. That means that in my twenties I was running a 2-program (rebellion) by being unorderly, and in my 30s I was running a 1-program by being orderly. So on the subject of order/chaos, I was never quite free, my behavior was always based on desire (to be like my parents) and resistance (to be different than my parents). Once you can actually see this (and it only takes a few minutes in Meditation to find examples from your childhood), you are free from it.

Once you have determined program-2 items, try to remember an instance from your childhood where you saw the opposite of that in your parents. Really try to look into this, it will surprise you. For example, I used writing books as a rebellion against my parent's narrow religious views. I did succeed in writing books, but it did not make me happy. Why did it not make me happy? Because at a much deeper level it was being run by the motivation of revenge instead of the joy of creative expression. I realized this when I was 25 (and had already written several books), and released my resentment. I then made the conscious decision to write only when I enjoyed writing.

After your Meditation, see if you either wish to Abort certain identities and realities or make a conscious decision to continue with them. The entire process may take a few hours or it may take a few weeks and even months to process **the full depth** of this issue. Don't rush it. Just realize that who you are may not be as self-determined as you thought it was.

Through absence, shaming or mistreatment by a parent, one may have subconsciously developed "mommy or daddy issues" that are operating one's adult life. **The mere recognition** of these prime motives from childhood can cause a jump in levels of consciousness.

The mommy-polarity represents female/mother/nurture/safety/approval; the daddy polarity represents male/father/discipline/freedom. Lack of love from mommy can create a hardened, uncaring, self-centered, choleric workaholic. Lack of love from daddy can create a whiny, entitled, please-hug-me, lazy phlegmatic. The hardened discipline-fanatic would require some hugs from mommy; the oversensitive and dissociated airhead would require some attention from daddy.

The love-seeking types tend to externalize their problems. When they have a personal issue they project it out into the world demanding "change" in others. They seek to blame and continually feel "inconvenienced" and "offended" by all sorts of external cues. If the father was either too strict/hard or not home most of the time, they might develop an aversion toward discipline as well as toward successful people.

The freedom-seeking types tend to internalize their problems. When they have a personal issue, they blame themselves, are shy of seeking external support, and also don't care to support others. They are preoccupied with separating themselves from the external world and community. The projected hurt of not having been nurtured by a mother figure (who may have not been home, not breastfed, or otherwise put the child to shame) can lead to lack of compassion, exaggerated individualism ("I can stand on my own feet, damn it!"), and an aversion toward unsuccessful or supposedly "lazy" people.

There are many ways to transcend these projections. You can do so by embracing both mommy and daddy wholeheartedly, as well as feeling the embrace returned. You can also do so by making good with them in real life. Above all, you can recognize the various polarities in life and transcend them. It is fine to be an individualist and yet part of a greater whole.

It is fine to be freedom loving, and yet also enjoy closeness and be togetherness loving. It is great to get approval, but to also *give* approval. It is quite educative to be poor, and also quite fun to be rich. The imbalance in your energy-field arises through one-sided outlooks. Becoming a whole, integrated (and thus magnetic and powerful) human being then means embracing the mommy-side, embracing the daddy-side, then moving beyond that to your true higher self.

The Illusion of Fame, Glamour, and Fortune

Fame, Glamour, and Fortune are overrated. Look at famous people in the 50s, 60s, 70s, 80s, and 90s. How many of them are still famous? How many of them are left? How many of them are happy? You wouldn't even recognize 90% of the "famous" people I showed you from the 70s, much less know their names. I recommend replacing the goal of "fame" with the goal of "spiritual enlightenment". That way you'll have something that lasts forever and never wears off.

And if you do have a higher state of energy and awareness, some material success and/or fame will naturally follow – not because it was your goal, but as a side-effect of the *energy you are*.

There is an old wisdom saying that goes like this: *"A camel went to seek horns, and its ears were cut off."* That is to say that if you try to be someone other than who you naturally are, suffering follows. But if you give yourself and your life to the truth of who you are, your most natural path follows.

People seek fame because of the positive emotions they associate with it, as opposed to their supposedly inferior now-state. If I gave you a bag with a Million Dollars, that might trigger some excitement. But that temporary "high" would only arise because of what you think the money *means*.

The truth is that you could summon that high-feeling regardless of the bag or its contents. You are able to come alive before someone promises fame and fortune. A reality-creator is someone who *comes-from-aliveness* and needs less external props to feel it. If you were given fame and fortune, how long would the good feeling last?

I assure you it wouldn't last too long because you see the cause of the high outside of you. What if fame and fortune were taken away from you again? Would your feeling go down? Have a week or two pass, and you'll become habituated to being a Millionaire. There is a finite amount to any reality. Anything that is not the Ultimate is finite. No matter how good or bad things are, that too will pass. Find that which is not temporary, but eternal, and you will be free from the Illusion.

Students of the Reality Creation Course have identified the exercise where I read from a random news-article in different levels of energy as one of their favorite because it directly demonstrates the idea that you can create ecstasy out of nothing. And as you increase your vibration, the mirror of life begins to reflect that. Fame and Fortune are merely a side-effect of high energy. Fame is not the main goal and purpose of any sane human being. If fame is the main goal, you will be disappointed because you will notice that you have been following the programs of the ultra-narcissistic world-self instead of learning of the goals of your higher self.

All desires are the desire for high energy. Once you identify the *real* desire you may not yet have achieved it, but you are one step smarter than before because you are no longer chasing shadows. What you really want is not fame or fortune, but energy. And energy is created by love. The side-effects of love are prosperity, health, and maybe even some fame. But those things are only the skimmed cream, not the inner milk.

Once you have examined the underlying motivations of wanting fame and fortune, you are ready to let go of them and then follow something you truly enjoy. Do you enjoy singing? Then sing, not to become famous, but because you love it. Do you like painting? Then paint. Do you like writing? Then write. If you do so with sufficient joy and energy, your work will become widely known – not because you wanted to be discovered, but because people like to gather around the warm fire of enthusiasm. Quit waiting to be discovered and start doing what is energetic and fun and what requires skill, passion, and persistence.

As WHO Are You Experiencing the World?

People ask me: "Is it a good book?" or "Is it a good movie?" or "Is it a good country?" The truthful answer is: "It depends on who is asking!" As WHO are you reading the book? A gardener notices gardens. A man desperate for Sex notices women he can't get everywhere he goes. A woman whose cat has died notices cats everywhere. A basketball player will more likely notice sports parks than the woman with the dead cat.

From which IDENTITY or viewpoint you view the world determines what you see and experience. The manifestation of your wildest dreams could be right in front of your nose and you would not notice it if you are not accepting of it. If the house burns down it might leave one person scarred for life and another person liberated to find a better house. The event itself is meaningless. Your **reaction** to the event is what creates reality. I keep repeating this concept throughout my Blog because almost every request for assistance I get from people conveniently glosses over this little detail.

Once you occupy a viewpoint you start looking for evidence to confirm it. And you will find that evidence. If you want to know what you really believe, deep within, look at what evidence you are finding in life. For example, I believe I am in a very happy relationship, and I find evidence for it every day.

Here's an exercise to commit this idea to memory:

1. Look at something you are experiencing, seeing, or feeling.

2. Ask: Which **version of me** is experiencing this?

3. Ask: How would a higher version of me experience this?

Life is 10% about events and 90% about your reaction to them.

The remainder of this section addresses the advanced concept of "Play-Acting as a Self-Improvement Method".

Play Acting as a Self-Improvement Method

Here's a fun and playful method of self-improvement. Begin by choosing some real life person you very much admire who you would enjoy modeling (imitating). Small children learn new skills by imitation, and there is no reason you shouldn't make use of this skill. Imitation requires empathy and imagination. Empathy to put your awareness into the other person, and imagination to think about what that person thinks, speaks, acts, and feels like.

The aim now is to model yourself after that person. First consider outside appearances: What does s/he dress like? Do you have similar clothes? Might you get some? What is his/her hairstyle? How does s/he walk? Could you copy and practice his/her stride? How does s/he use his/her eyes? What makes his/her facial expressions different from others? Could you practice new mimics and gestures in front of the mirror? What vocabulary does s/he like to use?

To make this method work you will have to study some videos of him/her more attentively.

S/he is then no longer a mere face for entertainment but an energy-field to be scrutinized and learned. If you use this, then assign some daily practice time, for instance 15 minutes, for being this person. That means you actually go ahead and schedule "being _____" (name of the person) into your time-planner or calendar.

A new role needs to be rehearsed many times. Once you have rehearsed some, go a little deeper. What culture and family was this person brought up in? Are his/her mannerisms of a certain country, creed, or culture you could adopt? What are the beliefs and statements of this person? Could you adopt some of those beliefs, just for fun, just to test-drive them? Remain playful throughout all of this. You are not "trying to be someone you are not", you are play-acting a new identity. As you do so, remarkable things will happen. One of those remarkable things is that your thought-processes, your presence, and emotions will change. Your appearance will change.

Going even deeper, ask yourself how this person would react to various situations you encounter in daily life.

Be assured that s/he would react differently than you react. If you want to take this to a higher level, write down some of the typical situations you encounter in life. Besides that, write down how you normally react and beside that write down how s/he would react. And then practice reacting how you imagine s/he would.

Finally, realize that this is you. The soul can take on many different identities. You don't have to be stuck with the same ideas, viewpoints, the same job, the same goals, the some concerns, the same attitudes, and the same problems all your life. Go ahead and adopt the traits of this person you like and discard the ones you don't like. (To more deeply get into the role, initially you should also take over some of this person's negative sides, but in time you can drop those.) Take your own best qualities and mix them with the new ones you have practiced. Realize that all of your practice actually had nothing at all to do with that person. It was all in your imagination and how you imagined that person to be. You created it all in your mind. With your mind you created an entirely new reality.

If you enjoyed this you can continue to experiment and switch roles. And as you do so, you become increasingly aware of who you really are. You are none of those roles! There is something more essential that is always there no matter which role you adopt. But you would not have found out if you hadn't become just a little crazy and experimented. The real you is that which is always there, behind all the roles.

I enjoy visiting places I used to live a long time ago because they reflect who I really am. How so? Well, when visiting those places I can feel, sense, and remember what has changed and what has not changed. The stuff that changed wasn't really me. The stuff that is still the same as back then is more essentially me, more basic, more real.

What life comes down to is this: If you want to be more successful you can identify with the role of being a success. There are various mannerisms, behaviors, words, and attitudes that go along with it. I have studied successful people all my life, which is why

I am quite aware of what those things are. When you find yourself in a difficult situation, ask yourself "How would _____ (fill in name of successful person) handle this?" Your imagination – which is one of the most powerful tools you have – will give you much better answers than if you ask: "Why do bad things happen to me?" Exploring the mystery of identity and its relation to reality is fun. Feel free to explore it.

3
Realms of Bliss and Ecstasy

The Lighthouse in Search of Light

*Once upon a time there was a Lighthouse in search of Light. With his ray of light he swept over the lands and waters looking for light, not noticing that what he was searching with **is** light. His beam fell on various objects. Some of the objects reflected the light and the Lighthouse exclaimed, "Ah! I found it! That is the Light!", still without noticing that he himself was providing the light. After a while the Lighthouse realized that the light of the physical objects was not permanently there, that he had not yet found the ultimate source of Light. And so he continued his restless search. Then, one day, he discovered another Lighthouse. And the other Lighthouse discovered him.*

And then he was bathed in the Light of the other tower. "That is IT!" he exclaimed. "I have never seen that much light!" And he fell in love with the other Lighthouse. But because he still did not notice that he himself was a source of Light, he became dependent on the other Lighthouse, dependent on its Light. And every time the other Lighthouse put its light elsewhere, he missed the warmth and comfort of its Light and felt cold and lonely. One day a wise old sage visited the Lighthouse and told him that he already is what he is looking for. That the tool with which he is searching is what he is searching. "God cannot be understood because God is what understands," and "The eye cannot see itself, because it is that which sees," the sage said. Then the Lighthouse noticed its own radiant light. And he learned the ability to consciously direct his light and warm others and himself with it. He learned to change the intensity of the radiance according to the situation. And the Lighthouse became enlightened. Or more precisely: He finally noticed what he had already been all along.

Note: Replace the word "Light" with Attention/Energy and the word "Lighthouse" with **you** and re-read the story.

Experience Ecstasy out of Nothing

In one of my last email-coachings I asked a student to choose a boring or normal part of town and go sit there. His task was to sit there without phone, book, or object. How long? Until he felt ecstatic. "No matter how long it takes, stay there until you feel fantastic," I told him. The only breaks he was allowed to take were for the restroom and food.

The reason he was given this task was because he had lost the childlike ability to feel awesome independent of circumstances, surroundings, and substances. The further away you move from the soul, the more "stuff" you need to feel anything.
This exercise might go a number of ways. In the first hour you might feel OK with it, relieved to finally cut yourself lose from the bombardment of TV, Internet, Coffee, and Voices telling you how it is and how it is not. The second hour might bring up some agitation because deeper, suppressed emotions arise. But as you allow these to come up and keep sitting, they will dissipate and take you to a higher level of energy. In the third hour you will begin noticing things about your surroundings you may not have clearly noticed in years…such as how beautiful the trees are.

It does not matter whether this exercise takes 3 hours or 30 hours. The aim is to feel ecstasy out of nothing and with no help from anything.

If you can feel Ecstasy no matter what is happening around you and especially when nothing is happening, you have regained your soul and transcended the constant need for input and events outside of the here-now. You will then bring elation into your life instead of expecting to get elation out of your life.

Consciousness and the Good Life

A body cannot experience itself. Only consciousness can experience things. A mind cannot experience itself. Only consciousness can. The aspect of you that is witnessing and aware of the body and the mind is Consciousness. Without consciousness, the body and mind amount to nothing. Your left arm, for instance, does not have the capacity to observe and experience itself. There is something else that is experiencing the arm and that is Consciousness. Mind and body are tools of Consciousness to experience physical reality.

Consciousness is the part of you that is unimpressed, undisturbed, and unimprinted by life.

Someone could indoctrinate you and manipulate your actions by imprinting various desires and resistances onto your mind, but throughout it all, consciousness remains innocent. We enjoy the company of children so much because they're unmanipulated and therefore, unmanipulative consciousness shines brightly and innocently. The essential aspect of you can never be indoctrinated because it simply observes. The mind desires and resists and can easily be programmed by anyone.

Consciousness is the context in which mind and body happen. Consciousness is larger than mind and body; is aware of mind and body. Because it is closer to the real you it is worthwhile to study consciousness itself more than studying mind and body. Consciousness holds no opinions at all. It is the mind that holds opinions. Your opinions and whether you agree or disagree with something are of secondary importance to actual experience. If you state your opinions toward another human being, his/her mind will usually react and state his/her opinions which either agree or disagree. One of the narcissistic mind/ego's motives is to have superior opinions to that of another mind/ego. When you state your opinions toward Consciousness itself, there is no reaction, only observation.

Here is an experiment: Go outside and state all of your lamentations, complaints, desires, and opinions toward a tree or toward the stars of the night sky. What is their reaction? Nothing. Opinions and points-of-view may be important to the world-mind and life on earth, but they aren't essential to consciousness. Consciousness observes and experiences, but it does not have to retain a file cabinet where these experiences are recorded for later use as an opinion. That means it is able to view things as if it is viewing them for the very first time, with no judgment whatsoever. It "just knows" what something is and what its energy-level and purpose are by pure perception, without the need for drawing upon pains and survival-needs to form a view of reality.

If you closely observe your mind, especially in social situations, you can see its narcissistic behavior: It asks itself if it's looking good. It asks if it can come up with a better joke than someone just told. When the group is putting someone down who is not present, it joins in to put that person down even more. However, when it gets criticized it becomes reactive and defensive. Putting others down comes easily, having itself be put down is strongly resisted. Merely noting what the mind is doing tends to lessen its influence so more of the witnessing and opening aspect of yourself can shine forth.

Sometimes I sit in a social situation and simply label what it is doing: "Now it's trying to show off." "Now it wants to impress that person," "Now it wants attention," "Now it's getting bored and wanting to leave," "Now it feels hurt because its self-importance was questioned." This type of meditation gradually reveals part of the mind's neurotic state. But rather than becoming judgmental of the mind and seeing the ego as an "enemy" (which is the mind judging itself), amusement ensues. Releasing exaggerated thinking-ness and approval-seeking elevates your state to a more humorous and loving mood and more spontaneous self-expression.

Is there an even bigger context than Consciousness itself, one that is aware of Consciousness? I believe there is. There is a larger context which is experiencing consciousness. It is a sort of hyper-consciousness within which consciousness is. Some people call it God. Other names have been:

Source

Creator

The Infinite

The Ultimate

Essence

The Absolute

The Omniscient

The Omnipresent

The Omnipotent

The Primary Force

Allah

El

Ain Soph

The Uncaused Cause

The One

The Original Light

The Unspeakable

Brahma

The Beginningless And Endless

Elyon

The Most High

Om

Presence

I Am That I Am

The Timeless Being

Bhagavan

Father

Lord

Cosmic Controller

and countless others. Whatever you call it, it is the only real cause, its presence permeates everything, and it is both my experience and my teaching that to lead "the good life" all you require is awareness of this super context. Put in more simple terms, things such as Awareness, Meditation, Intention, and Prayer are quite sufficient to be, do and have all that is good for you in life.

Any type of overwhelm, confusion, fear, doubt, and worry is of the mind, not of Consciousness. It can all be released by sitting back and resting into the observer-mode, resting back into the part of yourself that is unaffected by the ever-changing winds of mind and life. You can submit all desires and resistances to the cleansing power of this super source.

An uneducated mind can easily be manipulated into hate and fear. Mis-emotion is the result of manipulation, of having been manipulated into a distorted view of overall reality. When feeling mis-emotion, it means you have either manipulated yourself or have been manipulated into certain beliefs, plans, and actions that are not aligned with Source. Because you have free-will, you have the capacity to choose between that which is life-nurturing and that which isn't. You choose many times a day, thereby creating your reality piece by piece. The mind, being like a naive sponge that can be programmed with anything, is easy to manipulate.

All I'd have to do is drag up a few statistics that show all the wrongdoings of a particular group or person, then link it to your own life being less worthwhile because of that group or person. With that trick I could get some people to hate. But the more consciousness (and thereby spiritual energy) that permeates the body/mind, the more one's intelligence goes up and the less easy it is to manipulate you. In fact, most contemporary TV-and-Internet advertisements do not work above a certain level of consciousness. Above that level advertisements have no effect at all because consciousness itself has neither desire nor resistance; the TV-ads mean nothing to it. An ad might imply that owning a certain shower-gel or car means you will be sexy and attractive. But while you view that ad from the observer mode, from consciousness instead of from mind, it will have no effect on you because you have no desire to be attractive (you already are), and you easily see that having the car or shower-gel has nothing at all to do with how attractive you are.

You want the good life in every way and every day? Then simply always refer to the most high context, the most high source in everything you do. Submit your entire life to that which is the most high. In every case of doubt or concern, I habitually look first and foremost to the all-pervasive source and presence to guide me, to send support, ideas, and resources, without exception. When you have had a fight with someone, to whom do you first look? Source. When you have had an accident, to whom do you look first? Source. When you seek inspiration, to whom do you look first? Source. When beginning an important job, to whom do you look first? Source. And there is only one source. And this one Source provides for everything. If you are looking for a job it's OK to place reliance on the classified ads in the paper. It's OK to place reliance on the advice of friends. It's OK to place reliance on a job interview. It's OK to place reliance on what you see and hear. But if you truly prefer The Good Life, always put your primary reliance on the Creator-of-all-things, secondarily on Consciousness, and only as a third option, on your mind and that of others.

Do You Realize Just How Good/Bad You're Doing?

Do you realize just how good/bad you are doing? Compared to the lowest ebbs of anguish, you are doing great. Compared to the highest realms of Enlightenment, you are doing terrible. So what is better – to compare yourself to the highest states and say, "I am doing terrible," or to compare yourself to the lowest states and say, "I am doing great!"? I think it is an interesting philosophical but also practical question to ponder. I use both, depending on the situation, context, and mood. When I see arrogance in someone I can remind him/her of his/her mediocrity compared to the higher. When I see someone drowning in self-pity, I can remind him/her of his/her greatness as a human and his/her relative well-being compared to the lower. And that is how understanding the levels of energy is so useful. You quit looking for "the right method" and see that it depends on where you are. It's easy to see how you are really doing terrible.

You are in many respects just another idiot, one of many, a face in the crowd. You have hardly anything to show, and before you know it, will return to the dust in the ground. And if you are a certain type of person or of a certain mood, this way of seeing things will push and motivate you to move upward. Some people really do have to put themselves down; to belittle themselves, in order to self-deprecate to achieve anything. It's easy to see how you are really doing great. You are in many respects valuable and worthy, a unique and beautiful human being. You have your own unique contribution to the world, and you are an ever expanding soul. And if you are a certain type of person or of a certain mood, this way of seeing things will push and motivate you to move upward. Some people really do have to put themselves up, to love and appreciate themselves to achieve anything. Do you realize just how good/bad you are doing?

Lojong Mind Training

One of my favorite ancient practices is "Lojong" which, in Tibetan Buddhism translates as "Mind Training". Lojong Practice consists of "59 Slogans" which are organized into "7 points". Most of the 59 slogans don't even require explanation or interpretation to a modern context...they are immediately grasped, even though they were written down a thousand years ago and based on much older writings. I am not a practitioner or follower of Lojong as in a formal discipline or religion (I am a practitioner of the 2-minute-enlightenment-technique). But I do think it's valuable to at least have read or be aware of some of its slogans because each one – in and of itself – can raise one's level of consciousness. I find it remarkable how I – through Meditation Practice – have arrived at many of the same conclusions as the authors of this text. The following translation is taken from here. If there are slogans you don't understand, please refer to the text source.

Point One: The preliminaries, which are the basis for dharma practice.

Slogan 1: First, train in the preliminaries; The four reminders, or alternatively called the Four Thoughts.
1. Maintain an awareness of the preciousness of human life.
2. Be aware of the reality that life ends; death comes for everyone; Impermanence.
3. Recall that whatever you do, whether virtuous or not, has a result; Karma.
4. Contemplate that as long as you are too focused on self-importance and too caught up in thinking about how you are good or bad, you will experience suffering. Obsessing about getting what you want and avoiding what you don't want does not result in happiness; Ego.

Point Two: The main practice, which is training in bodhicitta. Absolute Bodhicitta.

Slogan 2: Regard all dharmas as dreams; although experiences may seem solid, they are passing memories.

Slogan 3: Examine the nature of unborn awareness.

Slogan 4: Self-liberate even the antidote.

Slogan 5: Rest in the nature of alaya; the essence; the present moment.

Slogan 6: In postmeditation, be a child of illusion; relative Bodhicitta

Slogan 7: Sending and taking should be practiced alternately. These two should ride the breath (aka. practice Tonglen).

Slogan 8: Three objects, three poisons, three roots of virtue - The 3 objects are: friends, enemies, and neutrals. The 3 poisons are: craving, aversion, and indifference.
The 3 roots of virtue are the remedies.

Slogan 9: In all activities, train with slogans.

Slogan 10: Begin the sequence of sending and taking with yourself.

Point Three: Transformation of Bad Circumstances into the Way of Enlightenment

Slogan 11: When the world is filled with evil, transform all mishaps into the path of bodhi.

Slogan 12: Drive all blames into one.

Slogan 13: Be grateful to everyone.

Slogan 14: Seeing confusion as the four kayas is unsurpassable shunyata protection. The kayas are: Dharmakaya, sambhogakaya, nirmanakaya, and svabhavikakaya. Thoughts have no birthplace, thoughts are unceasing, thoughts are not solid, and these three characteristics are interconnected. Shunyata can be described as "complete openness."

Slogan 15: Four practices are the best of methods. The four practices are: accumulating merit, laying down evil deeds, offering to the dons, and offering to the dharmapalas.

Slogan 16: Whatever you meet unexpectedly, join with meditation.

Point Four: Showing the Utilization of Practice in One's Whole Life.

Slogan 17: Practice the five strengths, the condensed heart instructions.

The 5 strengths are: strong determination, familiarization, the positive seed, reproach, and aspiration.

Slogan 18: The mahayana instruction for ejection of consciousness at death is the five strengths: how you conduct yourself is important. When you are dying practice the 5 strengths.

Point Five: Evaluation of Mind Training

Slogan 19: All dharma agrees at one point — All Buddhist teachings are about lessening the ego; lessening one's self-absorption.

Slogan 20: Of the two witnesses, hold the principal one — You know yourself better than anyone else knows you.

Slogan 21: Always maintain only a joyful mind.

Slogan 22: If you can practice even when distracted, you are well trained.

Point Six: Disciplines of Mind Training

Slogan 23: Always abide by the three basic principles — Dedication to your practice, refraining from outrageous conduct, and developing patience.

Slogan 24: Change your attitude, but remain natural. – Reduce ego clinging, but be yourself.

Slogan 25: Don't talk about injured limbs — Don't take pleasure contemplating others' defects.

Slogan 26: Don't ponder others — Don't take pleasure contemplating others weaknesses.

Slogan 27: Work with the greatest defilements first — Work with your greatest obstacles first.

Slogan 28: Abandon any hope of fruition — Don't get caught up in how you will be in the future, stay in the present moment.

Slogan 29: Abandon poisonous food.

Slogan 30: Don't be so predictable — Don't hold grudges.

Slogan 31: Don't malign others.

Slogan 32: Don't wait in ambush — Don't wait for others weaknesses to show to attack them.

Slogan 33: Don't bring things to a painful point — Don't humiliate others.

Slogan 34: Don't transfer the ox's load to the cow — Take responsibility for yourself.

Slogan 35: Don't try to be the fastest — Don't compete with others.

Slogan 36: Don't act with a twist — Do good deeds without scheming about benefiting yourself.

Slogan 37: Don't turn gods into demons — Don't use these slogans or your spirituality to increase your self-absorption.

Slogan 38: Don't seek others' pain as the limbs of your own happiness.

Point Seven: Guidelines of Mind Training

Slogan 39: All activities should be done with one intention.

Slogan 40: Correct all wrongs with one intention.

Slogan 41: Two activities: one at the beginning, one at the end.

Slogan 42: Whichever of the two occurs, be patient.

Slogan 43: Observe these two, even at the risk of your life.

Slogan 44: Train in the three difficulties.

Slogan 45: Take on the three principal causes: the teacher, the dharma, and the sangha.

Slogan 46: Pay heed that the three never wane: gratitude toward one's teacher, appreciation of the dharma (teachings), and correct conduct.

Slogan 47: Keep the three inseparable: body, speech, and mind.

Slogan 48: Train without bias in all areas. It is crucial always to do this pervasively and wholeheartedly.

Slogan 49: Always meditate on whatever provokes

resentment.

Slogan 50: Don't be swayed by external circumstances.

Slogan 51: This time, practice the main points: others before self, dharma, and awakening compassion.

Slogan 52: Don't misinterpret. The six things that may be misinterpreted are patience, yearning, excitement, compassion, priorities, and joy. You're patient when you're getting your way, but not when it's difficult. You yearn for worldly things, instead of an open heart and mind. You get excited about wealth and entertainment, instead of your potential for enlightenment. You have compassion for those you like, but none for those you don't. Worldly gain is your priority rather than cultivating loving-kindness and compassion. You feel joy when you enemies suffer, and do not rejoice in others' good fortune. [10]

Slogan 53: Don't vacillate (in your practice of LoJong).

Slogan 54: Train wholeheartedly.

Slogan 55: Liberate yourself by examining and analyzing: Know your own mind with honesty and fearlessness.

Slogan 56: Don't wallow in self-pity.

Slogan 57: Don't be jealous.

Slogan 58: Don't be frivolous.

Slogan 59: Don't expect applause.

4
Enlightened Consciousness

"Life, like sex, needn't be understood or made sense of. Simply enjoy it and its meaning will reveal itself."

– Fred Dodson in "The Infinity Course"

*Ask yourself: Do you want to gather "Information" and "Knowledge," or do you want to **feel alive**? When you are into **Thinking** too much, know that you are running away from **Feeling**. Release Thinking and Info-Gathering and return to Feeling. In that way, you return to having more Energy.*

– Fred Dodson in "Levels of Energy"

Unlimited Being

Imagine a tiny dot on a white piece of paper. That tiny dot is what most people have narrowed their attention to and have identified with when thinking they are their body/mind. The rest of the piece of paper and beyond in all directions and dimensions is the vast expanse of all-that-is. Therefore, being more open in awareness rather than narrow and pinpointed, goes more in the direction of Unlimited Being and Cosmic Consciousness. Opening in this way, so that you are not only involved with the tiny dot, but at least the rest of the area surrounding it, allows you to more easily experience new realities.

Creating new realities would mean to create a new tiny dot. That is easier from a perspective outside the original dot. Otherwise, you'd only be creating over the already existing dot…which would look messy. So let's experience some of this Unlimited Being and not only read about it. As you sit there, relax. Let go of any tension on the outbreath. And as you sit there and read this, notice what you are aware of.

You are aware of these words, but become aware of a little more: the sounds in your surroundings, what the chair you are sitting on feels like... Become aware of your body, aware of your breathing, and aware of the objects near you. You have now opened your awareness a little and expanded it from that tiny dot to something slightly bigger.

You are not that which you are aware of. Anything you can *observe* you cannot at the same time *be.* You are not the cup, table, or the computer. As the observer, you are separate from them. Likewise, you are not your body and mind. Don't take my word for it, check for yourself.

Are you aware of your body as it is sitting there? Are you aware of what you call "mind"; that stream of thoughts coming and going? Who is the one that's aware? You are identified with the body, obviously, and your awareness likes "hanging around" in or near the body and mind, but you are not that. Try pointing to where "me" resides. And if you now point to a part of your body, who is doing the pointing? The hand? Are you your hand? Not hardly. Your brain? Are you that piece of meat called brain? I doubt it. You are not a body or mind.

If you are having a difficult time experiencing this right now, then could you at least acknowledge that your awareness is not limited to the body/mind?

Feel the Body. Now expand your attention to all the empty space surrounding your body. And expand your attention to some tree or object outside of the building you are in. You are experiencing that awareness/attention is not limited to the body. Otherwise all you could perceive is the body.

It is as simple as that. Many, when I speak of Unlimited Being and of experiencing that think they are going to skyrocket to a state of enlightenment. But experiencing Unlimited Being is more natural, more relaxed, more normal, and also more attainable than that. You just did it. And rather than going for this thing they call "spiritual enlightenment," I'd recommend you relax into what you already are and gradually deepen this small bit of relaxation you felt.

You already are an Infinite Being; Unlimited Awareness; All-that-is. Actually there is nothing to achieve, nowhere to go, nothing to do, no program to go through, and nothing to solve. Beingness Just Is. The trees just are. Your body and breathing just are. None of it requires your maintenance. None of it requires your extra effort. None of it requires your achievement. None of it needs to be deserved. Feel that Beingness for a moment that is already whole and perfect, in the here, in the now.

If you could just sit still and aware and be present a few minutes a day, you'd open a bit and rejuvenate because of that. What keeps you narrowly focused on that small dot is resistance toward what-is. And the only time we're willing to let go of all resistance and "Just Be", is during sleep.

During sleep we allow ourselves to relax back into that vast expanse which we are. And because of that we regenerate during sleep. So if you could do this for a few minutes while waking, you would not need that much sleep and you'd also feel more refreshed throughout the day. *What-is* here and now requires no effort. So sit some minutes a day and just *Be*. Be that which is aware. Be that which is effortless and natural. And when you've accepted the state of being that has no resistances, no desires, no needs, no urgencies, no obligations…then, if you still care, focus on the realities you prefer or do the jobs and activities you prefer. It will be much easier from that state of rest.

Becoming Lighter and Lighter

Generally, the Ego resists everything and the soul embraces, everything. The negative that is resisted grows and the positive that is resisted disappears. The negative that is embraced disappears, the positive that is embraced, grows. This powerful lesson is easy to understand, but applying it in daily life is a lifelong exercise. And as you invest conscious effort into practicing this you become lighter and lighter, less and less dense. So just remember one thing: The Ego is always "away from" and the Soul is always "towards". The Ego is always "No"; the Soul is always "Yes". For the Ego it's always too hot or too cold. When in a Relationship, the Ego wants to break free, when free, the Ego wants back into a Relationship. It is never happy.

The Soul on the other hand, enjoys both. It embraces all. What happens when you embrace all is that you become more like the soul…light and tranquil. Negative energy more quickly moves out of your energy-field because you are not keeping it there with your resistance. You can begin saying "Yes" to life….including taking out the trash. That can be an enjoyable thing to do. You can embrace taking out the trash. And what happens? While you were taking out the trash, you were not projecting resentful energy into the Universe, but tranquility. The Universe never sleeps. It registers everything you signal out. All of your emotions are vibratory signals bringing back to you what you put out. The Universe cannot discern whether you are taking out the trash or making love. It will simply respond to whatever energy you put out. Your life, as you experience it today, is the sum total of all the vibratory frequencies you have put out.

Evaporate the Ego-Self

The mind or so-called "Ego-Self" is a recording machine. Its job is to record the experiences of life and play them back. The mind does its job perfectly, but it is not who you are. You are much more than that recording machine. Once you realize this, you gain peace of mind and are no longer terrorized by believing in all of the negativity the mind has recorded throughout life. You then no longer view things from the viewpoint of having recorded them thousands of times, but fresh, with new eyes, as if seeing them for the first time

This Meditation Process will evaporate more of the Ego-Self that makes your life feel restricted, narrow, and repetitive, and it will open your Awareness for more fluidity, surprise, and ease. Awareness, which is Infinite, limits itself through various "I am _____" statements. Write down all the "I am _____" statements that come to mind.

Examples:

"I am human."
"I am a soul."
"I am a man/woman."
"I am an employer/employee."
"I am a son/daughter."
"I am successful."

"I am a failure."
"I am overweight."
"I am athletic."
"I am good looking."
"I am boring."
"I am interesting."
"I am rich."
"I am old."

There is nothing wrong with all of these identities, except that most people have forgotten that they are deliberate creations of the soul, roles we play for a certain time, and not who we really are. With the support of this process you will loosen the rigidity of these various identities and viewpoints from which you create reality. You will still be able to be a soul, a human, an individual, a father, a daughter, or whatever you are, but it will not be the only thing you define yourself as. You will also begin to feel a more expanded self – a cosmic self, an infinite field – beyond all the "I ams". Once you have created your list of "I ams", state their opposite. Since everything can only be experienced in duality/contrast, when you state one thing you also state its opposite, whether you are consciously aware of it or not. Where your mind creates "hot" it also creates the concept of "cold", since no such thing as "hot" could exist without "cold". Your list items would then, for example, look like this:

"I am an employee/I am unemployed."
"I am rich/I am poor."
"I am boring/I am interesting."
"I am smart/I am stupid."

The other side of the coin is either pushed down into the subconscious or projected onto other people. The projection then sounds something like this: "I am smart, they are stupid." "He is interesting. I am boring." "I am richer than him." "I am poorer than him." Whether the other side of an identity is pushed into the subconscious, projected onto others, or consciously assumed does not matter for the case of this process. What matters is to know that an "other" side does exist. *Every topic is actually two topics.* You have truly mastered and transcended a topic when you are OK with both sides.

Therefore, take your list and meditate on the first item as follows:

1. Feel or Imagine being side a. Release Resistance and Embrace.

2. Feel or Imagine being side b. Release Resistance and Embrace.

3. Go back and forth between a and b several times, until you are entirely OK with both sides. Finally, rest beyond the two sides as who you really are...pure, unlimited Awareness. If you wish, whisper, "I am" at the end of each round.

Apply this three-step procedure for each item on your list. If you have difficulty performing this Meditation by yourself, use the *Bliss Course* instead.

It's All Happening Right Now

Humans are peculiar Beings. If I say to someone, "We are going on a trip today, I want to show you something really, really special," s/he will be happy and excited the whole trip. If then we arrive at the Destination and there is supposedly "nothing really special" there, the average person will usually get a change of mood and not be happy and excited. The person decided to be excited because s/he *thought* something exciting was going on. This proves that a state of excitement and happiness is mostly subjective and does not have much to do with what is going on around you. It also shows how life is more about the journey than the destination. It is good to have a goal, but all the "real stuff" happens between now and the goal. Life is about the experiences you make between here and the destination. Your happiness lies not at your destination, but it is all happening right now.

There is a pretty advanced spiritual state that anyone can achieve within a few minutes. In this state one sees the world not through the mind but through the soul. When the mind looks at the here and now, it thinks, "There is nothing special going on right now, same old, same old." And for the mind it really is the "same old thing" because the mind has recorded what it sees thousands of times. It has seen the Moon thousands of times and thinks, "Well, that's nothing special. It's just the moon. I've already seen the moon."

The soul sees things differently. It can sit there and observe the current surroundings with awe, amazement, gratitude, astonishment, wonderment, and reverence – no matter what those surroundings are. Why? Because the soul sees without filters. It sees Infinity within every moment. Every moment and current situation has great depth and height. If you look around you right now, right there, where you are, and you sit and observe long enough, you will begin to realize that there is more going on than meets the eye. There is never "nothing going on". The mind-self is bored. That's why it retreats into its mind world and makes up problems all the time. But the soul is never bored. ANY reality is worthwhile for the soul. It pays off to just stop a few times during the day. Just stop everything you are doing and look around you. Return to the here and now and try to sense the Infinite within the Moment. See if you can sense the unfathomable beauty of the supposedly "mundane" objects and events around you. Artists and Photographers have an easier time "seeing things" in the "mundane". If you keep trying to get somewhere other than here and sometime other than now, you are missing the best parts of the overall journey. This is why all spiritual teachers worth their salt remind of the now-moment. What they are really talking about is the way the soul perceives things. Because the soul exists outside of time, there is no past and future, and everything can be accessed in this moment. This very moment contains doorways to Infinity. This is only mysterious to you if you have spent the greater part of your life in the recording-device called "the mind" instead of in reality.

The Beauty of Life

"Don't look for God," the Master said. "Just look – and all will be revealed."

"But how is one to look?"

"Each time you look at anything, see only what is there and nothing else".

The disciples were bewildered, so the Master made it simpler: "For instance: When you look at the moon, see the moon and nothing else."

"What else could one see except the moon when one looks at the moon?"

"A hungry person could see a ball of cheese. A lover, the face of his beloved."

Sometimes the incredible beauty of life is revealed even to the preoccupied eye. You might be walking down a snow-covered street at night when the beauty of the snowflakes reflecting in the streetlights on the background canvas of a black sky suddenly strikes you, and you stand in silent amazement. And for that moment in time, your mind is temporarily shut down and a new type of aliveness and energy fill your body.

This state of being does not have to be a rare one-time-thing. I teach higher planes of consciousness precisely with these types of experiences in mind. Below a certain gradient of energy, you are preoccupied to a point that you're not even aware that you exist. You are not "feeling yourself". Then, one level higher, in mid-range energy, you are not aware that anything other than you exists. At this gradient, the world is not actually really seen, but rather "perceived" in a conceptualized way. That is why so many of the spiritual sages of all ages refer to really "seeing" the world. In a "normal" state everything is filtered through thought and opinion. If you record an audio or video over and over, it becomes somewhat "lossy". Likewise, if you filter reality through too much thought, it also becomes "lossy", and loses some of its vivid brightness. Below a certain degree of consciousness everything is filtered through memory. Below a certain crucial level, you remember mostly bad things, and in those rare instances you remember good things, you remember them with a sense of lack and longing. One degree higher, in mid-range consciousness, there is a mix of good memories and bad memories but all is still filtered through all sorts of mentations. And then, another degree higher still, there is no thought or memory at all, only 360-degree total awareness. At this level everything looks beautiful.

"Is there anything I can do to make myself Enlightened?"

"As little as you can do to make the sun rise in the morning."

"Then of what use are the spiritual exercises you prescribe?"

"To make sure you are not asleep when the sun begins to rise."

So here is an exercise: Go take a walk. Look at something. As you look at it, reduce your expectations and impatience and become somewhat meditative. Look at it still and remove any label, opinion, or memory you have about the thing you are looking at. Don't "perceive" but "receive" whatever is there, as it is. With no opinion, memory, concept, belief, or idea about the object whatsoever: no idea what it means, no idea where it is "from", its actual nature, the truth of it will reveal itself. Continue your walk in this way, moving from object to object or space to space, gradually releasing your projections and expectations, releasing your habitual narrow focus and incessant thinking. After this walk you will notice that the world really does look brighter, more intimate, and more real. You see that the beauty of life is actually innate, not something conceptual you have to impose upon it.

(Quoted text from "One Minute Wisdom", Anthony De Mello)

The Ineffable Zone

This is a sublime meditation-technique to enter the ineffable-zone. You stand or sit in some public or private place and imagine you don't exist. The whole scenario with its objects and perhaps people is there, but you are not. Take note of what is there; take note of movements, colors, shapes, and sounds.

As you continue to do this there are numerous things you realize. Foremost is that the scene gets kind of a fluid or movie-like quality. Secondly that awareness is not limited to an "I"-viewpoint but rather omnipresent. Another thing you will notice is a new kind of felicity, as if a burden has been released from your shoulders. Where there is no more "I" there is no more body and no more mind, and that can be a huge relief. There is nobody reacting to anything, no tension, no resistance or desire but simply pure and complete awareness. There are no errands you have to run in this state, nowhere you have to go or be, no obligations, no aims, no criticism, and no labeling…you are not there, you are absent; gone; non-existent. You are in the ineffable zone.

Everything is Consciousness

In advanced Mind-Spirit training, a human being learns to observe thoughts, develop unique thought, focus thought, and change thought. But there is an even higher level which is beyond thought, a realm that creates, witnesses, and permeates thought – the realm of **Consciousness** itself. As a felt sense, this realm is vivid, beautiful, precious, and indescribable, and the ultimate aim of my work with people.

Glimpses of this realm are so rare that usually only practicing mystics refer to it. But if you have spent years developing conscious thought, it is only natural that you start to develop an interest in what is super-ordinate to thought, interest in that from which thoughts arise, and that into which thoughts disappear again.

To become aware of the all-encompassing field of Consciousness, first become fully human. To become fully human it is requisite that you stop fighting against life and your personal situation as it is. It can take some time and discipline to reach that point where you know that **everything is Consciousness** and you can feel just right in any position, any location, and any vocation. But once realized, the weight of the world drops from your shoulders and you are amused at how easy it is and how easy it could have been all along.

From here onward, thought itself becomes increasingly unimportant, like some remote Television babbling inane nonsense while awareness is expanded to the size of the Universe. If you compare the size of the Universe to that of a babbling TV you get a sense of just how super-ordinate Consciousness is to the world of thought. Thoughts come and go of their own. You no longer involve yourself with them, you merely note them, but they are no longer prioritized as special or "mine". This is the supreme state all Meditation-Practitioners reach along their path.

This wonderful and blissful state is like watching the waves of the ocean without trying to grasp at the waves. Consciousness is that vast ocean, thoughts and emotions are only the waves that come and go. In daily life, when a thought or emotion arises it is merely noticed but not tampered with, altered, changed, transformed, resisted, or desired. Those are things that were done on the previous consciousness level. At this new level "what you think" and "how you feel" are seen as the mere surface of the ocean, and Consciousness as the entirety of the Ocean in depth, height, width, and expanse.

The unraveling of the world of thought begins when you notice the mind's narcissistic fascination with itself and gradually release that. That is accompanied by increasingly less limitation. Any limitation left is purely voluntary (for the purpose of building lifestyle and context within which to live). You transcend the petty preoccupations of the world, release all limitations, and then re-assemble limitations according to your actual preferences.

This higher state requires no solace or hope, no entertainment, no exercise, no information, no formal practice, and no specific belief. It is a state of surrender to that which is most high and infinite: God; Consciousness; the essential Allness-of-Existence itself. The space beyond "mind" is beautiful and powerful and can be accessed through Awareness practice. There is nothing more precious or worthwhile than this. Almost everything is a mere thought. So what is not-thought? And what creates and permeates thought? Discover the answers to these questions and you become less dependent on the world of *form* and more at home in the ever-stable form-less-ness.

On this journey there is no "final goal" and there is no state of perfection. The search for perfection is just another mind-limitation. The Universe is already perfect as it is. You allow yourself to make mistakes and learn from them. You allow yourself to change and accept there is no "final state". You allow yourself to develop new interests. The experiences you make in this higher realm need have nothing to do with what the books say, what the teachers say, or what the mentors say. What they say is just further ocean-surface stuff, further waves, and not all-encompassing Consciousness. Life is an ever-expanding, pulsating, energetic, dynamic, and intelligent process that cannot be captured and put into a book, stored on a computer, or caught in a cup. And although it is one-with-all, it is also uniquely individual (dualities such as individuality and oneness not being contradictions in this realm). Any thought you have about this realm is also just another thought. All of these words are just thought.

There are numerous pathways to this state of consciousness. One of them is to keep gently and humorously questioning your positions and releasing them. Another is to take complete, full, and radical responsibility for your reality. Another is cease "window shopping" various teachings and belief-systems, and to dedicate yourself more fully to one practice. You choose a pathway, decide for it, and then you become intimate with it (and thereby yourself), rather than jumping from trend to trend and only touching the surface waves of that Ocean.

If you put your awareness only on thoughts for about 15 minutes, just watching the circus-show of your thoughts in a calm and mildly curious manner (like how you might look at art), you can actually catch a glimpse of this huge field of Awareness. The witness of those thoughts is part of this field. But that witness is not limited to one observer-position (that of observing thoughts), but rather is limitless. In my experience anyone is able to experience at least some of this within only 15 minutes of silent sitting, breathing, and observing. You sit down, put everything aside, disregard all past and future, and ask yourself, "What is it that is actually going on here and now?" And then you observe for 15 minutes. When you have reached a place of calm you will see that what is *actually* going on is that a bunch of thoughts are running. As you let them run out without intervention, behind those thoughts something deeper, fuller, and more real arises. As you familiarize yourself with this state, all fears, worries, and complications fade away because they were rooted in the world of thought. Fears are like wooden-planks floating on the waves. If you are a wave, they are cause for concern. But if you are the ocean, they are so small you don't even take note of them.

You Only Use 1.6% of Your Potential

"There are 60 levels between Eternity and Will" states the Zohar (foundational text of the Kabbalah). This means that as humans we live in the *realm of free-will* (the realm of choice between good and bad) which is sixty levels removed from the highest Realm (the realm of the Absolute). Hence, Jewish Mysticism says that many experiences in our realm are only 1/60 (one sixtieth or 1.6%) of the ultimate experience or what others would call Enlightenment or Cosmic Consciousness. They say that sleep is 1/60 of death, dreams are 1/60 of prophecy, honey is 1/60 of manna (heavenly

food), Sabbath (day of rest) is 1/60 of paradise, one visit to a sick person takes away 1/60 of the illness, etc. It also says that if something is less than 1.6% of it, you do not have "a taste of it". This is why Jews are allowed to eat non-kosher food if there are less than 1.6% of non-kosher ingredients.

I quote these ancient teachings because my own Meditation-practice finds them to be somewhat true. I usually say, "Mind sees only 1% of all of reality," or, "Life on earth is only 1% of all-that-is," but I use "one percent" only figuratively. Maybe the ancient mystics are more accurate in saying that it's actually only 1.6%. The aim of my Meditation-practice is of course to increase this fairly small number so as to bring more energy and higher frequencies into the experience of daily life. If the 1/60 principle is correct, then even just experiencing 2% of the Infinite Realm makes for a *very* blissful life.

If the 1/60 rule is true, then a sick person in a hospital would have to be visited many times or by many people, and given a lot of loving attention to positively influence their health. If the rule is true, then taking no "day of rest" would mean that you would not even be experiencing the threshold (one sixtieth) which allows for a little taste of higher realms. (And how many modern day people do you know that won't even take one full day of rest a week, a day without their smartphones, without work, and without any concern or urgency?)

If 98.94% of overall reality is not normally experienced, that would mean that in your normal everyday consciousness is shrouded in a sort of **Amnesia,** and there are many, many, many things you have forgotten about: Abilities, Ideas, Places, and Realms you have forgotten about.

That means if you allow yourself to think thoughts you have not thought before, think thoughts you normally don't think, and remember things that have slipped out of your consciousness, you begin the process of reclaiming that which was forgotten. It is my experience that in a higher state of consciousness nothing is forgotten, and one can access many incidents in this life as well as in other lives. Forgetfulness comes because we have the free will to suppress and repress our memories and experiences. The purpose of doing so is to limit our focus. The purpose of limiting our focus is to be able to experience one thing at a time. For the body-mind it would be overwhelming and chaotic to have to experience everything simultaneously (This is why multi-tasking and attention-splitting is not good for the body-mind.). Things you have forgotten about return to you in a state of rest. If you are constantly busy or distracting yourself, deeper-layered information cannot pass through your inner filters. So the message here is clear: Rest. Take your attention to places it has not been to in a long time or ever before.

Another helpful hint: Rather than assuming that you know a lot and are highly informed and intelligent, assume that you know almost nothing (less than 1%) and are in the process of finding out. This letting go of the hubris of the intellect opens perception to knowing more than you think you know. Most of what you "know" must be wrong, otherwise you'd be blissfully enlightened. There is something really good and exciting about the idea that you only use 1.6% of your potential: It means that things can get a whole lot better, and better, and better. The rediscovery of your full potential after it was lost is perhaps one of the reasons we wanted to lose it in the first place…because it's so delicious to find again!

Control, Surrender, and Duality

Some teach Control as a means of success in life. They say you have to be disciplined, focused, in control of yourself (and in this way control circumstances), take action, set priorities, reach goals, etc. Others teach Surrender as a means of success in life. They say you have to let go, release, let it flow, allow the Universe to take over, and give up all effort and struggle. Reality Creation Coaching is one of the few "schools of thought" that teaches both. If you only surrender all the time, you don't train your will and determination. If you only control all the time, you don't allow the Universe to work greater miracles than you'd be capable of. The art of living is knowing when to control and when to surrender, when to act and when to relax, when to fight and when to forgive. A Reality-Creator then is neither a control-freak who needs to dominate and prove his/her will all the time, nor a pansy who passively sits back and turns the other cheek all the time. The Reality Creator is balanced and recognizes both his/her own will and divine will.

The same applies to all other Dualities. As a Reality Creator you become both expert at Non-Doing, as well as Doing. If you can fully embrace one side of the coin, you can fully embrace the other. Notice how people who don't feel good about hard work don't feel good about total relaxation either. They might pretend they do, but deep down they feel guilty about letting it all hang loose and being lazy. And so they are stuck in a realm of neither-nor. They don't want to work and they don't want to not-work. A soul loves to work. And a soul loves to be lazy. A soul loves being together with someone. A soul loves being alone. Neither side of the duality poses a problem. A soul loves being rich. A soul loves being poor.

The Ego loves neither. The Ego always dislikes both sides; the soul always likes both sides. For the Ego the room is too warm or it's too cool. From the perspective of Higher Self, everything is unfolding perfectly as it is. If you wish to master any subject in life, just practice loving both sides. If you want to master calm, then master both tension and calm. If you want to master prosperity, master both prosperity and poverty. If you want to master fear, master both fear and courage. All issues come in pairs of two but we often only recognize one side of the coin...and therefore, only live half of our potential. If you remember only one thing from reading this, let it be: Every issue is composed of two sides. Sometimes the other side is not clearly seen.

The Irresistible Power of Love

Did Gandhi really defeat the British Army through the power of love only? Did Jesus really heal the sick through the power of love only? Did the Berlin Wall really fall through the power of love only? Did the Beatles really gain their entire fame through Love only? That's what me and others have been claiming. In Levels of Energy I say that Love can generate more energy than anything on Levels below it – more than force, more than violence, more than massive action, and more than campaigning.

Handling Kundalini Attacks

As you experience higher levels of consciousness a

whole new set of challenges come up. You'll have problems you didn't even know existed. I usually coach people on money, relationship, career, and well-being issues, but once in awhile someone will bring forth something more exotic.

One of those problems is referred to as "Kundalini attacks" in Buddhism and Hinduism. Such experiences come about when the body is carrying more energy than it is trained to process. Just in case you are one of the few lucky ones to have had such a problem, I will now describe how to handle the energy. These "attacks" manifest as involuntary body jolts. These involuntary body jolts are not to be mistaken with demonic possession, which comes from too little Meditation. (Just kidding…well…half-kidding). The first time I had such jolts they were so extreme that I really scared my girlfriend. I was lying in bed and the energy surged so intensely through my spine that my body was lifted and jolted almost hitting the ceiling. Any researcher of the paranormal would have had a field day with me. Too bad these things always happened when there are no scientists around measuring and recording the event.

My girlfriend jumped out of bed stunned and disconcerted asking, "What's going on here?" or something to that extent. "You tell me what is going on here!" she yelled after I sat there for a minute not knowing what to say. The problem was I did not know what was going on because I hadn't read all the far-eastern literature on the side-effects of Meditation. School hadn't taught me. Parents hadn't taught me. The media hadn't taught me. Science hadn't taught me. I did sense it had something to do with the walking Meditations I had been doing all day, causing me to overflow with energy. The jolts were not unpleasant; they were more of a shock to my girlfriend. How did I handle the issue? I handled it by cutting down on my Meditation. I quit Meditating for a few months and eased back into a normal everyday-life state. It normally is as simple as that. The idea is not to over-strain your body. On the Levels of Energy Scale this stuff starts at around 570, and if you are not well-trained or used to a lot of energy, jolts happen, indicating extreme and swift changes in energy-level. Since my lifestyle back then was coffee, cigarettes, and fast-food, and my energy-level 270, the shift was too rapid. Had my energy-level been higher, the jolts would not have been as extreme. You experience energy-jolts almost every night when you go to sleep. They merely indicate a vibratory shift or a cleansing.

It's Not Life That Gets Better, It's You

Have you noticed how quickly you can change your mood when you meet someone you consider important? You may have been walking around uninspired. Then that *special* someone comes around the corner and says, "Hi!" and suddenly you put on your best face and all tiredness has disappeared from your face. You feel and look different sitting in front of your computer at home than you do standing in front of Mr. or Mrs. Important.

Things like this reveal several things. One of them is that we are good actors. But it also reveals that **states of low-energy are only acts**; illusions we walk around in. When situations call for it, we can discard bad vibes as easy as taking off a hat. We naturally rise to the occasion. When in a low state, check what **pretense** or act you are into. When hanging around at home, it's not really necessary to be in super-high-energy. But neither is low energy needed, even if that has become habitual. And it does become habitual with many: The employee who is surrounded by bored co-employees, who doesn't want to draw attention, so he pretends to be bored too… Soon he becomes bored. The guy who is fed up with his wife and *pretends* to be too tired to have an elaborate and unexpected night out with her, soon *really* becomes tired. The woman who is bored of conversing with her mother or playing with her kids, and pretends to be too tired for that, soon becomes tired for real. But if you work in terms of consciousness and energy, you are aware of these things and won't allow yourself to get into those habits. Then every day is an important day, and every person you meet important enough for you to stay in a good state.

I remember a time in my early thirties where I did so many coachings…several a day…that I started getting really complacent and careless. My performance and results dropped as a consequence. I had to remind myself how blessed I was to be doing what I was doing, and how important each and every student was. Reducing my number of students also helped.

Throughout life you learn that it's not life that gets better, it's you. Life pretty much stays the same.

Sure, places and faces may change, a car and house may be added or removed, painted or sold, but life's basic vibe is pretty much the same anywhere and anytime. What changes and evolves is **you**. You experience life according to who you have become. Once you realize that it's YOU who improves, you quit waiting for better times, quit living your life as a line or a circle, and you start living it as a spiral. The following picture illustrates what I mean more clearly:

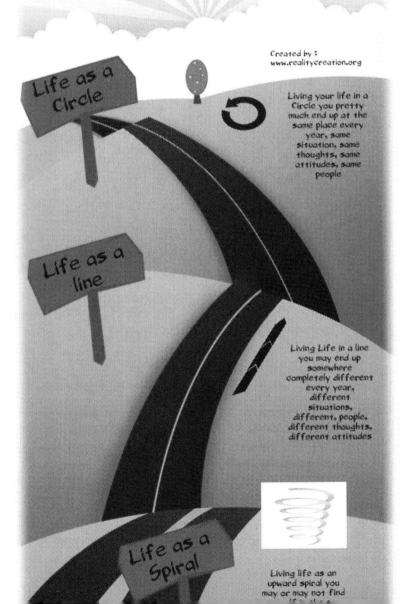

Living consciously, you notice how life repeats itself. But that doesn't mean you have to repeat yourself. You can be someone new with every repetition-variation of events. By the time you are 30, or if you are less conscious, by the time you are 40 or 50, you'll notice (for example) how every Presidential Election is the same as the last one: High hopes, followed by disappointed hopes. That's the *nature* of that particular game.

I have been watching it ever since the early 90s, across 4 Presidents. In every instance there was the silly belief that this new President would fundamentally transform reality and then great disappointment when that didn't happen. Neither the high hope in a new President nor the disappointment in the current President has anything to do with reality. *Your* reality has nothing to do with who is President. Which politician happens to be in "power" is irrelevant to a reality creator and only marginally relevant to society as a whole. People overestimate the meaning of politics because they have been conditioned to.

Another example: If you've been in a few relationships, you'll notice how certain problems that were not solved in the last relationship, carry over to the new one. Leaving a relationship for a new one will be stunning for three days, fresh for three weeks, and unique for three months.... But then, both partners real vibration, beyond the acts and pretenses, come up again. Mature people won't leave quite that quickly, but will first try to work through their own issues with the partner that is present. For the same reason, mature minds don't commit suicide because they know that's no escape from anything. Life goes on after suicide, and you will still have the very same issues you were trying to run away from.

The more consciously you live, the more you notice the repetitiveness of life. And as long as you are still the same person reacting the same way to life, nothing changes. Once you change, everything changes. Something romantic I recently heard someone say:

"I've looked at you in millions of ways, and I've loved you in each."

That's how stuff works. The person does not change, but the way you look at him/her can change – by which the person *does* change!

Consciousness is timeless. It observes the passage of time that life presents. It appears as if this time passage is linear, but what's really happening is that certain concepts are repeating over and over, in different variations, until you transcend them. Then, the next concept is delivered and repeated over and over until you transcend it. If you don't notice that the same thing is being given to you over and over – in different versions – it just keeps repeating until you **get it**. Earth is like a school where some cosmic teacher keeps repeating a lesson, until the student shows she has gotten it and can go to the next level.

The timelessness of consciousness becomes especially apparent in Déjà Vu and Déjà Reve. Déjà Vu and the less well known Déjà Reve are French words that are defined as follows:

Déjà Vu: *a feeling of having already experienced the present situation. Literally: "Already Seen"*

Déjà Reve: *a feeling of having already dreamed the present situation.* Literally: *"Already Dreamed"*

Mainstream researchers have tried associating these phenomena with mental illness, anxiety, delusions, and "temporal lobe epilepsy". Consciousness researchers see it a little differently. When you have the feeling you have already experienced something…it's because you have! Consciousness is outside of time. Therefore, what appears to be happening in the present moment might as well have already happened – from the perspective of the timeless aspect of self.

Forget Everything You Know

"Forget everything you know," is one of the techniques reserved for long retreat-style workshops. It is rarely used because it requires some experience in focus-and-release meditation. If you are unfamiliar with these practices, do not use the technique. The aim is to **let go of all conceptual thinking**, to temporarily drop the ego-self entirely. The result is that you experience your **essence and core…beyond** all thought, concept, and belief. Here I publish it for the first time

for the general public. In this exercise you are not letting go of these things in and of themselves, you are letting go of your concepts and thoughts about them. If, for example, the exercise instructs you to "let go of your body", you are letting go of your ideas about the body. No worries – your body will still exist after the exercise. Also: Anything you let go of, you can re-create later. When you are asked, for example, to let go of wanting happiness that does not mean I am asking you to let go of happiness. I'm asking you to let go of *wanting* happiness. Big difference.

What we are removing here are the many layers of "film" put on the "movie-projector" so that the pure light of consciousness can shine through – unobstructed by concepts... Don't make it a chore, use it lightly and playfully, and work with **whatever comes up** during the meditation, regardless of what comes up. The end-result is the so-called "no mind" state talked about by so many spiritual teachers. But rather than only hearing teachers talk about it, you are going to go ahead and experience the state yourself. The mode of the exercise is easy: You focus, then you de-focus. Then you focus again, then you de-focus. That's another way of saying you look at something, then you let go of it. All of this deliberate thinking and then letting go of thinking relaxes the mind deeply and thoroughly, similar to when you tense and relax your muscles for a period of time. Only here you are "tensing and relaxing" your thoughts, until the mind itself, is relaxed.

You can stream or Download the audio recording here:

Forget Everything You Know

Why Thoughts Keep Repeating in the Mind and How to Stop Them

Have you ever wondered why certain thoughts keep repeating in your mind? Do you know how to stop inner chatter?

The simple answer is: As long as your mind is full of thoughts, worries, memories and future-projections you are not fully **present**. If you want your mind to calm down and repetitive thoughts to dissipate, you need to intensify your awareness to the present or a specific object, person, place, thought, emotion, or thing. Without presence or a specific focus, the mind simply wanders all over the place. You need to either become very relaxed and at ease, or you need to become quite busy…too busy to think or too relaxed to think.

Thoughts keep repeating in the mind because they were recorded at a time you were more present than now. They keep repeating when an issue is incomplete, uncommunicated, unfinished, or there is a suppression of emotion. The mind becomes turbulent when we are worried about what happened or what will happen next. **Over-analyzing and over-thinking things is a symptom of fear.** When you trust the plan the universe has for you, there is relaxation of the mind.

Many people resort to entertainment in order to become fully present. That is, they are not strong enough to will presence from within, and they are dependent on external stimuli. So for the duration of a movie, a show, or a spectacle, their attention is fully drawn into the present moment and there is emotional relief. But once the show is over, their attention might drift back to the troublesome issues and their fearful emotion will return. Your emotions are created by what you focus on. Strong willed people, on the other hand, do not require entertainment to enter the here-now. They could be staring at a white wall all day and be present without becoming bored or distracted. The higher your level of consciousness is the less external stimuli you need to be present and feel well. At very high levels of consciousness you can even remain calm and present under difficult circumstances and personal attacks. At low levels of consciousness, not even the most beautiful sunset or woman will awaken you to the present.

Being attentive to the here-now and to the people around you will make you more interesting. When my own attention and energy are low, I stop being attentive and caring to the people around me. I might treat the shop assistant or hotel receptionist with disregard. I don't have that attention-energy left for him because it's depleted. Whereas, if I am fully attentive to the shop assistant, he will remember me and perceive me as friendly or interesting. Interested people are interesting. I have conducted dozens of seminars with hundreds of students and wondered why I do remember some of my students and not others. What is it that makes them memorable? I discovered that it's their level of attention and interest. I have all these peering eyes looking at me. The ones that are the most attentive appear to be more shining and present. The ones who are preoccupied with their own thoughts or distracted by their smartphones appear to be more dull and uninteresting. Whether they really are is secondary. Very present and caring people simply appear more attractive and magnetic.

Moreover, when you are very attentive to either a positive thought, the present moment, or a task or job you are doing, the mind ceases to exist. Thoughts cease to exist. Ask any professional person whether s/he does a lot of analyzing and thinking while s/he works. If a pro tennis-player starts thinking, he'll lose the game. Ask any two lovers whether they are thinking and analyzing while they stare into each other's eyes. They aren't. They are more present than ever…which is why there are almost no thoughts. Many people attempt to calm their mind through observing their thoughts while breathing calmly. This is Meditation. But another way to accomplish the same state is to merely become fully attentive and aware, fully caring and dedicated to what is happening now, or to which thought you wish to focus on.

Further calming of the mind is achieved by communicating something that you have suppressed. Many worries can dissolve by simply communicating a bit more, asking more questions, and resolving unspoken issues with people. If partners develop too many taboo subjects, lies, and unknowns, the mind becomes more turbulent and keeps repeating the suppressed thoughts over and over. A deepening of your mind's calm comes with completing unfinished tasks and letting go of asking yourself what is going to happen next. Nothing is going to happen next. The present moment is all you
have. And from the present, you can control what is going to happen next rather than being worried that something will "happen to you". Nothing happens to you, it all happens through you.

Not Confined by the Mind

Here's an experiment: Try being thought-free for 3

minutes. Not having any thoughts at all. No thoughts. Zero. Nothing.

OK, maybe that's too optimistic. So let's start out with 30 seconds. Can you stay thought-free for 30 seconds?

Alright, maybe I first have to explain why it's a good idea to do so. I have nothing against mind. The tool can come in handy when living on planet earth. It can tell you to wear a raincoat when it's pouring, how to solve math problems at the grocers and collect information from Wikipedia. As long as you are the Boss, it's a nice little tool to have. The thing is that as humans we tend to allow the mind to run too much of our lives and even decide stuff outside of its jurisdiction. The mind is a recording and playback device. It records events, words, and images, and then plays them back when it thinks these recordings will be helpful in various situations. So you are going on a date with a new potential partner, and your mind plays the records of when you got dumped by your ex and what a traumatic experience that was. See what I'm saying? The mind's suggestions are not always helpful. You needn't be confined by mind. In fact, regaining a little governance over your mind will give you more energy and aliveness, and a new sense of clarity and inner peace. Why? Because you are not the mind and you can more easily discover what you are: A much lighter, more free, more humorous and loving being. When you silence the mind a little you reduce the voice in your head and enter the choice in your heart. Life is not that voice, it's a choice. Confined by the mind, you don't make any choices but just let the mind run your day.

Some people are so overwhelmed by the mind they say, "Alright, just tell me what to do and I'll succumb." When the normal mind is silent, the higher mind comes in. The higher mind does not access only what was experienced in the past, it can imagine things not yet experienced. It can put its attention out into the universe and retrieve information not recorded by the mind-device.

Silencing the mind does not equal stupidity, but rather being henceforth run by intuition. "Intuition" is the soul, the higher self seeing and speaking. If there is too much mind-overlay, you can't hear that gentle and playful voice of higher self.

Let me put it differently. Imagine a light projector, projecting light on the wall. The wall appears as a white canvas. Then you put a slide on the projector and a picture shows up on the wall. That's all well and good, now you are experiencing this picture. But the mind goes overboard by putting dozens and even hundreds of slides on the wall, like some kind of nervous child. What then happens is that you don't see any picture anymore, just a blob of chaos and darkness. Silencing the mind is like removing those slides bit by bit until the pure white light of Consciousness shines again. Well…it doesn't shine "again", it was always shining, but now you can see it. You feel lighter and freer.

Your soul is the Projector projecting the light (attention/energy). The light moves through various filters (slides) that are added by the mind. If there is chaos in your life it's because there are too many slides and the slides don't match. So rather than getting the slides to match, it would be more en-light-ening to just remove a whole batch of them. **Isn't it interesting that the word "light" in English means both shining energy and something non-heavy?** Another benefit of a clear canvas is that when your mind does project an image, it more easily and clearly manifests. Nothing much can manifest if you already have 10,000 slides piled upon each other.

I have been teaching an awesome, wonderful, delightful little exercise for the past ten years called "Copying Thoughts". When I teach it, the minds of many people go: "So what? I don't understand how that exercise might be useful." Of course the mind would not understand what goes beyond it. "Copying Thoughts" works like this: You simply think every thought that comes up consciously or deliberately. No, no, not all day. Just now and then.

This is especially awesome when you are feeling emotional pain. Do you know where emotional heaviness comes from? It comes from piling up way too many thoughts. The heaviness of the slides-pile feels like emotional heaviness. "Copying Thoughts" is like taking the many slides into your hand deliberately, which makes it easy to let them go. Thinking your thoughts consciously helps you release them.

You will notice when you are in emotional pain that your mind is going crazy. And as you think every thought consciously, that speedy, panicky craziness subsides and the turbulence recedes. You will notice that the thoughts you are thinking are quite insane and wonder where the mind picks up all this garbage. It picks this garbage up from the collective subconscious and from certain negative energy-levels. So you notice that many of these thoughts aren't even yours! Notice what your mind does, for example, when your spouse criticizes or attacks you. It goes:

"S/he is criticizing me again." – "That's awful." – "What did I do wrong?" – "S/he is wrong. Definitely wrong." – "Did I make a mistake?" – "My life is miserable." – "When will this ever end?" – "I want to leave him/her. Just be free." – "Or do I?" – "If I leave him/her I will be lonely." – "Should I be OK with being lonely?" – "Being lonely is bad." – "Being lonely is good for me" – "But I am not gone yet, so I am not actually lonely." – "I just need a day to myself." – "I don't need to be gone altogether, just a few days for myself." – "Or one day." – "But what about our planned trip tomorrow?" – "OK, I'll have to create an argument the day after tomorrow so that we can still do the trip together." – "I don't want to actually leave, I just wish s/he would stop assaulting me." – "S/he is aggressive and mean." – "Marriage is not all that it's cooked up to be." – "Maybe I should just take a walk." – "I feel hurt." – "No, I don't feel hurt, I feel fine." – "I could feel fine if I wanted."

– "But I feel hurt." – "It's OK to just feel hurt." – "Or is it?" – "No, it's not OK to feel hurt because hurt indicates a problem." – "Houston, we have a problem." – "Nothing to do with Houston." – "Whitney Houston had a problem though." – "This has happened before and it will happen again." – "Oh God, s/he is going to attack me again." – "Fuck him/her." – "I am just going to do whatever I want." – "Or am I being unfair?" – "This needs some serious discussion." – "I forgot to go shopping." – "Are shops open until 6 or 8 today?"

If people could actually hear how the mind sounds, it would be like listening to a mental patient. And all of that just because s/he criticized him/her for not doing the dishes. Now when you consciously view your thought-process with the help of techniques such as "noting" or "copying thoughts" all this silliness ceases to be, and there is just peace.

So let me ask you again: Can you be thought-free for 3 minutes? Or at least thought-reduced? You are over-thinking things. I am not talking about suppressing thought here. That would make you a dullard. Instead I am asking you to observe; to look, and to take out the turbulence; to use the mind to calm the mind.

These thoughts on the screen point to a place beyond thought, beyond opinion, beyond heaviness, and beyond turbulence. Further afield you discover pure awareness. That which is aware of mind. Later on you discover that this observer/witness self was also part of the mind, and that there is an even more super-ordinate consciousness/presence, and so forth, all the way to enlightenment.

Transcending the Approval/Disapproval Game

You can experience some psych-spiritual relief by spotting and releasing the childlike approval/disapproval racket of the Ego-Self.

The Ego-Self (mind-mechanism, small-self, survival-self) thinks that if someone disagrees with it, s/he must be inferior, wrong, weird, or dislike you. Sounds ridiculous when you read it, right? But if you observe the mind-mechanism from a higher, more relaxed perspective, you can see this tendency in yourself and others clearly. *"He disagreed with me? What a fool!"* or *"She disagreed with me? Something is wrong!"* Of course disagreement does not mean something is wrong, it does not mean you are under attack, and it does not mean the person is weird. It just means s/he is occupying a different viewpoint, born out of his/her own experience. The soul-self sees disagreement with you and thinks, "Interesting. Maybe I can learn something here." Or, "So I wonder how they arrived at this view?" It's felt as more of a matter of interest than as of an attack. Ego-Self thinks that if someone agrees with it, s/he must be good, right, and smart. *"He agreed with me! He must really know what he is talking about!"* Or: *"She agreed! That means she is on the right track!"* Spelled out like this, it sounds ridiculous, I know. And of course someone agreeing with you does not make him/her good, special or smart.

They could just as well be completely ignorant. While we all feel better when we are acknowledged and relieved when there is consensus, the soul-self is not addicted to consensus, and it can easily tolerate a wide variety of apparently contradictory views without becoming uncomfortable. Its tolerance-margin is above planetary average. It can also integrate and harmonize many "conflicting" views. For example, higher-self has no problem at all seeing parallels in hundreds of belief systems.

These issues with approval/disapproval derive from **narcissistic tendencies** of the Ego-Self that wishes to be admired, loved, and acknowledged, and shies away from criticism, disapproval, and disagreement. This narcissism stems from the hard-wired drive for survival. But too much preoccupation with agreement and disagreement, praise and criticism, is unwholesome and leads you away from your core-self; your soul. When you live your life from higher-self, you are not that very in whether you are praised or criticized. You are more interested in "doing what your heart tells you".

Being of such friendly disposition solves all planetary wars and conflicts in time. A war or physical conflict comes from two sides being unwilling to occupy "the other side's" viewpoint. Instead, you will hear a lot of blame at what the other side "did wrong" in the past and is doing wrong now. In war situations you will see a lot of demonizing of "the other". It is then always "the other" that is at fault, responsible, bad, flawed, and uncompromising. Any conflict mediator knows that when there is too much talk of "the other", the sides have failed to assume responsibility for their situation and can therefore never resolve it.

The Ego-Self thinks that if you disapprove of someone's lifestyle, you must fear or hate them. This utterly false belief is played out on every social and political platform of this world. "This group of people disagrees with our lifestyle. Therefore they hate us." "This group of people lives differently than us. Therefore they are evil and in need of change." Every conflict happening in the world today is a result of the Ego's narcissism and its insistence that "the other" needs changing rather than oneself. The soul, on the other hand, prefers difference and uniqueness. Someone being different or disagreeing is not an existential threat. It only becomes a threat when the "other" begins physically attacking. But prior to the physical attack there was the false belief that the "being different" from the "other" must mean that the other is somehow strange, evil, or wrong.

The Ego-Self also thinks that if you love a person, you must agree with and believe in everything s/he does. Similarly, small children believe that if you admonish them, that "you don't love them anymore". Of course loving someone does not entail agreeing with everything that comes from him/her. It's important not to mix up the two and **not to compromise your integrity just because you love someone.** This kind of thing is especially prevalent in couples that have freshly fallen in love and then, with their rose-colored glasses, tend to embrace *everything* the partner says or does. What you see at work here is the desperate Ego-Self that is afraid of "losing love" if s/he disagrees. But if disagreeing with your partner means "losing his/her love", then there was no love in the first place.

The Ego-Self approaches the world trying to collect agreement and avoid disagreement. If not enough agreement is collected, it will modify its views to collect more agreement. So if you live in "neighborhood X" and all people there politically vote party X, the Ego-Self will tend to modify its political views in that direction. This strange consensus-phenomena has been demonstrated in plenty of social experiments. Unless of course you live from integrity; live from the soul…then your views and choices come from within, not from social-group consensus. The weaker your sense of inner self is, the more you will "flip" your opinions to match the people surrounding you or those employing you.

Sometimes the Ego-Self "switches sides", rebels, and tries to collect disagreement by being provocative, non-consenting, rebellious, and disagreeable. So it will start saying and believing just the opposite from what everyone else thinks, or their parents think, or their neighborhood thinks. This again can be seen in children who, to form their own stable identity, first seek agreement with parents, and then flip over to disagreeing with *everything* their parents say. A mature adult personality will be neither all-pro nor all-anti, but will simply respond appropriately to each situation **out of integrity rather than others' expectations**.

You can make a good step in the formation of an authentic and upright personality by checking within yourself whether you are operating from need-of-approval or fear-of-disapproval, or simply responding and being from the soul according to each new here-now situation. My book "The Leadership Course" contains several exercises in this regard. You could ask yourself:

What have I said or done, or not done in order to get others' approval or avoid disapproval?

What would I be saying or doing if I **lived my truth**, regardless of what the world thinks?
It may not always be easy to live your truth, but it always feels the most real. And by feeling **real**, the most is achieved in the long run. For example, I sometimes work for companies that consider themselves "serious and reputable". However, some of my views and methods could be deemed a little "far out" or unconventional. But I express them anyway because I prefer living my truth to "playing it safe". "Playing it safe" won't get you anywhere. If you want to experience something you have never experienced, do things you have never done. In any case, none of these "serious and reputable companies" have cancelled their business with me. But even if they did, so what? Not my loss. And I am not suggesting that one should be provocative and outrageous. When you follow your heart, your work easily harmonizes and syncs with the rest of the Universe without shocking or disrespecting others. The heart is naturally of a harmless and kind disposition and does not normally cause "twitter shit-storms", "media scandals", "public outcry", or any other hyped-up artificial constructs.

Much of the "outrage" and "scandal" you hear about in the media are actually the Ego-Self playing its approval/disapproval games on a mass-scale. Not a day goes by without there being some kind of "outrage" or "scandal" being exaggerated in the news. But much of it is actually selective-outrage. The journalist will be "outraged" by something that comes from a group of people s/he disagrees with. But if the same behavior comes from his/her preferred group, you won't hear him/her being "outraged". Higher-self normally does not participate in games of outrage, shock, and provocation. It does not seek to enrage or exaggerate, distort or emotionalize just to sell newspaper or ad-clicks. It seeks to soothe, humorize, play, harmonize, support, heal, learn, and educate.

The Point of Pointlessness

In my late twenties I spent three weeks getting up every morning at 4:30 to shovel snow outside and carry rocks from one hill to another. This was in summer, when there was no snow...

"What? That's pointless!" they exclaim.

"Yes, it is!" I answer.

Those accustomed to Zen-style mindfulness training will understand why I did what I did. For those who are puzzled, I'll try to explain a little, although even just explaining it kind of ruins the spirit of the exercise.

One of the problems the world-mind has is with the mundane. Another problem is with the pointless. You'll find that the more you try to avoid the mundane and the more you resist life's pointlessness, the more it haunts and taunts you. The id/ego always wants the novel, the special, the fun, the fascinating, the interesting, the joyful, the loving, the sexy, the spiritual, and the purposeful, and it tries to avoid the mundane, the boring, the normal, the tedious, the empty, and the pointless. But life is polarity and you cannot experience one without the other. But in embracing the mundane side of life it becomes easier to experience the non-mundane. In embracing the pointlessness of it all, the point of it all becomes clearer.

So now and then I do exercises as the one described above. The whole point of it is that it's pointless. It's devoid of purpose and devoid of meaning. It was a daily act of deliberate folly. It brought up numerous resistances:

Impatience,

Frustration,

A sense of living a meaningless life,

Sadness,

Boredom,

Anger,

Fear.

I just kept on, and kept on, and kept on the pointless practice until all such emotions were transcended and I was able to simply "do for the sake of doing", no purpose, no mind, no agenda involved – until external circumstance no longer dominated my inner state. I continued until there was only a sense of:

Peace,

Joy,

Fun,

Wonder,

Serenity.

At 4:30 in the morning, under the beautiful starry sky, feeling the cool breeze, the rich smell of pines at night. At 4:30 before the minds of the neighborhood awaken with their mind-chatter, with a shovel in my hand, sometimes shoveling air, sometimes hitting dirt, sometimes lifting the dirt, pointlessly carrying rocks to another hill, and on the next night, carrying them back.

The mind seeks out that which it enjoys, and avoids that which is not enjoyed. That is quite alright. It is natural to follow one's heart; to follow that which is inherently interesting. But to **only** be able to develop interest or joy as dictated by external circumstances is a limitation. So I sought to turn something I did not enjoy into something I enjoy. I had never enjoyed mundane work, much less getting up at 4:30 in the morning. Nor had I much enjoyed pointless action. So all three were practiced until enjoyed. No longer resisting mundane work, no mundane work is asked of me, nor has it been in years.

I believe it's important to learn that BEING is independent of DOING. That your inner state is not directly linked to your actions, but rather to the meaning-you-give-your-actions. One way to teach yourself this lesson is through "controlled folly". You develop a completely pointless habit or discipline. But you do so consciously (most people already have completely pointless habits by the way. But they never consciously chose them. Or is there any point in smoking or watching soap operas?) You can carry it out over a predefined period of time or until you are happy with it. You will learn a lot in the process. Humans have an existential fear that "life is pointless" or has no meaning. I personally don't feel or believe that, but I think it's an important part of your philosophical training to entertain or consider the idea and to liberate yourself from being afraid of it. As children we enjoyed pointlessness, did many things that were senseless, but caused great laughter within ourselves and those watching us. So there is a point in the pointlessness somewhere

Reflections of Light

A man is crawling through a dark tunnel at the end of which he sees a light. He follows the light until he finally reaches a cave opening in which there is a small pond of water. As his eyes adjust to the new situation, he becomes aware that the source of light was not actually the end of the tunnel but the pond of water. There is a light in the water. So he now walks toward the pond some distance ahead. As he comes closer and his eyes adjust to the new situation, a new awareness dawns on him. The source of light is not actually in the water. The water is only reflecting the light of the moon! And all this time he thought the pond was the source of light! He now thinks he has found the true source of light and becomes a follower of the moon. He is determined to leave the cave, steps outside into the night, and marvels at the shining light of the moon, a glow much greater than that at the end of the tunnel or in the pond. Generations pass until his descendants finally build a flying device to travel to the moon and reach that apparent source of light But as they approach the moon and observe it carefully, their eyes adjust to the new situation and they awaken to the fact that the moon is not actually the source of light. It merely reflects the light of the sun.

(Based on a parable I once read somewhere, source forgotten.)

The Eye of the Storm

I recently went skydiving with the aim to remain completely calm. I wanted to feel what it's like to fall out of an airplane at 16,000 feet without an accelerated heartbeat, without drama, without fear...just observing. With that intention in mind, I achieved my aim. It was an amazing and revealing experience. Normally, when we do something new or unusual there is tension. To override the tension we might scream, become chatty, or over-think. But as I dropped out of the plane I was at complete peace. Sure, it was quite cold, and the spinning of my body made my stomach a little queasy, but other than that there was only quietness. A quiet mind and slow heart rate doubles the intensity of any experience. Up there it felt as if I was temporarily "not part of the matrix" and free of the games being played on earth. As I drifted through the clouds, the peace and serenity were overwhelmingly beautiful. As my parachute opened, the peace deepened, and I experienced the world as "not external to my mind". It was actually the first time in my life I thoroughly enjoyed an "extreme sports" activity. It was not adrenaline-based but something higher. It reminded me of the fact that fear is regulated almost exclusively by one's inner intentions and thoughts and not at all by what's happening on the outside. It also, again, showed that by setting an intention prior to entering a new context, place, or space changes the experience. Moreover, staying calm in extreme situations can be a gateway to very high spiritual states. It is interesting too that on the same day I had read about an "illness" called "solipsism syndrome". According to the Wikipedia entry:

Solipsism syndrome refers to a psychological state in which a person feels that the world is not external to their mind. Periods of extended isolation may predispose people to this condition. In particular, the syndrome has been identified as a potential concern for individuals living in space for extended periods of time.

The state has especially been linked to astronauts. It is said that astronauts begin believing that they create the whole world in their minds and as a consequence "suffer from loneliness and indifference to the outside world". This was, however, not my experience while skydiving. Yes, I did experience the world as "not external to the mind". But rather than loneliness and indifference, I felt a deep sense of connection to all-that-is and an eagerness to participate in life. Maybe it's a habit of the psychological field to look for problematic rather than joyful states, but I am sure that believing the world is created in your mind is not an illness. Nor am I claiming that it's "all just in the mind". There are many other minds out there interacting with me.

This of course goes back to the question of: "How much of reality is subjective?" How much is objective?" Or: "How much of it do I create?" "How much is created by external circumstances or others?" Reality Creation Coaching teaches that you improve your life if you believe that at least 50-75% of it is subjective; created by you. It may be more, it may be 100%, but since that may be too much for people to swallow, I usually put it at, at least 50%.

This becomes entirely obvious when you start or re-start modifying your thoughts and emotions, and subsequently have new things happening to you.

So do reality-creators and law-of-attraction-practitioners all suffer from "solipsism syndrome"? My answer: Not if you are enjoying your life and succeeding in manifesting your intentions. Whether you are being delusional or metaphysical is measured by your results.

The skydiving experience got me thinking about the eye of the storm. If there is a cyclone or hurricane raging, no matter how chaotic, intense, and violent it is, the eye of that storm is entirely peaceful and silent. When you connect to your innermost core, you too can be entirely peaceful and serene, no matter how much is going on around you. You can enter a challenging business meeting, a relationship fight, a test of courage, or even a skydive with the intention of staying calm "no matter what", and your intention will set the tone of what happens. Your calm will make you immune to the storm and you will walk life in faith and optimism.

"Breathing in, there is only this present moment. Breathing out, it is a wonderful moment."
– Thich Nhat Han

A Cosmic Introduction to the Enlightenment Technique

A student of "The Enlightenment Technique" created the following Comics to introduce it. The first Comic Image depicts four very different people sitting on a park bench. Because of who-they-are, they filter their attention completely differently from the others, and will therefore perceive and ultimately experience a vastly different world:

The following depicts the basic version of the Enlightenment-Technique for your regular use and benefit:

The most basic version are the following three questions:

1. What do you notice?

2. Who sees it that way?

3. How would love see it?

A more detailed description of this method can be found in my book "Illumination of Consciousness.

The Enlightenment of Huang Po

There are only very few authors and teachers where, while reading, you get a glimpse and a sense of Infinite Consciousness. One such author is in fact Huang Po. He was an 8th Century teacher of Zen, teaching spiritual freedom long, long before modern new-agers watered it down for western consumption and marketability. While Huang Po did not write any books, his best teachings are collected in the booklet "The Zen Teachings of Huang Po". It's one of my more well-worn books as my fingers have been flipping its pages it for the last decade. Some people I have lent the book to have returned it to me saying, "This is useless nonsense," I return the comment with a smile because...they are right! To the world-mind of daily life, caught up in its endless rigmarole of wants and aversions, ups and downs, and lefts and rights, Huang Po's writings really *are* "useless nonsense". But seen not from the Ego's-Eyes but the Eagle's-Eyes, there is more to it than that. The Essence of his teaching is simple enough: "All the Buddhas and all sentient beings are nothing but the One Mind, beside which nothing exists. The One Mind alone is the Buddha, and there is no distinction between the Buddha and sentient beings."

"This mind is beginningless and endless, unborn and indestructible. It has no color or shape, neither exists nor doesn't exist, isn't old or new, long or short, large or small, since it transcends all measures, limits, names, and comparisons. It is what you see in front of you."

This is of course a familiar reference to the absolute "Oneness" of all things. Infinity cannot be divided, separated, polarized, or categorized into Levels. And while this type of experience is considered "Enlightenment", ultimately there is no difference between enlightened and unenlightened Beings because the Ultimate Being is both. About reaching this state Huangbo (alternative spelling) says:

Not till your thoughts cease all their branching here and there, not till you abandon all thoughts of seeking for something, not till your mind is motionless as wood or stone, will you be on the right road to the Gate." Start to think about it and immediately you are mistaken. It is like the boundless void, which can't be fathomed or measured. The one mind is the Buddha, and there is no distinction between Buddha and ordinary beings, except that ordinary beings are attached to forms and thus seek for Buddhahood outside themselves. By this very seeking they lose it, since they are using Buddha to seek for Buddha, using mind to seek for mind. Even if they continue for a million eons, they will never be able to find it. They don't know that all they have to do is put a stop to conceptual thinking, and the Buddha will appear before them, because this mind is the Buddha and the Buddha is all living beings. It is not any less for being manifested in ordinary things, nor any greater for being manifested in Buddhas." "Here it is – right now. Start thinking about it, and you miss it.

In my live-coaching work I actually teach of three distinct states.

1. Focused Attention

2. Open Attention

3. Thinking

I usually draw the three states on a piece of paper for students depicting focused attention or intention as a dot, open attention as an ellipsis, and thinking as a scribbled muddle. An exercise I then send the student to do is to focus attention on one thing or spot, and then to open it and just observe and be aware of the general ambiance, and then to go into thinking and worrying mode. My students are asked to repeat this three-cycle process over and over again until they have a firm grasp of the difference between the three. This is usually a one-hour walk. Focused attention, or Intention, is a narrow state that can lead to the ceasing of thought as Huang Po describes. Open Attention is also a thought-less state that can produce states of great joy. And the thinking state is…well…nearly useless in this context. Focused attention is for the creation of a reality, open attention is for release, and thinking is for existence in daily life.

Huang Po further writes: "Do not permit the events of your daily lives to bind you, but never withdraw yourselves from them. Only by acting thus can you earn the title of 'A Liberated One'."

This refers to the peculiar state of non-attachment that must be discerned from a state of dissociation. Non-attachment is not dissociation. While the semi-enlightened person is not attached to certain outcomes, people, places, or things and can let go of them at any time, it does not mean this person "doesn't care" or "doesn't feel anything". In my book "Levels of Energy" I say that this is the difference between the low state of apathy (dissociation) and peace (non-attachment). And to complete this section, one last Huang Po classic:

"Men are afraid to forget their minds, fearing to fall through the Void with nothing to stay their fall. They do not know that the Void is not really a void, but the realm of the real Dharma."

The Enlightenment of Nisargadatta Maharaj

Another one of my all-time-favorite teachers is Nisargadatta Maharaj who lived from 1897 to 1981. Maharaj taught Enlightenment (or Cosmic Consciousness) through maintaining a sense of "I am" with no adjectives added. In the following I will quote a selection of his thoughts, which speak for themselves.

My advice to you is very simple – just remember yourself, "I am", it is enough to heal your mind and take you beyond, just have some trust. I don't mislead you. Why should I? Do I want anything from you? I wish you well – such is my nature. Why should I mislead you? Common sense too will tell you that to fulfill a desire you must keep your mind on it. If you want to know your true nature, you must have yourself in mind all the time, until the secret of your being stands revealed.

A quiet mind is all you need. All else will happen rightly, once your mind is quiet. As the sun on rising makes the world active, so does self-awareness effect changes in the mind. In the light of calm and steady self-awareness inner energies wake up and work miracles without effort on your part.

There is nothing to practice. To know yourself, be yourself. To be yourself, stop imagining yourself to be this or that. Just be. Let your true nature emerge. Don't disturb your mind with seeking.

When you demand nothing of the world, nor of God, when you want nothing, seek nothing, expect nothing, then the Supreme State will come to you uninvited and unexpected.

By shifting the focus of attention, I become the very thing I look at, and experience the kind of consciousness it has; I become the inner witness of the thing. I call this capacity of entering other focal points of consciousness, love; you may give it any name you like.

Love says, "I am everything." Wisdom says, "I am nothing." Between the two, my life flows. Since at any point of time and space I can be both the subject and the object of experience, I express it by saying that I am both, and neither, and beyond both.

The mind craves for formulations and definitions, always eager to squeeze reality into a verbal shape.

What is wrong is that you consider yourself to be limited to this body and shape. What knowledge I try to give is given to the knowledge 'I am' in each of you, which is the same. If you try to get the knowledge as an individual you will never get it.

Quotes taken from his book "I Am That":

When you know beyond all doubting that the same life flows through all that is and you are that life, you will love all naturally and spontaneously. When you realize the depth and fullness of your love of yourself, you know that every living being and the entire universe are included in your affection. But when you look at anything as separate from you, you cannot love it for you are afraid of it. Alienation causes fear and fear deepens alienation. It is a vicious circle. Only self-realization can break it. Go for it resolutely.

In dream you love some and not others. On waking up you find you are love itself, embracing all. Personal love, however intense and genuine, invariably binds; love in freedom is love of all….When you are love itself, you are beyond time and numbers. In loving one you love all, in loving all, you love each. One and all are not exclusive.

All the universe will be your concern; every living thing you will love and help most tenderly and wisely.

I find that somehow, by shifting the focus of attention, I become the very thing I look at, and experience the kind of consciousness it has; I become the inner witness of the thing. I call this capacity of entering other focal points of consciousness, love; you may give it any name you like. Love says, "I am everything." Wisdom says, "I am nothing." Between the two, my life flows. Since at any point of time and space I can be both the subject and the object of experience, I express it by saying that I am both, and neither, and beyond both.

Once you realize that the world is your own projection, you are free of it. You need not free yourself of a world that does not exist, except in your own imagination! However is the picture, beautiful or ugly, you are painting it and you are not bound by it. Realize that there is nobody to force it on you, that it is due to the habit of taking the imaginary to be real. See the imaginary as imaginary and be free of fear. What begins and ends is mere appearance. The world can be said to appear, but not to be. The appearance may last very long on some scale of time, and very short on another, but ultimately it comes to the same. Whatever is time-bound is momentary and has no reality.

By all means attend to your duties. Action, in which you are not emotionally involved and which is beneficial and does not cause suffering will not bind you. You may be engaged in several directions and work with enormous zest, yet remain inwardly free and quiet, with a mirror like mind, which reflects all, without being affected. All that happens is the cause of all that happens. Causes are numberless; the idea of a sole cause is an illusion. The world is like a sheet of paper on which something is typed. The reading and the meaning will vary with the reader, but the paper is the common factor, always present, rarely perceived. When the ribbon is removed, typing leaves no trace on the paper. So is my mind – the impressions keep on coming, but no trace is left.

We are the creators and creatures of each other, causing and bearing each other's burden.

The sweetness is the nature of sugar; but that sweetness is there only so long as the sugar is present. Once the sugar has been consumed or thrown away, there is no more sweetness. So this knowledge "I am," this consciousness, this feeling or sense of Being, is the quintessence of the body. And if that body essence is gone, this feeling, the sense of Being, will also have gone. This sense of Being cannot remain without the body, just as sweetness cannot remain without the material, which is sugar.

What remains is the Original, which is unconditioned, without attributes, and without identity: that on which this temporary state of the consciousness and the three states and the three gunas have come and gone. It is called Parabrahman, the Absolute.

This is my basic teaching.

Put your awareness to work, not your mind. The mind is not the right instrument for this task. The timeless can be reached only by the timeless. Your body and your mind are born subject to time; only awareness is timeless, even in the now.

Nothing troubles me. I offer no resistance to trouble – therefore it does not stay with me. On your side there is so much trouble. On mine there is no trouble at all. Come to my side.

Look at your mind dispassionately; this is enough to calm it. When it is quiet, you can go beyond it. Do not keep it busy all the time. Stop it – and just be. If you give it a rest, it will settle down and recover its purity and strength. Constant thinking makes it decay.

You are not in the body, the body is in you! The mind is in you. They happen to you. They are there because you find them interesting.

Time is in the mind, space is in the mind. The law of cause and effect is also a way of thinking. In reality all is here and now and all is one.

Because of your existence, because you know that you are, you know also that the world is. So this consciousness, because of which you experience the world, is not unimportant; in fact, it is very important. So why not stabilize there? Meditate on that consciousness itself, and find out how this "I-am-ness" has appeared. What was its cause? And from what did this consciousness develop? Try to find out, go right to the source!

To locate a thing you need space, to place an event you need time; but the timeless and spaceless defies handling. It makes everything perceivable, yet itself is beyond perception. The mind cannot know what is beyond the mind, but the mind is known by what is beyond it.

"I am" is an ever present fact, while "I am created" is an idea. Neither God nor the universe have come to tell you that they have created you. The mind, obsessed by the idea of causality, invents creation and then wonders, "Who is the creator?" The mind itself is the creator. Even this is not quite true, for the created and its creator are one. The mind and the world are not separate. Do understand that what you think to be the world is your own mind. All space and time are in the mind. There is only imagination. It has absorbed you so completely that you just cannot grasp how far from reality you have wandered. No doubt imagination is richly creative. Universe upon universe are built on it. Yet they are all in space and time, past and future, which just don't exist. It is you who are in movement and not time. Stop moving and time will cease. Past and future will merge in the eternal now.

Of all the affections the love of oneself comes first. Light and love are impersonal.

When you do not think yourself to be this or that, all conflict ceases. Any attempt to do something about your problems is bound to fail, for what is caused by desire can be undone only in freedom from desire. You cannot be rid of problems without abandoning illusions.

It's always the false that makes you suffer, the false desires and fears, the false values and ideas, the false relationships between people. Abandon the false and you are free of pain; truth makes happy, truth liberates.

If you could only keep quiet, clear of memories and expectations, you would be able to discern the beautiful pattern of events. It's your restlessness that causes chaos.

Realms of Bliss

One my personal frustrations is that I'd like to find pictures to show people higher realms of consciousness, but I can't find any. I'd like to recommend books that accurately describe that magnificent cosmic bliss, but I can't find any. I'd like people to hear the sounds of higher realms, but I can't find any. This has taught me that higher consciousness and states of bliss are not available in the world; they are only available "within".

I have spent countless hours image-searching on the internet with every conceivable keyword-combination. I have even paid artists to paint according to my description. I have watched every movie on higher realms, spirituality, astral travel, heaven, near-death-experiences, and higher dimensions. But it's just not there. **Not even close.** To my knowledge, not even a fraction of higher states has ever been shown on planet earth.

I and many others have had glimpses of higher planes of existence. Their defining characteristic is such a beauty that even the most vivid imagination might only get a modest piece of it. I type "higher consciousness" into the image-search and I get a bunch of tripped-out psychedelic images that look more like pre-school scribblings than higher realms. So I type in "heaven", and all I get is kind of naive-childish looking religious images (as if angels had actual physical wings). So I type in "astral realms" or "higher realms", and I get all these over-saturated new-agey pictures with inane and boring "think positive" quotes popped over them. So I try "surreal", and I get a bunch of sinister psych-ward stuff. So I type in "sci-fi worlds", and I get all kinds of

dystopian tech-and-gear stuff. So I try "higher dimensions", and I get pics of the college physics class. So I try "channeled art", and I get stuff that looks like it was painted in depression therapy class. So I type in "surreal sci-fi consciousness spiritual heaven higher dimensions enlightenment", and I get nothing.

It can be challenging to satisfy people familiar with cosmic consciousness. As explained in my book "Lives of the Soul", no matter how many paper coins you collect, they will never make a real coin. Parallel to this, no matter how many items of this three-dimensional earth plane reality you collect, they will never amount to a higher fourth-dimensional plane. But that doesn't stop me from trying. While perfection cannot be reached (otherwise stagnation), improvement can. So, daily improvement is a good philosophy for life. Seeking perfection on the other hand, usually leads to frustration. Replace "reaching perfection" with "making daily improvement" and all is well. So I accept that I can't write the perfect book that accurately describes these higher states, but I can improve and refine – and intend to do so for the rest of this life.

The key that opens the gate to these unspeakably rich realms of bliss and beauty lies not in pictures, movies, books, articles, relationships, jobs, riches, or anything else worldly, of course. You catch glimpses of them when the mind is silent. So I teach techniques and produce audio-programs to silence the mind, in the trust that such higher awareness will in due course, lead to visions, lucid dreams, and places of bliss.

5

Transcend the Ego and Be Free

I Am Totally and Completely Wrong

If you think you are not the soul but the body/mind you will waste a lot of time trying to be right, asserting your rightness, or trying to make others wrong. This is the mind/ego fighting for its survival. If it is proven wrong or incompetent it fears for its survival. After all, knowledge and competence ensure that it has correctly recorded events and can protect the body/mind in case of emergencies. This is all well and good, but too much of being-right and making-others-wrong in order to look good, feel reassured, or not leave one's comfort zone can become an obstruction to enjoyment of life.

If you always have to assert that you are right in one area or another, that is a tell-tale sign that you are not actually right but afraid of being wrong. If you were right about something you would not have to keep confirming and asserting it or waste your time trying to wrong people. Being able to consider the possibility that you are completely and totally wrong about something (or even everything!) opens a space and a clearing in which new things can be learned. Another word for this is openness or being receptive. It is linked to humility. The other side of that coin is to have the ability to be totally and completely right and convinced. Mastering one side helps in the mastery of the other side.

For example, I am willing to consider the possibility that everything I have learned, taught, and written in books and on the Internet is completely and totally wrong. I am willing to consider that everything "my life" is based on is a lie. I am willing to abandon all of it any time if it would turn out to be so. This type of open-mindedness requires some courage, but it breeds more knowledge. It is impossible to gain more knowledge in the belief: "I already know it all." Maybe everything I think I "know" is only one LEVEL of understanding that has no meaning at all on another level.

The willingness to be completely and totally wrong is extremely helpful in Business too. People who have succeeded in one thing or another create a mental file labeled: "This is how to succeed. First you must do A, then B, then C..." But what if the way you have succeeded in the past does not apply to the future? What if, in order to progress, you need to open up to new information, information that has nothing to do with how you succeeded in the past? Language Learning is a great example of this principle: You can't learn a new language by looking through the frame of an old language you have already learned. If you think you can learn French while thinking in English, and using English grammar and sentence structure, you won't be speaking good French anytime soon. In order to learn French you have to **forget everything you have learned in the past** and view the language as a little child...open and fresh.

Letting go of being-right is useful in resolving conflicts. If you are waiting on someone else to let go of being right, your attention is mis-directed. Nothing happens "out there", your only place of power is "in here". Is letting go of being right a sign of weakness? This depends what level-of-energy you are at. These are the levels of energy from which it is recommended you assert more of your right-ness:

Submissive

People-Pleaser

Grovelling

Approval-Seeking

Needy-of-Harmony

If you never dare assert your right-ness out of fear, it is recommended you practice asserting your right-ness. In my book "Levels of Energy" this would mean ascending from level 100 to 190. But if you constantly and only assert your right-ness, it is time to move beyond that level and go higher into the acceptance of sometimes being just plain wrong or both of you being right from each of your perspectives. Especially when there is a problem that keeps repeating itself in your life, look for instances of thinking you are "right" about something or "already know". If an unwanted pattern keeps repeating, then there is something you do not know, something that requires deeper looking that begins with saying, "I don't know."

Try this liberating exercise for a week, if you want. Allow yourself to think of, consider, whisper, or write-a-sticky note that says, **"I am completely and totally wrong."** Try to conjure up this attitude in various conversations and interactions you have with various people. Not as in putting-yourself-down or criticizing yourself, but as in the realization that just because you see it a certain way doesn't mean that's the way things are. What if you are completely and totally wrong about a certain person? What if s/he is not as bad as you thought? Or what if s/he is not as good as you thought? Can you take back the label you put on him/her and look at him/her in a new light? What if you are completely and totally wrong about your job? What if it is not as bad as you thought? Or what if it is much worse than you thought? Or what if it is much better than you thought? Could you open up a little and see things differently than your beliefs dictate? If you can see something from other viewpoints than only "your own", you will see more.

"Don't go searching for new landscapes, but see the ones you already know with new eyes."

I Look Totally and Completely Ridiculous

You know what people make the worst impression? The ones desperately trying to make a good impression. Because they are preoccupied with how they look to others, things becomes tense and unnatural. To some extent every human being has some of the "trying to look good". It's a basic survival-pattern of the body/mind. But it does not really help if your goals are being at-ease with others (the side-effect of which really does make you look good). These are some variations of this particular pattern:

- Wanting to make a good impression

- Needy of Approval

- Overly status-conscious

- Overly comparing yourself to others

- Trying to be special or different

- Trying to be the same as everyone

- Trying to assert your superiority

- Being afraid of someone being better than you

- Trying to resist conformity and fitting in

- Trying to conform or fit in

Seen from more honest eyes, all of these games people play look totally and completely ridiculous. Make peace with being a totally and completely ridiculous fool. Make peace with the fact that there are actually people out there that are more competent than you, stronger than you, more important than you, and better looking than you. Once you release some of your self-importance and "trying to be different", "trying to be superior", or "trying to be the same and conform", you will have dropped a lot of baggage and energy is freed up. With the energy that is freed up you will discover your soul…the part of you that really is wonderful, beautiful, powerful, and unique. Whereas the part that is always wanting to be unique and powerful never was and never will be. Study human nature and notice how the "making an impression" game is happening every day with everyone. Some preoccupation with vanity will straighten you out. But too much of it will create an extremely narrow mask-self that has nothing to do with your true nature that is spontaneous, funny, hilarious, relaxed, positive, joyful, and ready-to-go.

Narcissism Makes You Weak and Stupid

Ask yourself this:

Would you like you if you met you?

Think about it.

Narcissism is exaggerated preoccupation with yourself, with the way you look, with your supposedly superior intelligence, ability, and knowledge. It is self-admiration, self-importance, and the tendency to view everything and everyone only as it relates to you. The Ego-Self (as compared to the Soul/Spirit) is essentially narcissistic to some degree or another. It misses 99% of reality because its attention is continually preoccupied with itself.

Gradually letting go of your Narcissism will make you more aware, stable, and powerful...unless you again become narcissistic about being more aware, stable and powerful. The first step to overcoming Narcissism is firstly by knowing what it is, noticing it within you, and also being painfully aware of how unbecoming it is. You will also notice it in others and in how the entirety of their act, the entirety of their words, and the entirety of their behavior is geared toward making themselves look good. Some people are better at hiding it; their Narcissism is more subtle, but it is present in almost every human being.

Here's a test: Criticize someone. Question his/her self-importance. Then, a short time later, ask him/her to do you a favor or to put in a good word for you somewhere. Nine out of ten people will not do you a favor or speak well about you after you've criticized them. That is the extent of pettiness on planet Earth.

Ninety-percent of the "problems" and "limitations" in your life disappear once you let go of the inner narcissist. Yes, you are special and unique in the sense of being a magnificent and radiant energy-form. But the part of you that knows its specialness is not narcissistic about it. The soul is special, not the Ego-Self. There is nothing at all special about the Ego-Self yet this part creates itself as "special".

The second step to overcoming Narcissism is to put yourself into the shoes of the people around you; to extend more interest toward others. To sometimes do something, say something, or see something that has nothing to do with furthering of your own agenda. When was the last time you did something for someone else with no idea of personal gain whatsoever? Just for the sake of loving kindness?

It's easier to be selfless when you are not suffering. I teach people they should be selfish on energy-levels 0-400. But above those levels, too much self-centeredness becomes a limitation, narrowing your field of perception down to the little spot where your own body/mind stands. To progress on upwards, begin noticing that there is a whole wide universe out there to explore, a whole wide universe beyond the limited "body/mind" you call "me".

You Are Already Whole and Complete

You are already whole and complete. The struggle of life for many is to "get" completeness. Only very rarely does a human rise above this struggle and come from completeness rather than attempt to "get" it. Someone who enters a meeting in a state already whole and complete will have a lot more to give to that meeting than someone seeking to "get" something from it. Someone approaching the weekend already whole and complete will experience the weekend differently than someone hoping to "get" something from the weekend. Someone who is already whole and complete and drinks coffee will taste it differently than someone hoping to "get" more awake from that coffee.

What if you were already whole and complete before getting sex? Not only would that make you a more attractive sex partner, it would also fully transform the entire experience. You would no longer be requesting someone else to make you whole and complete. Look at all the techniques people try to use to "get" a better sex experience and to "get" ecstasy. What if they were to already come from ecstasy before sex had even begun?

Everyone is in a rat-race of "getting to", always on the run, always trying to "get" somewhere else, be someone else, try something more, try something better, and/or try something different. But what if you were to first accept things as they are, and then decide to come from those places instead of trying to "get" to them? That is what is really meant by living in the here-now. And that is an extremely powerful state. It is the state of flow.

We phase in and out of this state, depending on whether we are viewing life from the eyes of the soul (love) or viewing life from the eyes of the Ego-Self (resistance). Actually, life has nothing at all to do with your job, your money, or your partner. Life is not about what you can "get" from these things. It is about what you bring into these things, about what you give, and about who you are. This simple (and yet for many so mysterious) reversal is all that is needed for 100% flow.

People take their cues on how to live life from you. Can you sense the responsibility you have? They take their cues from you. Your partner, employees, children, bosses, friends…they take their cues from you. Understanding that opens up a sense of responsibility but also possibility. If you come from a state of completeness instead of want (lack), everything changes. To come from completeness instead of going toward it, only two things are required:

1. Accept what is as-it-is fully and totally. Your current surroundings and situation are not lacking. They are exactly where you are supposed to be and full of opportunity.

2. Decide who you are or which state-of-happiness you are in or coming from. It's only a Decision. Decide to come from that state instead of striving for it.

Ocean of Consciousness

The following illustration provides a map of consciousness and helps the viewer discern between "higher consciousness", "conscious mind", "subconscious", and "unconscious".

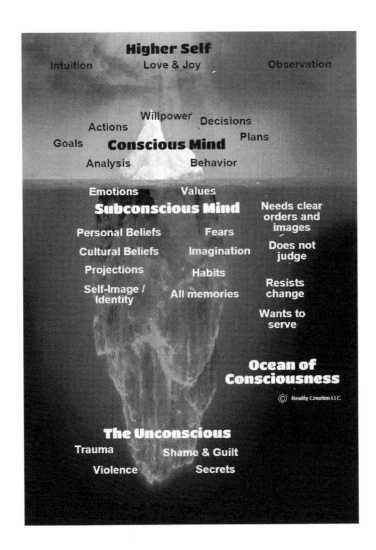

Your "higher consciousness" can also be called "the soul", and at an even higher level, "consciousness" itself. It is your essence, the source of "intuitive insight" and high positive emotions such as love and joy. When you are in a peaceful "observer mode" you operate at this level. Your conscious mind (also called just "mind" or "ego"), is the realm of conscious choices, will, action, and analysis. While conscious and deliberate action is required to "program" the subconscious, that which you are aware of consciously is only the "tip of the iceberg", and most of your life and reality are actually regulated by the Subconscious.

From this illustration you can see that your Imagination as well as your self-image have a much deeper root than your conscious thoughts and plans. Goals and Plans will help you move in the right direction, but they would be more effective if you first create change at the level of identity and imagination. In order to serve you, your subconscious needs clear orders in the form of values and emotions that are linked to images. As you repeat your emotionally loaded images, they eventually become subconscious. From there you radiate a new "vibration" and begin attracting a new reality. Your subconscious resists change and requires proper emotional convincing to shit to what you prefer.

The "Unconscious" is like the sub-sub-conscious in which suppressed experiences are stored. Applying emotional processing to the unconscious can cause some emotional pain but also great release. Once your life is going exactly as you like, you can assume that your subconscious is properly programmed. In that case you'd rather not meddle with it. But until then, work with your subconscious, your emotions, and mental images
to create that which you prefer.

Advanced Energy Breathing Techniques

"Inhale, and God approaches you. Hold the inhalation, and God remains with you. Exhale, and you approach God. Hold the exhalation, and surrender to God." ~ Krishnamacharya

Ready to change your overall physical, mental, and spiritual state for the better? Look no further.

The following breathing techniques can also improve the lucidity of your night-dreams (if performed before sleep), your health (if performed softly), and allow inner visioning to be more vivid.

Technique 1. Breathing the Universe

1. Lie down and come to rest.

2. Imagine the entire Universe is dark violet or purple.

3. On the in-breath, imagine breathing in the entire Universe and this color into your body. Also imagine not only breathing in through your mouth and nose but through the skin-pores of your entire body.

4. Hold the breath for a moment

5. On the slow out-breath (which should be twice as slow as the in-breath), breathe out of the open mouth with a "Haaaaaaaaaaaa" sound. Do not imagine anything specific (the color-energy stays in the body).

Repeat at least 10 times.

And how do you feel? Quite wonderful I suspect!

Technique 2: Breathing 1-4-2

This is the 1-4-2 Breathing-Technique which will result in an increase in clarity, wakefulness, and calm. It works better than caffeine and also supports the removal of toxins and stale energy from the body.

1. Breathe in 1
2. Hold the breath 4
3. Breathe out 2

That means you hold the breath 4 times as long as you breathed in, and breathe out twice as long as you breathed in. So if you breathed in for 3 seconds, you hold for about 12 seconds and breathe out for 6 seconds. If your in-breath was 4 seconds, you hold for 16 and breathe out for about 8 seconds.

Repeat once for a little relaxation, repeat five times for a boost in energy, repeat ten times for feeling high as a kite.

Technique 3: Toning Vibration

1. Breathe in.

2. On the out-breath slowly and gently sing the letter "A".

Repeat this for a few minutes, and then, when your mind is sufficiently relaxed and your body energized, add a visualization of something you wouldn't mind experiencing while sounding the "Aaaaaaaaaaaaaaaaaaa". This is a way of energizing a thought-form (for more on energizing thought-forms so that they influence reality see The Reality Creation Course).

Technique 4: The Breath of Life

1. Breathe in through the nose and into the stomach

2. Breathe out twice as long through the mouth with a "Haaaaaaaaaaaaa"-Breath sound (not using the vocal chords in this one).

Repeat at least 10-30 times to feel more energized, clear, and ready to roll.

Technique 5: Spatial Breathing

For the improvement of spatial perception:

1. While looking at something far away, breathe in.

2. While looking at something near you, breathe out.

Or:

1. While looking at something big breathe in.

2. While looking at something small breathe out.

Repeat for a few minutes until you notice an improvement in mood and perception.

Technique 6: Emotional Clearing

For clearing mis-emotion:

Using the 1-4-2 technique combined with focusing on a feeling of mis-emotion (apathy, sadness, fear, anger, boredom, etc.)

1. Focus on the mis-emotion in the body and breathe it in (release resistance).
2. While holding the breath, hold the issue in focus.
3. On the out-breath release attention from it, let go.

On the next in-breath re-focus on the mis-emotion. Repeat several times until it has dissolved.

Isn't it great how easy this is?

Technique 7: Intensifying Feelings

Using the 1-4-2 technique combined with focusing on something you like. The result will be an increase in energy and awareness.

1. Focus on something you like (visible mentally or in your surroundings) while breathing in.

2. While holding your breath, hold your focus on that nice thing.

3. On the out-breath, let go, release your attachment/attention to that.

On the next in-breathe re-focus your attention to that nice thing or another nice thing. Repeat several times until you notice a shift in mood and lucidity.

Technique 8: Whole-Body Breathing

As you breathe, notice how the mouth and nose are actually not the only places you breathe in. You breathe in through your whole body. Most of us limit breathing to the mouth and nose, but feel for a moment what it feels like to be breathing in through the pores of your skin of the entire body, breathing with your entire being.

If you don't believe that in and out-breathing happens through the skin, focus on the middle of the palms of your hands for a moment. And now breathe in. Usually you'll feel a pulling sensation there when you pay attention to it.

Whole-body breathing for a minute or two can feel extraordinarily refreshing.

Technique 9: Circular Breathing

This one creates a slight "buzz". Do not overuse.

"Circular Breathing" means that there is no pause between the in- and outbreath. So that this does not become hyperventilation it is done slowly, gently, and through one nostril only. Nostrils are open and closed with a finger:

a) Breathe in through nostril 1.

b) Breathe out through nostril 2.

c) Breathe in through nostril 2.

d) Breathe out through nostril 1.

e) Breathe in through nostril 1.

f) Breathe out through nostril 2. etc.

Repeat 10-30 times. While doing so keep your eyes "soft", that means not focused on anything in particular. Remain aware of the distance and the peripheral. Breathing can be done consciously or unconsciously. As such it serves as a gateway between the conscious and the subconscious. It is good to breathe unconsciously most of the time. But it is also good to breathe consciously some of the time.

Breathe In Breathe Out

Life is breathing in and breathing out. The Universe is expanding and contracting. The tide is coming and going. The best way for a human to flow with the tides of the Universe is through "Welcoming and Releasing".

Sit down and make yourself comfortable. Begin to **Welcome** your thoughts, feelings, bodily sensations, memories, impressions, and sense perceptions that are happening here and now. Other words for "Welcoming":

Embrace It

Allow It

Welcome It

Let It Be Here

Open to It

Stop Resisting It

Love It

This will immediately put you in a state of poise and presence, no longer at the effect of the unruly monkey-mind. You can focus on a single issue, thought, or emotion and welcome anything that goes along with that, or you can just welcome anything in general. Fully feel any emotion coming up, no matter if it's pleasant or unpleasant. Gradually release judgment, resistance, and aversion. Let go of labeling anything "fear", "anger", or a "problem", and just allow yourself to see it as energy, as a feeling, or a thought.

As you continue to meditate, notice how everything just happens all by itself. Feelings, thoughts, images, sounds, perceptions, breathing…it all just happen, no effort required. No resistance required. No self required. No goal required. Notice how feelings and thoughts just pass by, just come and go, just arise and fade away if you do not do anything with them, resist them, or hold on to them. Get used to just observing your thoughts and feelings without trying to do anything with them. Let them be there.

Once you are very good at welcoming realities, welcoming impressions, welcoming things, and breathing them in, you may start breathing them out. Actually, just welcoming feelings can dissolve them, but if some are not dissolved from welcoming, then practice deliberately letting them go. You could do 10 minutes of thought & feeling welcoming and then 10 minutes of letting go. Or you could be focusing on just one topic and welcoming it for a few minutes to then let that go. The whole point of "Welcoming and Releasing" is so you can only let go of what you have. That's why "welcoming" means taking something in; taking it into the "hands" of awareness. Releasing or Letting go is not actually a push against something or a clinging to something but just letting something be. Just letting a feeling be. No longer investing importance, attention or intention to the memory, thought, or feeling.

How to Release Pain

Once you learn "welcoming and letting go" you can easily practice it with emotional and physical pain or ANY sort of undesirable reality, including hardly tangible ones such as "an undefinable dullness of life" as someone recently told me. Simply zoom in on the pain in your body. Release wanting to get rid of it, wanting to understand it, wanting to change it, and wanting to transform it. Instead, welcome it as it is. Fully embrace and accept whatever is there. Go to the very center of the feeling.

Call it "energy" or "feeling". Be with it and breathe with it softly. Optional: In some cases you may want to ask: "What do you want?" And if the feeling responds with some intuitive thought, then visualize the fulfillment of that thought. Then "release" it by just letting it be. No longer invest attention into it. Stop reacting to it or interfering with it. Let go.

Circular Breathing

One way to center and elate yourself is through circular breathing. To practice this mindfulness and meditation method sit in a straight-back chair.

a) Begin by noticing your breathing; watching your breathing.

b) Once you've spent at least a minute calmly noticing your breathing, gently allow your breathing to fill the stomach (which naturally also allows it to fill the lungs). Do not force your breathing; simply guide it to be a little slower, softer, and deeper. Do not hyperventilate.

c) Once the former becomes comfortable allow your breathing to become **circular**, with no pause between the in and out-breath. You are breathing all the way in, but rather than pausing, as you naturally do, you simply continue to the flow of air with the out-breath. Breathe all the way out, but rather than pausing, as you naturally do, simply continue to the flow of air with the in-breath. Continue to do so for at least five minutes, ten minutes or, if you enjoy it, for much longer. The result is stress relief and more energy.

Because breathing normally happens subconsciously/automatically, circular breathing may bring up some subconscious material that wants to be released and surrendered. This releasing happens naturally if you do not interfere with the process, if you do not suppress any of the emotions that come up, and if you do not abort the breathing technique until you feel better again.

Circular breathing is not natural, but neither is suppressing deep breathing as so many people do all day. Circular Breathing therefore counterbalances the habitual suppression of breath that goes along with the noisy and stressful "lifestyle" of modern mankind. The bottom line is: GET OUT OF YOUR HEAD AND FEEL!

●

6
Infinite Awareness

Infinite Awareness

Care for a sip of enlightenment? Then come in, read, be amazed.

As humans we narrow our focus to perceive and experience only a tiny dot, a small part of the whole. To experience anything in particular we have to limit and contract awareness to the extreme. Otherwise we remain in our native state of **Infinite Awareness**. Returning back to Infinite Self from lifetimes of limitation and contraction is the most exhilarating experience in this Universe and makes up for many lifetimes of limitation. Without having those limitations in the first place we wouldn't feel Liberation as intensely. Any preoccupation, desire, object, resistance, life, planet, galaxy, emotion, identity, persona, body, or self is a tiny dot compared to Infinity. You are an individualized version of Infinity. You are created in the image of Infinity; a mini-universe. Infinity is creative; you are creative. You are a viewpoint of the whole. The following images give you a sense of the vastness of Universe. Take a few moments to look and feel.

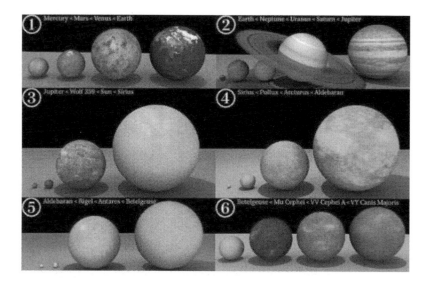

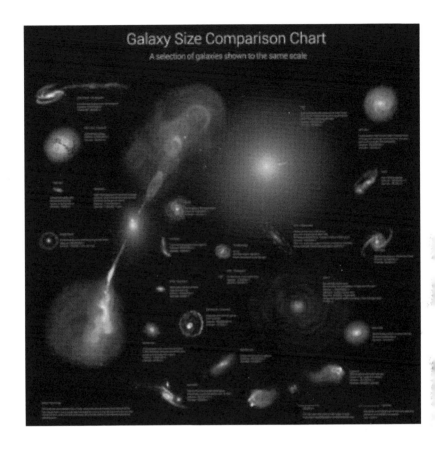

In an Infinite Context, what is big and small depends on what you are used to. What is difficult and easy depends on what you are used to. What is left, right, up, down, important, and unimportant depends on the viewpoint you occupy within this vast infinite space. If you take Infinity as your absolute; your guiding light; your context-for-life, then you understand that "Everything Belongs". You also gain some perspective and calm when facing the challenges of daily life. I'm in a pretty humorous mood most of the time because my own context-for-life is Infinity. My reliance is on the Absolute, not the limited, the never-changing, not the ever-changing. The moment you place your reliance and trust in something less than the Infinite and Eternal, you are setting yourself up for disappointment because everything but the Infinite and Eternal is limited in time or space.

The purpose of Reality Creation Coaching is to loosen the fixity and extreme preoccupation with the tiny dots just a little bit so that you more remember who you really are and allow your abilities and perception to be expanded.

An aspect of Infinity is its holographic nature which is described with phrases like: **"As above, so below,"** and: **"As in the big, so in the small."** In this sense, Infinity is contained in a grain of sand. If you define yourself as a human, the sheer vastness of the Infinite may overwhelm you. But if you define yourself as an integral part of the whole, as a spirit and as an individuation of Infinity, you will be awestruck with appreciation and excitement at being alive.

Infinity is not only an intellectual concept. It is something you can sense and touch experientially. As you read these words, relax your body and take note of the Is-ness of what-is. That means: Notice what you are perceiving right this very moment. Maybe there are birds chirping nearby, maybe raindrops. Maybe you notice your breathing. Maybe you notice the shapes and colors you are surrounded by. Everything is in constant flow and motion.

Your hearing, seeing, feeling, sensing, breathing…it is all happening by itself. There is no goal, no intention, no action, no patience, no waiting or work required to perceive. These are already a given, already a birthright, already simple and effortless.

Let Infinity be your point of reference and your guide. When there appears to be a "problem" in your daily life, contrast it with Infinity. Compared to Infinity it is not a problem, but merely a matter of curiosity.

Infinity and Eternity are all that was, all that is, and all that ever will be. It is everything and nothing. It is both ever changing and never changing. As a guide it teaches humility. It teaches that there is a creative force that is more powerful than anything we have imagined. It teaches that there are limitless possibilities and worlds. It teaches us that in order to expand we are to stop focusing on that tiny dot and become aware of more. It teaches us that anything we can imagine does exist somewhere in some way.

As you sit in the present moment notice that there are trillions of paths you could be taking today. Trillions of things you could be doing, seeing, thinking, and hearing. And it's your choice. You are a viewpoint of Infinity and therefore connected to all that is. And from all-that-is and has been created, you chose what to dedicate yourself to.

Infinity is All-Inclusive

"Trying to get rid of something is like trying to get rid of a part of Infinity. By definition everything that is a part of Infinity will exist forever and ever. Therefore, trying to get

rid of something is a complete waste of time and energy. What you can do is stop fighting it...by which the relevance of that thing decreases and your attention is freed up for all the other things going on in the Universe."
– Fred Dodson, Parallel Universes of Self

I initiate people into the mindset that **Everything Belongs**. You cannot exclude anything from Infinity. The reason I teach this philosophy is to support people to lessen their suffering. Almost anyone who experiences any suffering at all believes that something is happening to them that *doesn't belong*. But the idea doesn't make any sense. If it wouldn't belong, it would not be happening. Since it is happening to you in life, it does belong to life. It belongs to your life. Every aspect, part, point, scene, scenario, issue, person, place, thought, emotion, object, state, idea, and concept that you are experiencing, belongs. Nothing is an interruption of life. A few examples:

- If you have to commute an hour a day, you do not have to treat this as "dead time". This one hour a day is also an integral part of your life. There is no benefit at all in fighting it. Change it or embrace it.

- You are never in a Relationship with the "wrong" person. Whoever you are in a Relationship with right now is the exactly right person, exactly matching your energy-state, and the lessons you have yet to learn. Love them or Leave them, but don't waste your energy thinking it's the "wrong" person.

- You were not born on the "wrong planet". You came here intentionally with a set of visions and goals.

- An accident or mishap is not an interruption of your life. It is a wake-up call, your higher-self trying to tell you something it could not otherwise communicate. There are no "interruptions". Things may seem like interruptions to the desires of the Ego/Mind, but there really are no coincidences. Everything that happens is supposed to happen and is just right for your life plan. You are always getting back the overall energy and intentions you are radiating.

- A traffic jam is not hindrance to reach your goal, it is an integral part of the path to the goal. I know it takes some discipline to see things this way, but seeing it this way (and everything else) is incredibly empowering.

- An unhappy customer is not a problem, but a chance for you to get better. The "everything belongs" attitude is the only real option. It does not mean that you have to forever put up with traffic jams, unhappy relationships, and mishaps. But by no longer treating them as extraneous, you begin to become more tolerant and accepting of life, while at the same time no longer losing energy by fighting the things you don't like. There are other aspects of Infinity you could be focusing on. But by fighting unliked aspects, you keep focusing on them. By no longer fighting them, you quit activating them over and over again.

Welcome everything that happened and did not happen today as it was. Quit hassling yourself with how life is "supposed to be". Once you want what you get, you get what you want.

Omnipresence

A good subject of Meditation is Omnipresence. Omnipresence means to be everywhere at the same time. So I will sit down for 15 minutes or so and consider omnipresence. This puts me in touch the totality of things and with the aspect of Self that is already omnipresent. Omnipresence means **you can access any time and place** in this Universe and beyond. It means you are aware of everyone and everything simultaneously. The state traditionally known as "spiritual enlightenment" has something of omnipresence. Meditating on Omnipresence loosens the rigid and narrow ways of everyday life. Beyond the focal point of mass-attention there is a vast and wide universe waiting for its discovery. The Universe was created for the enjoyment and benefit of incarnated physical beings, yet we haven't even begun to look at 0.00000001% of it.

Are you God-Like?

"You are Gods; and all of you are children of the most High." - Psalm 86:2

"I am God," spoken as Ego/World-Self this is a statement of grandiose megalomania. Spoken as Soul/Higher-Self it is a statement of self-realization. You are a miniature god, equipped with the same abilities as the Supreme Being. You have the ability to…

…start things
…change things
…stop things

You have the ability to make decisions. One decision leads to another and so on, which means you are creating your reality piece by piece. This process may have been going on for eons. Even if you cannot control 100% of your reality due to karmic influence, you can get hold of what you can control and create and start from there. As a coach I always recommend you start with things you can control, not with the far-out.

Ancient Tradition teaches the following scale of Consciousness:

The Infinite (God)
Pure Awareness (True Self)
Ego/Will (I am)
Identity/Mind (I am this/that)
The Senses

The Reality Creation Tools are designed to help you discover and later re-discover your part in creating your reality. Your influence over reality increases the higher you go on the scale.

Some people ask me about how to get the reality creation techniques to work better or how to get them to work at all. A better approach than getting the tools to work is to ask yourself whether the **user** of the tools is willing to change. How willing are you to change? If you are willing to change, the tools work. I will try something unique here. I will try to help you get a sense of the state called Pure Awareness/Zero Point/Free Attention while reading this, so that by the time you are finished reading this section you will be closer to that state. Right now, as you sit there, bring your Awareness to the present moment. Stop resisting the present moment and be fully here. Notice your surroundings. Notice the room you are in. Take a few deep breaths. Acknowledge the present surroundings, the present objects, your body, your senses, and everything that is going on here and now. As you stop resisting, you transcend whatever you were resisting. As you cease doing anything you will notice there is still a lot happening. Seeing, Hearing, Feeling, Thinking, Breathing, Swallowing, Sensing, and a number of other things are happening. Become present of what is happening now as if it were the most important thing in the world.

Now bring your Awareness to the sounds you hear. Be aware of all the sounds. You might be hearing the sound your computer makes. You might be hearing the voices of others, maybe birds and cars outside. Become very aware of sound. Notice how the mind labels or builds images or associations around every sound, as in: "That is a bird." "That's the computer." "Those are people." As you listen to the sound, try removing the label and association if you can. Remove any label and simply be aware of the sound itself, without any back-story. Even remove the label "sound". You are now more purely aware of sound, without any filtering going on. You may notice that this practice is deeply relaxing.

Now bring your awareness to the chair you are sitting on. Put your consciousness into the chair. Act as if the chair is the most important thing ever. Become one with the chair. See if you can pinpoint where the chair stops and your body begins, or where the body stops and the chair begins. And be fully present with the chair. Next, retrieve any labels, ideas, and associations you have about the chair. Find the state prior to labeling the chair. Be aware of the object as it is, without even calling it "chair". You will notice a shift in attitude, where your awareness is merely with energy rather than a physical object. Stay with the chair for awhile. See if you can be perfectly happy just sitting on that chair and feeling it, without the need to go anywhere, to do anything, without desire or resistance. Just you and the chair, minus the label "chair". Breathe softly. Breathe with and as the chair.

Next, bring awareness to your thoughts. Develop curiosity about the thought-process itself. Observing your thoughts right now, relax and just let your thoughts think whatever they want to think. Every person on planet earth doing this exercise will notice thoughts. Some thoughts will be nice. Some will be not so nice. Some will be neutral. Who is the witness of those thoughts?

Just like you did with the sounds and the chair, remove your resistance, labeling, pushing or pulling from those thoughts. So that you are no longer one who reacts to the thoughts, but only one who witnesses them. The thoughts are then neither good, bad, nor neutral, they are just thoughts coming and going. And even remove the label "thoughts" so that you are simply observing "something" but you have no prejudice as to what it is you are observing. Be pure awareness of thought. And remain like that for some time, maybe even several minutes before you continue to read.

You will have noticed that the mind has slowed down and your attention is beyond the narrow band of everyday concerns, appointments, and expectations. You are a broader, calmer, wider, clearer version of yourself. You are no longer limited, contracted, and/or constricted to some desire or resistance. You have peace of mind. From this "zero point" there are no intentions, no plans, no analysis, no efforts to get something, and no efforts to avoid anything.

You will take a break from reading this and in a minute, stand up and walk to the other side of the room you are in now in slow motion. Every movement you make and every step you take must be done in full awareness. You will notice that conscious standing, walking, and moving; deliberate acting, will give you a sense of full control over your reality. So go ahead and walk to the other side of the room and back to your computer in full awareness and in slow motion. I'll see you in a few minutes.

Welcome back. What does it feel like to be pure awareness? If you have been doing this correctly, you'll feel more at ease and at the same time more powerful. More God-like because you control your starting, changing, and stopping of things. That is the purpose of mindfulness, the purpose of Meditation, and the idea of purposeful action.

Now bring awareness to objects in your room that you have never brought proper awareness to. Choose any object, say "Hello" to it and acknowledge its existence. Bring your awareness to it as if it were the most important thing in the world. Examine it. Lose yourself in that object. Go inside the object with your attention. You might intuitively sense that as you are truly connected with only

ONE thing in the Universe, you are connected with everything in the universe. This full awareness can be brought into anything...a problem you wish to dissolve, a person you wish to improve communication with, and/or a job you would like to improve... Things go wrong because people do not bring full awareness into them. If you have an accident, it was because awareness was missing. If you are short on money, it was because awareness and attention to detail was missing. Impatience is the ultimate lack of awareness. Give the object you are looking at some patience and be with it until your impatience recedes, and you are fully and totally present.

Notice how the label of that object, the name of it, your opinions about it, and other information about it do not allow you to fully grasp the energy of it, and do not allow you to get into this focused and light state you are currently in. So bring your full awareness to your body. Notice your body and feel it fully. And remove labels and identifications with the body and just sense what is really there. You are experiencing your body instead of intellectualizing about it, thinking about it, and abstracting about it. The moment you are experiencing the here and now, all past and future fades away, and with that, all problems fade. I have said before that all worries and fears indicate lack of awareness. Fear and worry mean that you are identified with the content of your mind rather than slowing down and becoming mindful of what is going on.

Bring your awareness to the empty space around the body. Bring your awareness back to the body. And back to the empty space around the body. Where does one start and the other stop?

Bring your awareness to some painful memory or emotion. As with the other things, become intensely curious about it. Remove all labels so that you are no longer judging it as "painful". Be aware of the energy itself. With a wide open mind, observe. You will notice that as you no longer push or pull the energy, it starts to develop and dissolve by itself, in the light of your awareness. Gently put your awareness away from this memory and notice something nice in your room, a picture for instance.

Become aware of its details. Perceive things you have not noticed about it before. (Yes, it is possible to have a picture in your room for years and still have things you have not noticed about it – that's how blind one can become.) As you perceive detail, the world gets more beautiful.

Now finally, just be fully present, without any specific task of where to put awareness. When you are fully present, you are not trying to assert yourself. You are not trying to make someone wrong. You are not analyzing or judging the situation. Presence is a peculiar state, not native to the normal physical-reality-earth state. You are not putting yourself down, not putting yourself up, you are just present. Being present does not mean being spaced-out or zoned-out. That's dissociation (subtle resistance), not presence. A present person is naturally kind and loving…s/he is god-like.

The Mystery and Immensity of the Infinite

Ancient sages referred to God's voice as "the voice without Echo". This was interpreted by some, to be a reference to: My God is the only true God, your God isn't. But I believe the phrasing means something different entirely.

Echo is created when a sound-wave travels through space and time and hits upon an object that resists it and reflects it back. A "voice without Echo" would therefore be a voice that permeates everything in the Universe, without the sound being repelled or bouncing back. The idea of a "voice without Echo" therefore refers to the **Infinite**. And that which is Infinite and Limitless would then really be the "only true God". Any God depicted in less than Infinite terms is not the real thing.

Much psychological and spiritual progress can be made by remaining aware of the Infinite. Why? Because it puts everything else – including your daily life activities and musings, problems, and considerations – into the proper context. It can also be very exciting and inspiring to stay aware of the sheer *immensity* and *mystery* of the Infinite.

Here are some synonyms to help you along in considering it:

Inexhaustible

Bottomless

Everlasting

Eternal

Total

Absolute

Perpetual

Limitless

Vast

Myriad

Countless

Unfathomable

Immortal

Boundless

Indefinite

Omnipotent

Omnipresent

Omniscient

Immeasurable

Unending

All-Inclusive

Comprehensive

The Being that is Infinite is not bound by time or space, not within or without the Universe, not limited by height, width, length, or depth, and not restricted by past, present, or future. This Being has no limited resources, no limited capacity, no limited understanding. Its presence is everywhere, in every Universe that ever was, ever is and ever will be.

The finite earth-mind asks, "If God can do anything, can he make a rock so big that he can't pick it up?" This is supposed to be a paradox or an unresolved riddle, or a logical impossibility to somehow debunk the idea of omnipotence. From an infinite perspective however, the answer would simply be "Yes!" Whatever question begins with "Can..." the answer would be "Yes". Yes, he is able to make a rock that big. And yes, he is able to pick it up anyway. "But...that doesn't make sense!" the finite-mind would say. And of course it doesn't make sense from a finite perspective. It violates the laws of physics. But these laws and this logic apply only to our realm, not to the Infinite.

And in fact, that's precisely what we did with this planet earth. We created a realm so dense and mysterious that it's too difficult to transcend the burden and get out of it...but we will do it anyway! Because in an Infinite Context, nothing is impossible.

Awareness of the Infinite is of practical use to daily life, especially in terms of what people call "Abundance". The more aware you become of the immensity of it all, the more you, for example, understand that **there is not much difference between 10 Dollars and 10 Billion Dollars. If Infinite Abundance is the standard, what's the difference?** That's like talking about the difference between 20 Degrees and 21 Degrees Celsius. World Poverty ends once people awaken to the ridiculous ease with which it is possible to draw upon this Unlimited Abundance.

Some people are actually offended by such ideas because they seems disrespectful of the poor, cruel even. But I'll have to keep on telling them because what is required is a Revolution of the Mind, not a Revolution of the World. Every possible external method of world poverty reduction has been tried and failed because the solution is not external. It doesn't matter how much funds I donate to the poor, as long as there is no fundamental change in Consciousness, the money I give them will soon be used up and they will be back to their default state. Anyone who went from poverty to riches owes that to a fundamental change in Consciousness.

Just like there is not much difference between 10 Dollars and 10 Billion, there is not much difference between the super-rich and the poor. Once this is understood, poverty will cease to exist. There is only a very *slight* difference in Consciousness, 21 degrees instead of 20. The press keeps painting the super-rich as "very different" than all the rest of us, but it's just not so. The slight differences in Consciousness are referred to "odd quirks of the super rich" by the press. But they are not odd quirks at all. They are slight differences in Consciousness. A few very simple examples:

Jeff Bezos, owner of Amazon.com and one of the wealthiest people alive, often keeps a seat free in meetings for an imaginary customer sitting in that free seat. Meeting attendees are meant to imagine a customer sitting there. The public calls this a "weird quirk". I call it a good exercise in conscious customer visualization and care. His top managers periodically have to go down and work at the telephone-hotline. The press calls this an "odd practice". I call it a good exercise in authentic customer connection. With a Boss of this kind of Consciousness Amazon will remain successful for years to come.

Rupert Murdoch, one of the most powerful media Moguls alive, practices Transcendental Meditation. The press calls it "an odd quirk of a bored old man". I call it "practicing Infinite Awareness".

Louis CK is one of the most successful stand-up comedians of all time. On stage he looks like a regular and lazy guy who spends most of his time sitting on a couch, watching baseball and eating pizza. In reality he is extremely industrious. He writes and rehearses his shows like crazy, for many weeks and months before performing them on stage. People call it "obsessed". I call it focused dedication.

Richard Branson, one of the most successful Entrepreneurs of all time, dresses up as different identities (most recently as a stewardess), for various marketing gigs. The press calls it "quirky". I call it vibrational-energy-shifting. Once an infinite-perspective is internalized, many other things follow from that. The main thing in regards to unlimited abundance is first to understand the Infinite Context in which you exist. That's really the first step of the way and all else follows from that.

Manifesting 10 Billion Dollars is just about as easy as manifesting 10 Dollars. This is where things get interesting. I'm sure I have your attention now...if you read this far! However: Are you sure you really want 10 Billion Dollars? I'm not so sure, not so sure at all. I'm not sure it would benefit you. I think you'd soon get bored and come complaining about something else. And that would be the secret reason you do not give yourself 10 Billion. Because you know it's rather meaningless once you view life from an Infinite Perspective. Once you realize how easy it is to get, it loses its meaning! The Ego only wants stuff it thinks it can't have.

I bet you don't care and would still like to know how to manifest your first 10 Billion. So what's the trick? How does it work? Well, if you are still asking, you haven't been paying attention to this book. The answer has already been given. You have to get yourself to believe that 10 Billion is not an "outrageous" sum of money, an "incredible" feat", or an "unbelievable" amount. You need to become aware of the how prevalent abundance really is. OK, it's sort of enjoyable to have 10 Billion, so even though it's an Illusion, I understand how you might want to experience a piece of the cake. So here's the deal: Spend, say three days, in an awareness of just how rich and abundant the Universe really is. Dress like it. Talk like it. Walk like it. Act like it. Request like it. Feel like it. Deal like it. Think like it. Give like it. Reject what is not-abundant. Be calm like it. Notice abundance everywhere and all the time. It's a universal rule that your own personal abundance will increase in this way. It's impossible to be aware of the sheer immense abundance of things and not attract some for yourself. How much Abundance will you summon? You will summon as much as you are really ready for.

Going away from money, how might awareness of the Infinite help you enjoy life more? Well, if you live in an Infinite field where everything is possible, everything becomes mysterious, fascinating and full of surprises. You start seeing the interconnectedness of everything. Then the person you are talking to is not just the person you know, but has an infinite amount of aspects you do not yet know. Then the apartment you dwell in is not just an apartment, but contains histories and energies you have not yet noticed. Then the walk you take is not just a walk you take, but one that can be taken in an infinite amount of ways. And what if the annoying person next door is actually an angel in disguise?

A Timeless State

Consciousness is timeless and there is a method to get an intuitive sense of this. The method is to **meditate on time-spans**. A time-span is from point A to Z. It could be your time in school, your time in a relationship, your childhood, your twenties, thirties, your time in a country, your job at a company, life from birth to death... Even small A-to-Z spans such as going out or driving to work qualify. Anything defined by a beginning and an end is a time-span. Such Meditation has the effect of perceiving time as limited and temporary, **enclosed by borders.** This naturally facilitates an awareness of that which is beyond the borders, beyond time, and that which is witness to time. Meditation on the finite calls forth the infinite. In just three to ten minutes of this you notice there is a part of you, the Observer, that remains unchanged throughout all of these phases and episodes of life. No matter where you were, who you were, and what was happening, there is a part of you that remained the same. You get in touch with that "real you", the soul that transcends time, space, and temporary conditions.

Another way to get a sense of timelessness is to become aware of the transience of all things; how all things come and go. You sometimes get this sense when looking at old white and black photographs. Who are the people in those photos? Nobody remembers them unless their work happened to transcend time.

You can also get this sense by noticing how patterns and cycles keep repeating throughout History. The same dramas are played out in new versions. Those who have studied History tend not to repeat the mistakes the current Generation is making. Every politician should actually be a student of History. The conflicts and dreams of today are not much different than those five hundred years ago, five thousand years ago, or twenty thousand years ago. Faces change but the earth-typical programs are exactly the same. Back then people gossiped in the market place, today they gossip on the Internet. Back then there were predictions of doom vs. predictions of glory, as there are today. Back then there were armed conflicts, as there are today. What's the difference?

Here's another way to get a timeless feel. This is a pictorial trip through Times Square from 1872 to 2013. People are generally fascinated by such pictures because it puts their Consciousness to the position of time-traveler. Plenty has changed in 130 years, but two essentials - the existence of humans and structures - have stayed the same.

"TIMES" SQUARE, formerly called Longacre, formed by the intersection of Broadway and Seventh Ave., extending from the "Times" Building, at 42d St., to 47th St., center of the theatre and hotel district, 37 of the foremost playhouses in America within 1500 yards, with seating capacity for audiences aggregating 45,000; Metropolitan Opera House two blocks below 42d St.; Hippodrome, largest playhouse in world; one block east; more people pass 42d St. and Broadway in 24 hours than any other point in world; are great restaurants, some of world-wide reputation, which give odd

Life, the Universe, and Everything

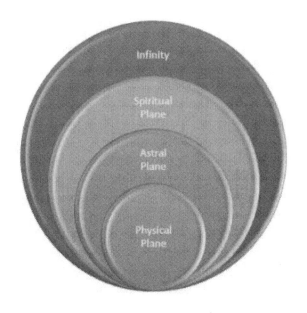

All spiritual traditions roughly categorize the planes of existence as shown above. There is our Physical Plane, which includes planet earth and all its objects, forms, and bodies as well as all other planets and objects in the Universe. I show the planes as circles within circles because while the next higher plane includes the lower plane, the lower plane does not include the higher. Someone existing on the spiritual plane can see the astral and physical plane, but someone residing on the physical plane cannot normally see the astral and spiritual planes (unless these qualities of "inner sight" are developed within oneself). Some traditions include a "mental plane" in between the astral and the spiritual. For simplicity purposes, I included that plane in the "spiritual plane". In-depth observation could split each of these planes into dozens of sub-layers (such as "lower and higher astral plane"), but I prefer to keep it simple.

Most of what passes as "spiritual" in our physical plane is actually astral. The difference is that spiritual energy is experienced as "light", "non-dual", and "clear", whereas astral-energy is more associated with what we call "weirdness", "mystery", and the "paranormal".

The planes of existence roughly correspond with the following "selves":

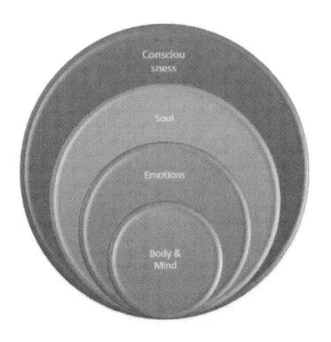

Your body & mind are your aspects of the Physical Plane. The mind has the capacity to reach up to and get information from the astral and sometimes even the spiritual plane. Survival-based thinking (worry) is locked into the Physical Plane. Imaginative thinking derives from the Astral & Spiritual Plane. Emotions correspond to the Astral Plane. Your individual Soul or Higher Self corresponds to the Spiritual Plane. You do have an aspect that is permanently at home there. To access your soul, all you have to do is imagine the highest-version-of-you. And Consciousness or Awareness itself corresponds to Infinity. For those worried about "losing their individual Identity" when they become Enlightened (when they become pure Infinite Consciousness).

As you can see, your individual soul is *included* within the highest level. So are emotions, and so is a physical body. The life-span of a body on earth is rarely more than a 100 years. The life-span of an astral-body is rarely more than a 1000 years. And the life-span of a soul can be Millions of years to Infinite. The "selves" roughly correspond to the following motivations:

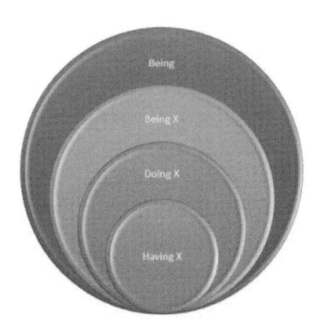

The physical-self is motivated by "having". "Having" a number of physical objects increases its sense of reality in the physical universe. One level higher, the prime motivation is not having, it's "doing". The person motivated from this level will not be talking about what he has and owns, but about what he does. Movement of energy then becomes more important than static objects. The spiritual level is motivated by being someone. The soul likes to slip into various roles and be those roles. A lifetime spent with different jobs and professions is a lifetime to the soul's liking. And at the highest level, rather than being this or that, one is content with simply Being.

The motivations and selves roughly correspond to the following "Modes of Consciousness":

At the lowest level life is all about reacting and surviving. At the mid-level it is about thinking. Lower-thinking is preoccupied with the past (remembering), higher-thinking is preoccupied with the future (imagination). At the spiritual level, thinking lessens and is replaced by intuition (simply "receiving" of information in the here-now) and mere witnessing, observing, and awareness.

The Universe itself consists of the following regions:

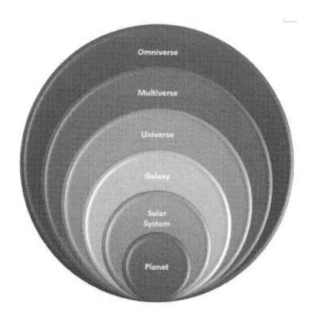

The "Multiverse" can be perceived from the Spiritual Plane and the "Omniverse" can be witnessed from the Infinite (I almost said "Infinite Plane", but the Infinite is not really a Plane, it is that which includes and creates all planes and more.).

The Omniverse does not correspond to simple cause-and-effect thinking. If you think in terms of: "Where did it all start?" and, "What was the beginning?" and then go on to theorize about the "Big Bang" or "Ultimate Origin"...the Omniverse does not work that way. The Omniverse always was and always will be, without beginning, without end. It did not "start" with a "big bang". The Universe may have started that way, but the Universe is part of the linear cause-and-effect reality. So those saying that "everything" started with a "Big Bang" are not wrong...they are just seeing it from the limited physical-universe perspective.

I have created these pictures to provide an easier visualization of "how stuff works", and how the levels-of-existence or levels-of-energy and consciousness correspond to each other. Once understood, this model is not only simple but easily *consistent with everything you will ever learn or experience*. It's the all-inclusive model philosophers, theologians, and academics have been arguing about for a long time.

The different levels are not a matter of being "better or worse". Sure, from a human perspective it feels extremely liberating to become lighter. But from an Infinite Perspective, everything has its proper place. There is actually no duality of "Light vs. Darkness". Instead there is one light that manifests in different levels of density (see my book "Levels of Energy"). In the following image you see that the entire Omniverse is "one color" (blue, in this example), in different density-levels, rather than being two colors (black and white, blue and red, etc):

The physical plane then, is not really "in opposition" or "the opposite" of the spiritual plane, but just another, denser expression of it. Therefore, embracing physical action, accepting one's physicalness, etc. are no contradictions to spirituality, they are extensions of it. *One of the unique qualities of a human being is to have an existence in each of the planes.* Normally you exist either on the spiritual, the astral, or the physical plane. But a human exists in all three! At night time while the body is sleeping, you are living an entire life on the astral plane. While waking, you live on the physical plane. And your spiritual-aspect (higher self) is present both day and night. You have three minds:

Subconscious Mind (corresponds to the astral-body and emotions as well as recorded events – memories – of the physical-self)

Conscious Mind (corresponds to the physical-body and your daytime life)

Higher Mind (corresponds to the Spiritual Realm)

The Subconscious Mind will give you much more information than the Conscious Mind can give you. It is accessed through relaxation, hypnosis, night dreams, question-techniques, inner imagery, lucid dreaming, and out-of-body-travel. The Higher Mind will give you even more information than both the Conscious and Subconscious Mind. It is accessed through Lucid Dreaming (rather than just Dreaming what the subconscious provides), Prayer (only if it is addressed to the highest source), deliberate inner imagery (conscious visualization), Meditation, and Awareness-Training.

The intention of this book is, of course, to inspire the reader to live life a little more from the spiritual plane. My advertisement for such is because humans have become just a little too caught up in the game of the physical universe. This has been the cause of undue suffering. So **lighten** up!

7
Life is a Spiritual Journey

To determine whether something is really important or not, ask yourself: Will it still be important in 1000 years? – Frederick Dodson

Life Is a Spiritual Journey

Most of the great wisdom traditions agree that:

1. Spirit, by whatever name, exists.
2. Spirit, although existing "out there," is found "in here," or revealed within to the open heart and mind.
3. Most of us don't realize this Spirit within, however, because we are living in a world of sin, separation, or duality — that is, we are living in a fallen, illusory, or fragmented state.
4. There is a way out of this fallen state (of sin, illusion, or disharmony), there is a Path to our liberation

*5. If we follow this Path to its conclusion, the result is a Rebirth or Enlightenment, a direct experience of Spirit within and without, a Supreme Liberation, which:
6. Marks the end of sin and suffering, and:
7. Manifests in social action of mercy and compassion on behalf of all sentient beings.*
– Ken Wilber

Intensify Your Experience of Life

There is a difference between just existing and actually living, a difference between just going through the motions and having a spirited life. One type of life is merely experienced in the mind; the other is experienced out there in life itself. One experience is worth a thousand books.

The entertainment industry with its endless books, websites, movies, and audio recordings portrays the adventures of other people and oftentimes these are fictional adventures. Once in a blue moon someone, having undertaken a real adventure, is portrayed. But it's still not the viewer's adventure. As such, all entertainment is merely borrowed adventure, where we can imagine having a fulfilled life for the duration of the book or movie.

One authentic experience supersedes a thousand books. In fact, after every real, deep, high, or intense experience, I've found myself losing interest in mere information for weeks and sometimes months. None of those words on paper are needed if the real thing is experienced. You can't taste strawberries from a book no matter how many books about strawberries you read.

All rapid learning is facilitated by experience. That's why I did not enjoy school that much. The best way to learn about another culture is not from a textbook but by living amongst that culture for a few months. The best way to learn to pilot an airplane is by spending time in the pilot's cabin beside an experienced pilot, and just doing it. The best way to experience the power of intention and inner will, is by practicing it. The quickest way to learn a language is by immersing yourself in it with no opportunity to resort to your native tongue. The best way to experience serenity is through meditation, not considering meditation. The best way to become an accomplished author is by reading and writing as much as possible. The best way to become an accomplished *anything* is by doing it many times. A romantic experience with another person supersedes a hundred romantic movies.

To experience something means to be present and engaged in an activity rather than thinking about it. You can intensify your experience of any situation by letting go of evaluating, judging, and labeling an event while it happens. Save the judgment for later. If you are rafting on a wild river, you don't need to consider the technical details of the boat, what you will have for dinner later, what the people there think of you, or when the trip ends. **All of that is thinking-ness...a habit taken from days when you are not experiencing life itself first hand**. Instead the splashing of water, the riding of waves, the laughter and surprise is quite enough to fill your soul with joy.

The mind is a peculiar thing. It replays images from the past, recordings made when you were more present and alive than you are now. To protect itself from the liveliness and excitement of the present moment, it focuses on these thought-patterns. Let go of that and instead pay close attention to what is happening right now. That will heighten your appreciation of what is presently happening, thus intensifying your experience.

This is a quote taken from my book Journeys in Spectral Consciousness:

When you record a piece of video or audio over and over again, like the mind does, it becomes, in technical terms "lossy", meaning quality is reduced. Soon you are no longer viewing the unfiltered, present moment in all its radiant brilliance and vividness, you are viewing a lossy copy of reality. You are viewing a highly processed recording, not the original reality. The processed and automated images eventually begin to decay, making life look increasingly more dull and boring. Once the filters of the mind are removed, the radiant aliveness of Divine presence begins to shine, and everything appears to be more three dimensional, deep, fascinating, and illuminated, with more texture and color. You are viewing reality unedited.

This is why, in my live workshops, I have people walking around outside staring at various aspects of reality while reducing their own labels and expectations, while slowing down enough to see reality as it is – as luminous energy. If you can slow down your mind, you begin to see it. If you have ever heard someone say, "I don't know what she sees in that guy," this is because the person who is in love sees the radiance of the Divine, whereas others don't see it. When the person stops seeing that divine spark in the other, the "being in love" will recede.

Quotes from the Ancient Kybalion

Some quotes from the ancient Kybalion:

"To destroy an undesirable rate of mental vibration, put into operation the principle of Polarity and concentrate upon the opposite pole to that which you desire to suppress. Kill out the undesirable by changing its polarity."

"Nothing rests; everything moves; everything vibrates."

"The possession of Knowledge, unless accompanied by a manifestation and expression in Action, is like the hoarding of precious metals - a vain and foolish thing. Knowledge, like wealth, is intended for Use. The Law of Use is Universal, and he who violates it suffers by reason of his conflict with natural forces."

"As above, so below; as below, so above. "

"Every Cause has its Effect; every Effect has its Cause; everything happens according to Law; Chance is but a name for Law not recognized; there are many planes of causation, but nothing escapes the Law."

"Everything flows, out and in; everything has its tides; all things rise and fall; the pendulum-swing manifests in everything; the measure of the swing to the right is the measure of the swing to the left; rhythm compensates."

"Everything is Dual; everything has poles; everything has its pair of opposites; like and unlike are the same; opposites are identical in nature, but different in degree; extremes meet; all truths are but half-truths; all paradoxes may be reconciled."

Science Fiction and Fantasy Are Closet Spirituality

When I was a child I had an intense interest in Science-Fiction. Looking back today I realize that this was a child-like expression of a deep longing for higher realms. Not being experienced in higher realms, the desire was projected into "other worlds" that mainly lie within the physical universe. Very rarely did science-fiction back then venture into the spiritual or metaphysical. At the overall lower level of Consciousness prevalent a few decades ago, 90% of all sci-fi was mixed with earthly ideas of violence and paranoia. I clearly recall asking my Dad about the Star Trek series, "Why do they only show ugly and mean aliens?" I knew there just had to be some really beautiful ones out there. I asked myself whether humans might have some inferiority complex which made it difficult to envision more beautiful beings (by human standards) from other worlds than their own.

Your own fascination with sci-fi or fantasy can be a reminder that you would actually like to experience some of these other worlds or higher states of Consciousness rather than only reading about them. A good way to experience some of those far journeys is Lucid Dreaming. However, keep in mind that you came to planet Earth in order to be on planet earth. If you can fully embrace normal life on this Planet, without trying to remove yourself into ascensionist and escapist fantasies, you become lighter…by which it paradoxically becomes easier to elevate yourself to higher states and travel to other realms. The way *through* is the way out.

Simplicity

"The Taoist symbol for simplicity is an uncarved rock; it is potential that does not carry any fixed definition. Shedding definition is letting go, not defending any idea of yourself, and not investing in a fixed viewpoint. When your mind is not forced into expressions of judgment or pretense, it will quiet and flow with what is present. Compulsive desires will disappear. Letting go of justifications and arguments will bring your mind back to the present. Ask simple questions. Give simple answers. Share simple pleasures. Enjoy the things that money can't buy. Observe. Be an uncarved rock (minus the rock). "
– H. Palmer

Karmic Coaching

Almost all spiritual traditions suggest that there is some kind of Karma at play, some kind of "what you put out, is what you get back", some kind of accountability, judgment, or boomerang-effect for your thoughts, words, and deeds. I believe this principle to be one of the few universal truths that applies to every soul. I can see the principle at work on a small scale over a lifetime. I can see how people who wronged others later got wronged themselves. How those who did good deeds in their life, sooner or later get good done to them. Because the small scale is a reflection of the big scale, I believe that the "law of karma" also applies to our existence as a soul over many lifetimes.

According to Buddhism and Hinduism there is a higher level of consciousness in which karma no longer has an effect. One can either balance one's karmic account by making up for bad deeds, or one can reach that higher plane in which all karmic debt is deleted. One then leaves the cycle of birth and rebirth. Abrahamic Religions have a similar concept whereby God has the power to render one's sins null and void when people pray for forgiveness.

When, in my coaching work, I encounter something that does not seem to resolve with the usual tools and wisdom, the next step is to look at karmic inheritance. About 10% of people's issues do not seem to dissolve no matter what is tried. It seems to stick no matter what they think, believe, or do. In this case it is wise to **assume** that you, at one point in your existence, have done similar to others. Most people you suggest this to will initially resist the notion of having caused harm to others. That's normal, as only very few people consciously want to bring harm to others, and if they did they would be quick to cover it up in very deep layers of their subconscious. But the alternative to the karmic view of life is not that appealing. The alternative is to believe that life is primarily random and pointless and that you can encounter suffering without rhyme or reason. Submitting to this life-view is ultimately more disempowering than admitting you may have made mistakes in the past.

My method of karmic coaching is as follows:

1. Spot an issue you have been unable to resolve.

2. Identify yourself as the **victim** of that issue and spot its **perpetrator** (this can be a person, event, or circumstance).

3. Look for a time in your life when **you** were the **perpetrator** of that thing. Look for times when **you** have **made others victims** of that. If you can find no such time during this life, then use your imagination to speculate on a

past life in which you were the perpetrator of that. Imagination, when used as a tool for karmic research, will either deliver information that actually happened, or as a symbolic representation or metaphor that can nevertheless have a healing effect.

4. Experience (Imagine/Visualize/Feel) being a victim of that and being a perpetrator of that. Alternate back and forth between the two for at least a few minutes or more. In your mind, merge the two, seeing them as one single energy-field that fed off each other. Release and let go on the out-breath.

5. Find a way in the external world to **help others** who are victim-perpetrator of this event. By helping them unravel their pattern and find forgiveness, you transcend the victim-perpetrator field, ascending to the helper-field.

A practical example: Let's say your life is going along quite well and you encounter inexplicable misfortune, even though you thought and did all the "right things". Your house was burned down by an anonymous group of villains. Since you were not radiating any fear and since you had not caused anyone similar harm, instead of immediately projecting yourself as the hapless victim of an evil and unpredictable world, you would **assume** that at some point in your existence you caused similar to others. You would sit down to meditate and imagine that you had done that to someone else. An image of you burning down someone's barn in a past life might come up. It does not that much matter whether the image and the past-life are real or not. Even if it is only a metaphor, this has the effect of leaving the victim-level and ascending up one step higher to the perpetrator level, in which you are **responsible** for the harm. In my book "Journeys through Spectral Consciousness", I describe the three levels as: **Victim – Perpetrator – Helper.** Then, in your Meditation, you move back between the two positions of victim and perpetrator several times, while noticing and feeling how they feed each other energy. It is my view that if one does not leave the victim-perpetrator cycle, it keeps repeating from lifetime to lifetime. You will become the perpetrator and then the victim and then the perpetrator and so on. To leave this cycle you would then chose to become the third level – the helper. In this example that would mean helping the victim of a house burning with his/her forgiveness or helping the perpetrator of a house burning make up for his/her damage. You might need a little imagination to come up with a way to help such people. If you cannot find an opportunity to help victims and perpetrators of your event in real life, then you can also transcend the issue by forgiveness of both sides and seeking to make some amends for your deed yourself. By doing so, you leave the victim-perpetrator cycle and no longer have to play that "game" over and over again.

I have experienced a few quite magical transformations while applying this process within my coaching work. When you look back and notice that "event X" just no longer happens to you, you only see it happening to others, you know you have left that "game" for good.

Life on Earth Is Perfect for Balancing Karma

Life on earth is a perfect mix of agony and bliss, light and darkness; an *opportunity* to undo negative karma and accumulate positive karma. It's as if this planet was designed for just that purpose, and most of us have plenty of time to fix our karmic account.

There is no need to be frustrated at life, no need to assume you're on the wrong planet. When you decided to come here you knew exactly what you were doing.

The game couldn't be simpler: An **act of kindness** adds to positive karma, an act of unkindness adds to negative karma. At the end of the game both sides are weighed and whatever outweighs the other determines the next game level. Does this sound too simple? Well, it's what all the great and ancient spiritual paths teach. So what if you undergo numerous hard knocks throughout life? Then why not assume you are making up for pre-life karma! That makes it easier and it puts you in the driver's seat, feeling responsible for your destiny. Becoming whiny and vindictive has not proven effective for anything.

From a karmic standpoint, life on earth is about choosing good and bad. It's not about getting rid of bad. That's one of the great misconceptions. The belief that: *"The world has to be perfect before I can be happy,"* is guaranteed to disappoint you. Does that mean you should no longer try making the world a better place? Am I discouraging activism?

No. But if it is your calling to be a world-improver, you are really doing that for your own karma, not necessarily to heal the whole world. You can heal parts of it. In fact: *You can heal some of the people some of the time, you can't heal all of the people all of the time.* You don't know what *their* karma is. Some people don't require the healing you think they do.

This insight can be especially hard when someone close to you is dying. Someone might ask me, *"How can I help him/her heal and stay alive?"* and my answer to that is that if it is his/her time to go, you can't do anything. You can intend, meditate, or pray for them and request as follows:

*"Allow him/her to experience **whatever is in the highest good.**"*

And if his/her healing is in the highest good, he/she will be healed. If passing on to the other side is in his/her highest good, then that's what will happen.

There are many tricks in which "the dark side" can keep you from practicing kindness. One such trick is to think that any kind of resentment is justified. But there is no justified resentment – at all. That does not mean you have to approve of the various things going on. Kindness does not equate to approval of negativity. It's the realization that those who commit evil are merely acting from ignorance. To forgive them means to recognize the basic *naïve predisposition of the human mind.* Everyone *thinks* they are doing the right thing, even if it's not. There is no merit in holding resentment within your energy-field because that presumes that feeling bad punishes others when actually you are only punishing yourself.

The world may not be perfect in your eyes, but for the purposes of karmic balancing and choosing, I couldn't imagine a more perfect environment. Planet Earth is a work of genius.

Don't Be "Spiritual", Be Spirited

The word enthusiasm is derived from en-theos, meaning god within. Those who are on fire with an enthusiastic idea and who allow it to take hold and dominate their thoughts find that new worlds open for them. As long as enthusiasm holds out, so will new opportunities.

Norman Vincent Peale

A mediocre idea that generates enthusiasm will go further than a great idea that inspires no one.

Mary Kay Ash

Knowledge is power, but enthusiasm pulls the switch.

Ivern Ball

Success is the ability to go from failure to failure without losing your enthusiasm.

Winston Churchill

The real secret of success is enthusiasm.

Walter Chrysler

I studied the lives of great men and famous women,

and I found that the men and women who got to the top were those who did the jobs they had in hand, with everything they had of energy and enthusiasm.

Henry Truman

The great accomplishments of man have resulted from the transmission of ideas and enthusiasm.

Thomas J. Watson, Sr.

If you can give your son or daughter only one gift, let it be – enthusiasm.

Bruce Barton

It's faith in something and enthusiasm for something that makes life worth living.

Oliver Wendell Holmes, Jr.

Enthusiasm – the sustaining power of all great action.

Samuel Smiles

Don't be "spiritual", be spirited. Real **spirituality** is to **be spirited** – or vigorous, vibrant, vivacious, spirited, animated, sparkling, energetic, dynamic, enthusiastic, passionate, irrepressible, lighthearted, and ebullient.

These modern times have many calling themselves "spiritual" without actually being spirited. People who are just going through the motions of some kind of ritual or religion out of habit or tradition rather than burning love, are not spirited. So called "spiritual seekers" who are only reading up on spiritual ideas to solve some problem are not really spirited. Spirited people are more players than seekers, creators than consumers, involved more in context than content, more curiosity driven than trauma driven. Method-shopping and workshop-hopping is not the primary activity, but exploration, experimentation, and extrapolation. Spirituality is not a trendy lifestyle-choice but a deep lifelong love affair. It is less of a doing, more of a **being**. This is why the **cultivation of character, ways of behavior, virtues and values is a quicker way of raising your consciousness than "having" and "doing".** Even your material success in life also largely hinges not so much on what you do, what you did, or how much, hard, and long you worked, but rather on **who you are and what value your being-ness brought to the world**. And what does it take to be more spirited? Well, to have more energy. And how do you have more energy? You have more energy with a good combination of physical movement, healthy nutrition, positive inner focus (attention-shifting, visualization, meditation, or prayer), a sound environment, and a right-for-you-career. The first three are under your complete control, the latter two are mostly under your control but may take longer to establish. Hence you could be more Available, Friendly, Considerate, Humane, Humble, Imaginative, Forgiving, Honorable, Reliable, Courageous, Envisioning, Benign, Easy-Going, Firm, Disciplined, Content, Cordial, Diligent, Open, Patient, Positive, Thoughtful, Stable, Appreciative, Respectable, Persistent, Conscious, Flexible, Adventurous, Authentic, Kind, Sensible, Tolerant, Supportive, Honest, Pleasant, Optimistic, Balanced, Equitable, Loyal, Joyful, Beautiful, Empathetic, Compassionate, Intuitive, Creative, Deliberate, Strong, Responsible, Trusting, Initiating, Aesthetic, Contemplative, Generous, Cheerful, Attentive, Interested, Caring, or any other trait you can pinpoint and remember to practice. You move not from external to internal but from an internal state and character to external expressions and results.

Night Swimming and Out-Of-Body-Travel

This is a praise of Night Swimming. As I recently worked in a place that has daytime temperatures of 104 Degrees (40 Celsius), swimming in the ocean at night is pleasantly warm. I recommend it to anyone who hasn't had the chance to do so. It is exhilarating and enlightening for many reasons. Floating in the black sea under a canopy of stars, away from noise not only provides a slight fun sense of "danger", but also mimics the nightly journeys of the soul. Let me explain: Every night, when your body falls asleep, your essence; your spirit, leaves the body. It would be bored to spend all night in the bedroom. The last thoughts you have while falling asleep determine where the journey goes that night (the last person you think of at night, by the way, reveals where your heart is). Actually, *everyone* practices "out of body travel" whether they know it or not. It's nothing unusual, you do it every night. What people mean by "out of body travel" however, is being *aware* that they are doing it. Usually the mind falls asleep with the body. But if the mind stays awake while the body sleeps, you will experience a jolt and become witness to your energy-self floating up in the air and traveling. When your energy-self, which is a part or aspect of your soul, leaves the body without any specific thought (and therefore without any specific destination), it simply "floats through space". The reason this space is dark is because most such journeys take place at night while the body is asleep.

People who have not had the chance to experience out-of-body travel can somewhat mimic this "floating through dark space" by night swimming. And if you are afraid of night swimming because you cannot see much and fear hidden dangers lurking in the water or air, then chances are high you would also be afraid of out-of-body-travel and secretly sabotage your ability to do so. By night swimming you can then in fact **test your readiness** to practice OBE. One who can night-swim without any fear is more likely to astral-travel (OBE) without fear. You see, if you harbor fear then that is the best indicator that you should not be astral-traveling (or night swimming for that matter), because your fear will only attract unpleasant experiences. Familiarity lessens fear.

When I had my first night swim in these pleasantly warm regions, I was at first a little skeptical. There was no lifeguard around, no hotel staff around, not even any other swimmers nearby, just me and the ocean. Because it was night, the wind had picked up and the waves were higher. I could not see the terrain under the water nor the creatures that swim there. But yesterday I was on my third night swim in a week and skepticism (fear) had been replaced by enjoyment, due to familiarity. So on this third night I tried venturing out further than ever before, beyond the barriers marked for hotel guests. I wanted to swim so far out that the hotel lights faded and it was only me, the water, the moon, and the stars. Of course I cannot and should not recommend this to anyone, which would be reckless and irresponsible…unless of course you have complete trust that you are protected.

Serendipity and Synchronicity

Serendipity
Some words evoke a smile merely by knowing their meaning. The dictionary defines "Serendipity" as follows:

"The phenomenon of finding valuable or agreeable things not sought for."

Isn't that a nice thought? Serendipity reminds of us a higher invisible force that delivers miracles when least expected, offers crossroads not deliberately willed, imbues grace when we have reached our limits, plays with synchronicity when we pay attention. The best things in life happen when, after long stretches of effort, we let go of trying to get them and give The Universe right of way. What then happens is surprise and usually much better than that which we sought for.

Synchronicity
As an adult I have lived at five different places. All of these places had the house number 5. Coincidence? I think not. What are the statistical chances of that? I take it to mean that the number 5

is somehow significant in my life, and I've based a number of decisions on it.

The first people to fly a plane, the Wright Brothers, came from Ohio. The first person to fly into space, John Glenn, came from Ohio. The first person on the moon, Neil Armstrong, came from Ohio. Coincidence? I think not. Somehow Cosmic Coincidence Control Center thinks that the pioneers of flight come from Ohio.

Synchronicity reminds us of some deeper layer of Cosmic Interconnectedness. I recommend you look at the names, numbers, and places of your life and notice some of the patterns. While it may not reveal anything directly useful, it will reveal that there are no coincidences, that there is some grander and more mysterious design underlying your life.

Just one silly example: These are some of the names of the people I have regularly booked Course and Workshop-Rooms with throughout my coaching-career:

Mr. Zimmer (Zimmer is the German word for "Room")
Mrs. Casa (Casa is Spanish for "House")
Mr. & Mrs. Albergo (Albergo is the Italian word for "Hotel")

No kidding! The names may resemble something from a cheap movie script but these were the main characters in my life that provided lodging for my seminars.

Synchronicity is only noticed if you pay *attention*. It's all around you. A fun game I sometimes play while driving down the highway goes something like this: "The next message on the back of a truck will be a message that applies to my situation." I'm using the ads on the back of trucks as my tarot-cards. I did this a few days ago regarding a decision of whether or not to make a certain trip abroad. I felt intuitively that the trip was not right to me. The next truck I passed had a huge Warning-Sign on it saying "Heavy Cargo. Be Cautious!" So I decided to cancel the trip. This may sound strange to you, but the Universe tends to communicate symbolically rather than directly. Sure enough, a few days later I learned that the meeting I was supposed to fly to turned out to be a disaster.

Another example: I was wondering whether to do a Business deal with one guy. In that moment a truck passed by featuring a company that had the *same name* as that guy. That was the Go! signal for me.

The Universe communicates in mysterious ways. Insight does not always have to come from deep books and teachers, it can come from the side of a truck.

There are no coincidences

A few months ago I had three jobs in Germany. The first one was in the "Linden Street" ("Lime Tree Street") in Munich. The second, a week later in a street called "Unter den Linden" ("Under the Lime Trees") in Berlin. The third gig was in a street called "Lindenspür Street (literally "Feeling the Lime Tree") in Stuttgart, Germany, **again exactly** one week later. So I was first at the Lime Trees, then I was Under the Lime Trees, and finally I was feeling the Lime Trees. These three jobs were, to all external appearances "completely unrelated" to each other, and I only noticed the amazing "coincidence" the third time this Lime Tree confronted me. What was the probability of being with Lime Trees three consecutive weeks, at different locations, and on vastly different jobs? The first job was a company seminar I was holding in Berlin, the second job was a TV-ad I was shooting, and the third job was a Seminar of my own. The chances of that occurring were very low as it's not *that* common of a street name. So I looked the tree up on Wikipedia to check what it meant and found this:

"In old Slavic mythology, the linden was considered a sacred tree. Particularly in Poland, many villages have a name "Święta Lipka" (or similar), which literally means 'Holy Lime'."

Apparently the cosmic-message being broadcast to me was that there was something about these jobs that was "sacred", and perhaps, that I should treat them as such. I am not that good at interpreting such "coincidences" and generally more fascinated by their occurrence than their meaning. But oftentimes interesting insights can be derived from a little bit of research.

If such example as above were a single event I'd probably forget about it quickly, but these things happen to me almost every month! Or more precisely: I suspect they happen every day, but I only notice them about once a month.

There are no coincidences. By that I mean that nothing happens randomly without purpose, cause, or meaning. The reason I teach this is because it has proven to me more effective than the common view that life is a series of random and meaningless events. The word "coincidence," meaning that something happens without a connection to something else, is nonsensical to me, just as the idea that existence "started" with a "Big Bang" out of "nothing" and "caused by nothing" makes no sense to me at all. (What makes much more sense is what Enlightened Sages tell us: That there was no "beginning" of existence and there is no "end" to it, as time is merely an illusory construct of physical reality.) Related words to "coincidence" are "by accident", "by chance", "by luck"…three more words that have (in my view) no basis whatsoever in reality. There are no accidents, nothing happens "by chance", and there is no such thing as "luck" in the sense of good fortune happening without a cause.

The words I use instead are *Synchronicity* (coined by psychiatrist Carl Gustav Jung and physicist Wolfgang Pauli), *Karma* (coined by ancient Eastern Spirituality), and *Attractor-Fields* (coined by modern metaphysicists). The word "coincidence" did not come into existence until around the 17th Century when it started appearing in France as "coincider" which meant: "A concurrence of events with no connection." Before that, the concept was unknown. And in fact, every time we use the word "coincidence" we intuitively feel that it's **not** a coincidence. We say "What a *strange* coincidence!" acknowledging that something mysterious is happening. But just because we do not understand how something happened, just because we cannot see the inter-connectedness of everything, does not mean an event happens without a purpose. Just like children only understand a small part of how the world works compared to adults, we too do not see the whole picture. **But we can intuit that there is more going on than meets the eye by the synchronicities that happen to us.** It can be a fun and revealing exercise to view *nothing* as a coincidence, to realize that *every* person you meet, every little thing that happens, everything you see, feel, hear, notice, and experience is connected to other things you see, feel, hear, notice, and experience. It is in this understanding that things begin to appear absolutely fantastic and baffling.

If you browse the Internet (or read C.G. Jung or Charles Fort) you will find numerous amazing synchronicities that have happened to people. But you will also find them if you **look at your life more closely**. Examine the names of the people in your life. Ask yourself what the deeper significance of their presence in your life is. Examine the numbers in your life (such as ages, house numbers you lived at, special dates, etc.). Look. Observe. Examine. And be **amazed**.

Humans Can Fly

Can humans fly with their bodies like superman? When I type "humans can fly" into Google, I find this answer from Yale University at the top position:

*"And now, scientists have determined that we never **will**: it is mathematically impossible for **humans** to **fly** like birds. A bird **can fly** because its wingspan and the wing muscle strength are in balance with its body size. It has a lightweight skeleton with hollow bones, which puts a smaller load on its wings."*

The scientific consensus is that we cannot fly and that it is "impossible". As you might guess, I disagree. First of all, I have issues with the use of the word "impossible". Only a hundred years ago flying with a plane, cars, wireless communication, and many other realities were labeled "impossible" by the "scientific consensus".

Secondly, in my experience, **humans are not given a desire without the inherent ability to achieve it one day**. Put differently: Where there is a will, there is a way. If you can dream it, you can do it.

Humans desire to fly has been so deep and continual throughout History, that on some level we believe it must be possible. I have had many night dreams in life in which I flew with my body. These dreams have been so detailed and realistic that sometimes, upon awakening, I was convinced that I could fly. Therein I was even given specific training instructions on learning how to fly, how to focus, how to move my arms and legs, how to lift off, speed up, and land.

Our deep desire to fly is demonstrated in all kinds of sports and activities in which they mimic flying, such as Skydiving, Kitesurfing, Paragliding, Air-Pressure-Hovering, Hoverboards, Flyboarding, Jetpacks, and Wingsuit Flying.

In my view we are already preparing and training for the day that humans can fly with their bodies. Every new reality first begins as a dream. Then it is mimicked and one tries to get as close to the "real thing" as possible. And finally, the new reality manifests.

Yes, of course flying with the body "defies the laws of physics" as we currently know them. That's why we should research more thoroughly into the hidden and untapped capabilities of the human body, mind, and soul. Rather than repeating the mantra: "It's impossible," and thereby shutting off all discussion, we should be saying: "It could be possible, let's find out how to do it." Our hearts have a yearning for the unknown, the amazing, and the incredible. Our soul wants to grow and expand beyond its previous limitations.

Our wish to fly might be based on the fact that our energy-body (soul) can fly. In order to mimic this ability, the future will be increasingly airborne. I believe that we will have shoes that allow us to float, flying cars, hovering boards on which to cruise around, mechanical wings, and floating bubbles for individual transportation within my lifetime…and that all of these inventions will eventually culminate in our ability to fly without tools.

8

Advanced Meditation & Non-Duality

Impatience Creates Time

In some workshops I deliberately implement exercises that test students' patience. They then might say, "How long will this exercise take?" There is a level of consciousness that exists outside of time, and the purpose of breaking the impatience (which is actually resistance toward the here and now and by extension resistance toward all of life) is to reach that higher level in which awareness is clear and lucid, and energy starts flowing in abundance.

People have noted that my presence and voice have a calming effect. That's because I've mostly overcome the time-paradigm. My patience is infinite, and they can sense I am willing to be-with-them eternally and never leave them behind. In levels of energy terms this state has been called "the 500s". Frequent questions people ask reveal their uneasiness (dis-ease) in being subject to time: "There must be a quicker way to achieve these results?" "When am I going to get ____?" "How can I manifest my preferred reality more quickly?" The answer to all of these questions is NOW. And if you can fully enter the now with infinite calm and equanimity, you do not really care when you are "going to get something" because all bliss is already here. Of course you understand that from this poised space, your intentions manifest more rapidly. Why? Because you're outside of time. You state an intention or a decision, then you stand back or let go. It's no longer matters "when" it will come true. Once you have stated the intention it has already come true, even if your physical eyes can't see it manifest. I know this is hard to understand, but you will get the hang of it with practice.

Of course those who claim to be "practicing patience" while gritting their teeth are still not practicing it. The kind of patience I am talking about knows zero resistance. It thoroughly enjoys what is going on right now. This timeless level is a real spiritual breakthrough, a totally different perception of reality, if you wish to step into it.

Flow Is the Best Time Manager

I had to postpone an important meeting with someone but calling it off would've likely caused a loss of opportunity. So I let go of the idea that there would be a loss involved and let go of the idea that I needed to call off today. A few hours later the guy called me and told me that he had to postpone the meeting, asking me whether or not that was OK. I told him it was fine, and we arranged for another time.

Stuff like this happens all the time. Almost every day. When you're in the flow, when you're in general well-being, all the puzzle-pieces of your life fall into place exactly as they should and exactly when they should.

How to Overcome Guilt over Wasting Your Time

One of the most common forms of guilt is the guilt over wasting time. You feel this guilt when you are not following the standards you yourself have defined. When you feel this guilt it's probably because you really are wasting time (according to your standards).

The bad news is that this feeling of guilt and self-pressure does nothing to solve the time-wasting feeling or activity. The solution would be to either no longer feel guilt over that thing you are doing or to quit doing it. But when you feel guilt you are re-creating the problem and will experience it again in a few hours, days, or weeks. The feeling of guilt may temporarily make you quit and do something more important, but in general, when you send out the energy-vibration of guilt over wasting your time that's a guarantee that you will do it again.

There are many factors involved in this and this process will help you liberate yourself from them. The issue is an inner conflict between the inner child-self and the inner parent-self.. Neither of those selves are YOU.

1. Visualize yourself doing the activity you think is a "waste of time". Since you are doing the activity, there is no point in putting yourself down for doing it, right? You either do it or you don't do it, what is the point of exerting resistance against yourself? So while you visualize it, gradually release the pressure

you have been putting on yourself. Gradually release the Judgmental Parent-Self within you. You are an adult now, and you allow yourself to play. While you visualize yourself playing, relax and release your muscle tension and resistance. Actually enjoy doing that activity fully.

2. Visualize yourself stopping that activity, not doing it and then doing something more important. In this case it is not your Parent-Self that is pressuring you, but your Child-Self. The Child-Self hates focus and discipline just as the Parent-Self hates play. So relax with the image of not doing the activity and doing something disciplined and sensible instead. Gradually give up any muscle tension or subtle Resistance. Continue to visualize and practice fully enjoying that activity. You are an adult now and you allow yourself to focus. You take control of your Destiny.

Repeat Steps 1 and 2 several times until you have transcended the parent-self and the child-self on this issue.

After you have mentally and emotionally practiced this, try putting it to action by first:

a) Enjoying the activity, play or "time-waster" to its fullest, with a good conscience,

and

b) Enjoying not doing the activity, doing something disciplined and time-efficient to its fullest with a good conscience.

The inner parent and the inner child are masks of the Ego. You recognize the Ego in that it has a problem with everything. You recognize the Soul in that it loves everything. It loves playing, it loves working. You are not a child and you are no parent to yourself.. You are You. You are Consciousness.

Stopping Time

There is an easy way to meditate. And that's to just stop everything you are doing for 30 to 60 seconds. Just that once or twice a day will energize you. Try it out right now: Stop doing anything.

Just observe. Just Be.

Welcome Back. How was that? Nine times out of ten you will feel more refreshed afterwards.

Why is that? It's because the mind/body goes on "re-set" when you let go of the past and future, and become present; come to the here and now. Hardly anyone ever does that. People are constantly involved with one thing or another and think they feel uncomfortable at in-between times in silence or nothing-ness. But the opposite is true. Embrace nothing-ness and it will greatly benefit you.

What is going on here and now? When is the last time you examined an object in your surroundings for a full minute? Try that right now. You will feel stronger afterwards because you let go of unreality (stories about past and future that are running in your mind) and return to what's really here.

What is really here, right now? Could you just be-with-what-is?

Memories of the Past and Imaginations of the Future can serve us well...unless it's all on automatic. That is why it is such a great relief to become present. To become now. I recommend you do that at least once a day. Wherever you are, stop in your tracks and just stand there, motionless. Or, sit down somewhere and just observe the people. Or, take a piece of fruit into your hand and look at it consciously for a whole minute. You have stopped time and become present. You have regained control of your reality.

Expanding-Time

You can expand time and reduce stress if you do what you are doing when you are doing it. That's the simplest and easiest way. When you are talking to someone, talk to him/her instead of looking at your blackberry or iPhone or waiting for another person to show up. The habit of eating while watching TV is widespread but it does not actually expand your sense of time, it contracts it. When I do sports I often listen to Audio-Recordings at the same time, but if I want to relax and expand my sense of time, I only focus on the sports. When you watch a movie, only watch the movie. Our multi-tasking society believes that "time is saved" by scattering attention, but that's not true. Test it out for yourself. If you are driving your car a long distance you will want to spend some of the time listening to music or audiobooks. But then there also comes the time where you just want to turn it off and actually be-with-the-driving. And that is relaxing and time-sense-expanding in a special sort of way. Reduce the tendency to not be fully present with what you are doing and your sense of time, space, and well-being will improve

Picking Ideas from the Air

A peculiar trait of human consciousness is the ability to "pick thoughts out of the air". I have been on the road recently, with hardly any access to news, internet, or radio and this is where I notice this phenomenon the most. Yesterday, while driving down the highway the following completely foreign thought popped into my head: "AC/DC just finished a new album." I don't listen to the music of AC/DC, nor do I follow their career, nor had I picked the information up from news or internet or the radio. But today, for the first time in a week, I happened to browse a news-site and read the headline: "AC/DC is bringing out a new album."

So how did I know that? Where did I pick this information up? This kind of thing happens to me on a fairly regular basis – I just get thoughts that are completely unrelated to my interests but later turn out to be accurate. There seems to be a "field" in which all the thoughts and ideas of mass-consciousness float around. My mind having been relaxed and not attached to anything in particular (the state one gets into on long highway trips), I simply "picked it up" as if my mind were a receiver of radio signals. The news-item was put into mass-consciousness or some consciousness near me, and I picked it up.

A skeptic might say, "You probably subconsciously heard it at a Service Station and then forgot that you heard it." But I hadn't entered any gas stations for days because I got all my fuel by credit card. "Well, then you must have heard it in a passing car," says the skeptic. To which I say, "But I had my windows up because I was using air conditioning." And then the skeptic says, "Well, you picked it up somewhere, you just don't know it. The brain has no extrasensory capabilities." And I say, "But I have received thoughts like these while lying in bed and falling asleep too. Without having had external influences for days."

A lot of new ideas and inventions seem to be received this way too. I sometimes feel that if I don't write about a new idea, someone else soon will. Inventors have often mentioned getting their ideas in dreams, in half-sleep, while gardening, while driving, while idly sitting around, or while doing something unrelated to their work. They typically focus on their work for some time and thereby program consciousness to find solutions to specific items. Then they let go or get distracted for some time, and the solutions suddenly "pop up" as if out of nowhere.

I have practiced similarly in my own work. For instance, I like reading books that are unrelated to my work. Not only does that bring fresh thoughts to mind, it has the effect of "letting go" from my normal focus so that the subconscious can "work stuff out". I work on something for a while, then let the subconscious do the rest of the work. Sometimes I give the subconscious the command to find something out for me. Then I go to sleep. When I wake up the next day, I know the answer to what I have asked. With the last book I wrote, I practiced this a lot: I'd stumble upon a mystery that I couldn't solve; an unanswered question. I'd focus on it while I fell asleep, then wake up with the answer – or the answer would just come up throughout the day.

I have also used this to find items that I have lost or misplaced. Once when I lost my car keys, I simply told my subconscious to go to work on it, let go of looking and then, a few hours later, when I had forgotten it all, the thought of where I had left them came into consciousness. The keys were on the floor of a garage in another town and my subconscious was showing me that! I would have never otherwise found them. So this "field" or "subconscious" - or whatever you'd like to call it - can more effortlessly solve problems than the

conscious mind can. It has larger resources, a larger bandwidth and knowledge to draw from. The supposedly "unproductive" and "lazy" times are at least as valuable as working times because these are the times your subconscious works for you, delivering creative ideas you wouldn't have come up with while working.

The Non-Duality Course

"The best way to win a game is to be both sides."
– Frederick Dodson

Definition: *Duality Surfing* is a method to re-experience both sides of a mental (and emotional) polarity or dichotomy. This results in a natural (non-forced) change of viewpoint to a level beyond both sides. This state is one of non-duality regarding a topic. It is a state of **freedom** and of **choice** to either decide for one side, the other, or neither of the two. Because every topic comes "in twos", Duality Surfing can be applied to everything. Hot can only exist in contrast to cold. Rich can only exist in comparison to poor. Happy and Unhappy arise together. With most people, one side of the coin is conscious (they are aware of it) and the other is unconscious. The minute you say, "I want to find a good partner," the concept of not finding a partner, or the partner not being good arises, consciously or subconsciously. In other words, without that goal, there is no problem. If you don't want to climb the mountain, the rocks on the path are no problem. Duality Surfing heightens your ability to accept the negative side of things. Having accepted one side of the coin, it becomes much easier to claim the other side. Therefore, Duality-Surfing heightens your ability to focus on the positive.

Application: When using Duality Surfing you define either a Desire, Resistance, or Topic to work on. Then you define the opposite of that. Then you merge your awareness with one side and then the other side, back and forth, until your attachment to either side releases, and you are able to view the subject non-dually. This is usually accompanied by a sense of relief and lightness and a "being OK with both sides".

Duality Surfing is practiced to increase mental energy (Attention, visual Imagination, Concentration), to increase Intuition (insights, hunches) through letting go of trying to solve things with the limited world-mind alone, to free oneself from mental records that are running on automatic, repetition-loops, for the increase of well-being and the general expansion of Consciousness. Duality Surfing is a "next Generation" psycho-spiritual Technique that is not yet widely known or used but speedily effective in terms of self-therapy and spiritual advancement.

It is important to learn that our world is built on polarity. One side cannot exist without the other. You can only perceive light in contrast to dark. Without a mountain there would be no valley. You can't have one side of the coin and not another. Otherwise it's not a coin. And yet, so many live as if a topic were only one thing instead of two. Man-Woman, Life-Death, Summer-Winter…all polarities are concepts that depend on each other. I keep referring to "most people" in my writings, as this is why "most people" are not enlightened or at source of their reality. Almost everyone that approaches me so that I help them to reach a goal, will say to me, "I do want THIS, but I do not want THAT (the opposite)." Well, I've got news for you: **If you want to have one thing, you will also have to experience its opposite**. And that's what Duality-Surfing is for: So that you don't have to experience its opposite in real life and not for long. You can do it all mentally. But sooner or later, in some way or another, you are going to have to accept "the other side"; your shadow; the dark side. As long as you have not accepted the factual reality of that side, you are still behaving like a little child in denial. In that mode you are forever running away from your shadows.

But you can't escape your shadow.

You can accept it though. And once you accept it, it will become your **companion** rather than your adversary. Most of what a human does is aimed at feeling better and avoiding feeling worse. So they do what they think will achieve that. But what "most people" (again, those pesky 99%) are not aware of is that every Desire is also a Resistance. If you desire freedom, you resist imprisonment. If you resist imprisonment, you desire freedom. Too much wanting one thing not only creates a lot of lack of that one thing but even has the tendency to create more of its opposite. These are a few dichotomies people carry:

"I want more surprises in my life" – "I want more security in my life."

"I want to be closer to people" – "I want to be freer from people."

"I am unique and individual" – "I am just like all other people of my group."

The idea of Duality Surfing is to harmonize, synchronize, and merge Dichotomies like these, to understand that both Option A and Option B are completely valid and offer interesting opportunities to experience. And also to understand that one can experience Option A as well as B at the same time. Only the mind believes there are contradictions. In my relationship for example, I feel completely free and at the same time totally close and committed. Well, meanwhile it's more than that: Thoughts about freedom or closeness don't even occur anymore because I have mentally released the entire construct. What is or is not proper behavior presents itself from moment to moment. I don't need a mental construct to "prepare" for how to behave in the future. The question is not whether path A or path B are good, but whether I am good right here and now, no matter which path is taken. And guess what? You can be completely miserable or happy on either path. Knowing that reality is determined by you and not by the path is pure power.

Taking in "both sides of an issue" can seem difficult because we tend to not want to change our viewpoint or acknowledge other ways of seeing things. Why do we feel uncomfortable changing our viewpoint? Because keeping a fixed stand at one point makes us feel more stable. And indeed, fixed opinions and strong beliefs do enable us to feel more powerful. This is the cause of religious fanaticism. If I have a fixed and unchanging belief about something, that belief will begin to draw and accumulate energy and create a reality that accords to that strong conviction. If someone asks me to change my viewpoint, it's only natural that I resist that. The person is asking me to give up my power! However, *with beliefs and viewpoints that do not help or serve you, letting go of your position is only a temporary loss you go into for a much greater gain.* Yes, releasing negative mindsets and attitudes can be and is experienced as a loss by many. That's why they don't do it.

For things you would like to create in life, you should become an absolutist who knows no other truth. For things you want to de-create in life, you should become a relativist who sees many levels of truth. "Is it true or not?" "Aren't both true?" "Is that really true?" "How do I know it's true?" And, "That's only a matter of perspective," are very useful questions and statements when it comes to things you want to dissolve. What you are doing is dissolving your tight grip on a certain reality. Example: "Is it really true that I have difficulty talking in front of others? Isn't it truer that I only sometimes have difficulty? Does it not come easy to me when I talk about things I like?"

About 99% of the time when people ask me a "this or that" question, the answer is: "Both!" The dual-mind is incapable of seeing that and requires one side to be "true" and the other to be "untrue". "Are you for or against them?" some ask, as if those were the only two alternatives. What if I am neither for nor against? Or what if I am *for* in some contexts and *against* in others? Or what if I am for something entirely different than those two options?

One of the traits of duality is the Pendulum-Effect. Maybe you have already seen people who were intensely holding on to something and then, sometime later, holding on to the exact opposite of that thing. The stronger you push the Pendulum in one direction, the stronger it will strike back into the other. That's why Buddha and countless other spiritual teachers tell you to "stay in the middle", "keep calm", "remain poised", and "easy does it". That's why often the most rabid "anti" stances are usually by people who were previously fanatically "pro" for that same thing.

As an experiment, write something down that you

used to like but today no longer like. For example, I really used to love living out in the country and avoided the city. Now I love living in the city and am not really in the mood for the country. Also write something down that you used to dislike but now like. I used to dislike Cathedrals, seeing them as dark and oppressive. Today, I love Cathedrals and see them as beautiful and sacred. If you write down a few instances like this, you will see the Pendulum Effect in action in your life. If you used to love smoking, maybe today you are really annoyed by smokers. If you used to worship a certain teaching, maybe today you are "anti" that teaching. Simply be

careful not to hate or crave anything too strongly, it could swing to its opposite someday when you least expect it.

Duality Surfing is a reliable method of achieving mental and emotional freedom. You will notice this already after the first few sessions of doing it. You will feel the relief and the strengthening of the state of certainty that resides beyond the myriad mirror-halls of the mind. I do not recommend you use Duality Surfing too frequently or desperately in some attempt to "gain enlightenment". Allow yourself to change gradually, softly, and gently over time. Radical behavior is unnatural and may create sudden changes…but what about the rest of the days of your life? I'd recommend not doing less than one session a month, but not more than one session a day. One session can take anywhere between 2 minutes and several hours. Doing this for several hours will get you high as a kite and able to access deeper seated issues. But it's not necessary for creating gains. Even 2 minutes of this can have a great effect. Realize that any shift mentally/emotionally gradually also creates a shift in your "real everyday life". Don't be surprised if there are issues that just don't show up anymore.

There is one rule to this: Never break off a Session while you are in emotional turmoil or a problematic reality. If, for example, your Duality-Surfing Session brings up old wounds, please continue your session until those energies relax and dissipate. You don't want to stay stuck in a bad state for the rest of the day. You can save yourself this trouble if you simply follow through to your Session to the end, without distracting yourself.

Let's now look at an example. Let's say you choose the desire to be self-employed. So being successfully self-employed would be one side of the equation. The other is not-being-self-employed, perhaps in this case, being an employee. So you would sit down, close your eyes, and focus on "being employed". Then, after 20-120 seconds (not more!) you would focus on being self-employed. Then, after another 20-120 seconds you would invest all of your attention again into being employed. And then back to being self-employed. This alternating back and forth is Duality Surfing. It is often not enough to move back and forth only twice. A normal session alternates between both sides several, maybe dozens, and maybe even many dozens of times. Sometimes you will experience one side getting stronger or weaker.

Simply continue in the same way. Sometimes, when doing a Session with someone, I will say things such as, "Allow yourself to be X," or, "Release Resistance toward X," or, "Welcome X," or, "Merge with X," or, "Feel X," or, "Imagine X," or, "Experience X"... These are all just different ways to say "Focus on...". Focusing can mean to feel or imagine, but in the sense of Duality Surfing, it always means releasing your aversion and resistance toward something and just sinking into it.

Your Session continues until you can effortlessly and willingly be any of the two sides. The indicator that your Session is finished is that you can take on any of the viewpoints easily. That means you are in full control of both states, without having to get something, fix something, change something, or overcome something. **Why are you in control of both sides? Because you turned them on and off several times during your Session.** Something you keep turning on and off, you eventually gain control over. It would be impossible to have this level of power if you were still stuck in one of the sides of the polarity. The level beyond both sides is the level from which you can easily create and de-create both sides. Consciousness is now no longer the left or right side of the Pyramid, but its cap.
Thesis and Antithesis become Synthesis.

What follows are some topics and sessions you can use Duality Surfing on, just in case you did not know the endless possibilities it can be used for. And to be quite honest, each and every human being as some unresolved issues with any of the topics listed here. Therefore, any can be de-polarized to great energy gains. The list is not complete. These are only examples. There are many more things one could examine. Also, what constitutes "opposite" may differ a little from person to person. For example, "having friends" is not the opposite of "being lonely" for all people. Some would say that the opposite of being lonely is being in a relationship, feeling one belongs on earth, or whatever else. Use the opposites that apply to you. On the left side I listed things people might consider negative, on right side things people might consider positive.

Lack of Love – Abundance of Love
Being Lonely – Having Friends
Not Getting Sex – Getting Sex
Wanting Sex – Not Wanting Sex
Getting Attention – Not Getting Attention
Not Getting Attention – Getting Attention
Being Criticized – Being Praised
Lack of Money – Abundance of Money
Being Ugly – Being Good-Looking
Time Pressure – Having a Lot of Time
Being Stupid – Being Intelligent
Not Feeling Anything – Feeling Something
Being Unwell – Being Healthy
Being Overweight – Being Slim
Being Overweight – Being Athletic
Being Cold – Being Compassionate
Death – Life

Life – Death
Complacency – Discipline
Discipline – Comfort
Laziness – Work
Work – Laziness
Being Enlightened – Wanting Enlightenment
Boredom – Interest
Boredom – Enthusiasm
Panic – Relaxation
Freedom – Closeness
Closeness – Freedom
Controlled by Others – Self-Determination
Being Addicted – Being Free
I Can't – I Can
Grief – Calm
Unhappiness – Happiness
Tension – Relaxation
Stress – Relaxation
Uncertainty – Certainty
Insecurity – Security
Out of Control – In Control
Mediocrity – Adventure
Mediocrity – Something New
Mediocrity – Higher Achievement
Apathy – Lightness
Apathy – Pro-Action
Being Right – Granting Rightness

Being Wrong – Being Right
Needing Approval – Having Approval
Being Criminal – Being Legitimate
Serious – Funny
Feel Bad – Feel Good
Same as Group – Individuality
Being Different – Being Same as Group
Owning Nothing – Owning Everything
Being Important – Being Unimportant
Being Unimportant – Being Important
Being Burdened – Being Unburdened
Being Responsible – Not Being Responsible
Not Being Responsible – Being Responsible
Not Knowing – Knowing
Difficulty to Remember – Can Clearly Remember
Needing Something – Being Content With What-Is
Focused on Time – Being Here Now
Aggression – Peace
Inertia – Energy
Never – Always
To Be Something – Not to Be That
Not to Be Something – To Be That
To Have Something – Not to Have That
Not to Have Something – Not Have That
To Do something – Not to Do That
Not to Do something – To Do That
To Be Submissive – To Be Assertive

Nothing – Everything
To Feel Pain – To Feel Free
I Am – I Am Not
I Am Not – I Am

Cleaning up on these topics alone would give you a boost to the sky and beyond.

Multi-Polarity Sessions

As previously stated, everything comes in twos. But some deeper subjects can also be addressed in multiple polarities. Alcoholism for example may contain the following aspects:

Being an Alcoholic – Being Clean
Craving Alcohol – Rejecting Alcohol
Withdrawal Symptoms – Well-Being
Others Disapproval – Others Enjoying Drinking With You

This would be an example of an 8-pole session which certainly delivers more of a "clean-up" than regular duality-surfing. If you are disciplined enough you can create your own in-depth session. If you lack the focus, or are uncertain of how to proceed then these areas are best left to a professional coach.

The special sessions you create for yourself can also be coupled with other techniques and methods of your own. I sometimes create multi-polarity sessions out of nothing, while I am working with people. Here is one I designed recently with a person who lacked professional success:

1. Write down how you are similar to a successful person.
2. Write down the opposite of that.

Duality Surf that.

3. Write down how you are different than a successful person.
4. Write down the opposite of that.

Duality Surf that.

5. Write down what others say about how you are similar to a successful person.
6. Write down the opposite of that.

Duality Surf that.

7. Write down what others say about how you are different than a successful person.
8. Write down the opposite of that.

Duality Surf that.

9. Write down a Role/Identity you would like to be.
10. Write down the opposite of that.

Duality Surf that.

An example of just one item of a more extensive list:

1. I wear tasteful clothes.
2. I wear tasteless clothes.

3. I don't tend to my finances.
4. I tend to my finances.

5. He asks a lot of money for his services.
6. He is selling himself under value.

7. He's a loser.
8. He's a winner.

9. I enjoy people's company.
10. I don't enjoy people's company.

The student fully experienced both sides of all of these items and several others on his list, and left the session in a state of complete and total freedom from the subject.

If you would like an audio to guide you through duality-surfing sessions, the Bliss-Course and Infinity Course contain complete sessions.

A Mind Wide Open

It had rained heavily during the night and the day, and down the gullies the muddy stream poured into the sea, making it chocolate-brown.

As you walked on the beach the waves were enormous and they were breaking with magnificent curve and force. You walked against the wind, and suddenly you felt there was nothing between you and the sky, and this openness was heaven.

To be so completely open, vulnerable to the hills, to the sea and to man is the very essence of meditation. To have no resistance, to have no barriers inwardly towards anything, to be really free, completely, from all the minor urges, compulsions, and demands, with all their little conflicts and hypocrisies, is to walk in life with open arms. And that evening, walking there on that wet sand, with the seagulls around you, you felt the extraordinary sense of open freedom and the great beauty of love which was not in you, or outside you, but everywhere. We don't realize how important it is to be free of the nagging pleasures and their pains, so that the mind remains alone. It is only the mind that is wholly alone that is open. You felt all this suddenly, like a great wind that swept over the land and through you. There you were denuded of everything, empty and therefore utterly open. The beauty of it was not in the word or in the feeling, but seemed to be everywhere about you, inside you, over the waters and in the hills. Meditation is this.
– Jiddu Krishnamurti, Meditations

A Quick Trick to Empty the Mind

Because I teach Meditation, people are surprised to hear that I don't meditate myself. I haven't done a formal meditation practice in more than 10 years and yet, I tell people to meditate. A little hypocritical, no? No. One of the aims of Meditation is to allow for higher states of awareness…inner calm, peace, lucidity, and bliss. I meditated off and on throughout my 20s, learning to access these states. After some time I noticed I wasn't transferring the bliss to normal daily life outside of the meditation. So I progressed to the next step: Meditating with eyes open. Could I achieve those same wonderful states with open eyes? I could. And then the next step: Meditating while walking. Could I achieve the same mindfulness while moving around? I could. Thus it became easier to transfer high awareness to everyday life. Then the next step: Meditating without meditating… being mindful and aware in daily life. And then the next step: Being clear and calm in difficult situations. While being interviewed, while being shouted at, while in downtown traffic, etc. I achieved that a lot more often than I had before. I'm still sometimes caught off guard, but that's OK. **The "being OK" with not always being aware, clear,**

and calm is a part of that calmness. Demanding always to be calm is just another sort of unneeded tension. Then came the next phase: That in which it didn't even matter anymore in what state I was in. That put me into an almost permanent state of well-being. But you can see the stages I went through to reach that delicious state of true equanimity, where one is in a good state most of the time and when not…that is integrated and accepted. As there was no more resistance toward "bad states", "anger", "a cold" and whatnot, those "negative" states lessened dramatically. Formal Meditation is only needed at a certain stage of development, in my opinion. Furthermore, I know people who claim to be meditating but are still incredibly tense…subconsciously. They turn meditation itself into some rigid and tense form of practice, thinking they are "meditating", when they are actually just sitting there with eyes closed and trying to concentrate or "achieve" something. "Meditation is not a means to an end, it is the end itself," is one of my favorite wisdom quotes in this regard. Another one is: "Meditate at least 15 minutes a day. Except if you're busy or have little time. In that case, meditate 60 minutes a day." But once inner calm has become normalized, you'll want to meditate without closing your eyes.

One of the goals of meditation is to "empty the mind". One of my tricks for doing so...without having to actually sit down and meditate...is as follows: **I simply put my attention on empty spaces.** I have been using this little "trick" for many years. I originally learned it through meditation training. But it's such a brilliant trick because it does in a few seconds what some meditators spend hours trying to achieve. When you rest your attention on air, on empty spaces or on "nothing", that's exactly what is reflected in your mind: Nothing; Emptiness. And that state beyond the circus of the everyday mind is **so pleasant and soothing**. You see, humans have the conditioned habit to focus on objects and people...on solid things the eye can see. Putting attention in between those objects, to the empty space between them, instantly calms the mind (unless this is turned into another strict chore).

Consider a parked car. Consider another parked car. Now, consider the empty space in between those cars; the empty space in between two people who are talking; the silence in between the chirp of a bird. Have you ever considered the empty space between your right foot and your left foot? Or between your computer and the wall? Or between the left wall and the right wall? Or between the utterings of a person and his next uttering? Have you considered the empty spaces within your body? In your nostrils? Have you considered the empty spaces before and after an emotion? Around an emotion? What about the empty space around your body?

Next time you feel a pain, try this: Notice how you instantly zoom into that pain as if it were the ultimate thing and all else irrelevant. But then notice the empty space around the pain…the pain free areas. The empty space prior to and after that pain. While focusing on the center of the pain itself, remain aware of the wider empty spaces around it and also in the room you are sitting in. Diffuse your awareness to include more than just the pain. What you will notice, when doing this, is that the pain is much less pronounced and sharp. If you master your awareness just a little, you can even learn to dissolve pain. Just with the information presented here. But you'll have to experiment a little. This also goes for emotional pain.

Are you socially awkward? Then try this: While talking to a person, don't zoom in on him/her or try to get everything s/he is saying. Let go of trying to make an impression. Instead, become aware of the greater surroundings. Open your awareness. You are still interested, still listening, still with him/her, but you are not fixated. Like in classical music or in sex, you have found the perfect equilibrium, the perfect state between tension (focus) and relaxation (de-focus). Correctly applied, your demeanor changes and you are no longer quite as awkward, shy, or tense.

Are you trying too hard to do your job right? Then you're bound to fail. Trying hard (focusing) is fine, but trying too hard will limit your awareness-scope dramatically. You can be a tough cookie, but not so tough that you crack. Humans tend to be in one extreme or the other. Either a person is smoking a few packs of cigarettes a day, thus polluting himself like crazy or, the other extreme: He is a germaphobe who is obsessed with "cleanness", and won't even leave the house. But the ideal state is usually somewhere in between extremes.

Three methods for instant mind-calm:

1. Take a deep breath.//
2. Let go of everything you know.//
3. Put your awareness on Empty Spaces.

I recommend mind-calming as a lifelong practice. A racing mind is not perceptive, efficient, creative, or intelligent. If you have ever observed what society considers "dumb people" or "people who lack intelligence" is that many of them strain their foreheads. You see them wrinkle their foreheads, as if they are exerting a huge amount of effort in understanding or perceiving. My view is that many of them are not actually "dumb". They have merely been conditioned to objectify too much; to strain their awareness too much. People who don't have that many wrinkles on their forehead don't strain their brain. They are either lazy, or they let Intuition do the work for them. There is a fine line between laziness (dullness) and intuitive calm. Find that difference.

The practice of being aware of empty spaces can be done superficially, or deeply. When it is done deeply, you can release all kinds of subconscious tensions, many of which you won't even know you had. These tensions are stored in your muscles and nerves mainly. If you drink a lot of caffeine you may have noticed that it heightens your focus. But drinking too much of it, does not heighten your focus, it makes you irritable. You may start to have twitches, ticks, leg moving, finger tapping, and similar. Your heart may start racing. You may also notice that you then rarely breathe deeply, and you are keenly focused on non-spaces. I'm telling you this so that you notice these things and become more aware of how you function in daily life in various states of consciousness. Just look and examine. If you have these problems but do not drink caffeine or take other stimulants, then you ought to practice more relaxation. All this "stress" of daily life is not needed to move forward.

If you want an empty mind, look at emptiness. The Universe is full of emptiness. It is serene and peaceful. In front of, during, and behind every creation there is void. There is more emptiness, space, and silence than there are sounds, matter, and objects. It may seem to you that your mind is incredibly loud and full of thoughts, but if you look more closely you can also see that there is a lot of empty space in between your thoughts. As you put attention on that emptiness, the thoughts recede and the emptiness grows. Then your mind feels as if you are sitting in a huge empty stadium and the chatter of mind is merely a small TV running at the far other side of that stadium. Not all that relevant, and no longer that loud. The benefits of such a crystal clear mind are numerous. An increase in perception and well-being is only the beginning of it.

The following article appeared in the Harvard University Gazette:

Meditation changes temperatures: Mind controls body in extreme experiments

By William J. Cromie *Gazette Staff*

In a monastery in northern India, thinly clad Tibetan monks sat quietly in a room where the temperature was a chilly 40 degrees Fahrenheit. Using a yoga technique known as g Tum-mo, they entered a state of deep meditation. Other monks soaked 3-by-6-foot sheets in cold water (49 degrees) and placed them over the meditators' shoulders. For untrained people, such frigid wrappings would produce uncontrolled shivering. If body temperatures continue to drop under these conditions, death can result. But it was not long before steam began rising from the sheets. As a result of body heat produced by the monks during meditation, the sheets dried in about an hour.

Attendants removed the sheets, then covered the meditators with a second chilled, wet wrapping. Each monk was required to dry three sheets over a period of several hours.

Why would anyone do this? Herbert Benson, who has been studying g Tum-mo for 20 years, answers that, "Buddhists feel the reality we live in is not the ultimate one. There's another reality we can tap into that's unaffected by our emotions, by our everyday world. Buddhists believe this state of mind can be achieved by doing good for others and by meditation. The heat they generate during the process is just a by-product of g Tum-mo meditation."

Benson is an associate professor of medicine at the Harvard Medical School and president of the Mind/Body Medical Institute at Beth Israel Deaconess Medical Center in Boston. He firmly believes that studying advanced forms of meditation "can uncover capacities that will help us to better treat stress-related illnesses."

Benson developed the "relaxation response," which he describes as "a physiological state opposite to stress." It is characterized by decreases in metabolism, breathing rate, heart rate, and blood pressure. He and others have amassed evidence that it can help those suffering from illnesses caused or exacerbated by stress. Benson and colleagues use it to treat anxiety, mild and moderate depression, high blood pressure, heartbeat irregularities, excessive anger, insomnia, and even infertility. His team also uses this type of simple meditation to calm those who have been traumatized by the deaths of others, or by diagnoses of cancer or other painful, life-threatening illnesses.

"More than 60 percent of visits to physicians in the United States are due to stress-related problems, most of which are poorly treated by drugs, surgery, or other medical procedures," Benson maintains.

The Mind/Body Medical Institute is now training people to use the relaxation response to help people working at Ground Zero in New York City, where two airplanes toppled the World Trade Center Towers last Sept. 11. Facilities have been set up at nearby St. Paul's Chapel to aid people still working on clearing wreckage and bodies. Anyone else who feels stressed by those terrible events can also obtain help at the chapel. "We are *training the trainers who work there," Benson says.*

The relaxation response involves repeating a word, sound, phrase, or short prayer while disregarding intrusive thoughts. "If such an easy-to-master practice can bring about the remarkable changes we observe," Benson notes. "I want to investigate what advanced forms of meditation can do to help the mind control physical processes once thought to be uncontrollable."

Breathtaking results

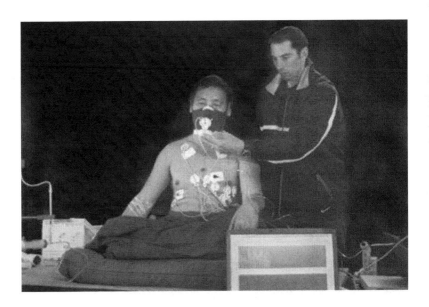

Image: A Buddhist monk has his vital signs measured as he prepares to enter an advanced state of meditation in Normandy, France. During meditation, the monk's body produces enough heat to dry cold, wet sheets put over his shoulders in a frigid room (Photo courtesy of Herbert Benson).

Some Westerners practice g Tum-mo, but it often takes years to reach states like those achieved by Buddhist monks. In trying to find groups he could study, Benson met Westerners who claimed to have mastered such advanced techniques, but who were, in his words, "fraudulent."

Benson decided that he needed to locate a religious setting, where advanced mediation is traditionally practiced. His opportunity came in 1979 when the Dalai Lama, spiritual leader of Tibet, visited Harvard University. "His Holiness agreed to help me," recalls Benson. That visit was the beginning of a long friendship and several expeditions to northern India where many Tibetan monks live in exile.

During visits to remote monasteries in the 1980s, Benson and his team studied monks living in the Himalayan Mountains who could, by g Tum-mo meditation, raise the temperatures of their fingers and toes by as much as 17 degrees. It has yet to be determined how the monks are able to generate such heat.

The researchers also made measurements on practitioners of other forms of advanced meditation in Sikkim, India. They were astonished to find that these monks could lower their metabolism by 64 percent. "It was an astounding, breathtaking [no pun intended] result," Benson exclaims.

To put that decrease in perspective, metabolism, or oxygen consumption, drops only 10-15 percent in sleep and about 17 percent during simple meditation. Benson believes that such a capability could be useful for space travel. Travelers might use meditation to ease stress and oxygen consumption on long flights to other planets.

In 1985, the meditation team made a video of monks drying cold, wet sheets with body heat. They also documented monks spending a winter night on a rocky ledge 15,000 feet high in the Himalayas. The sleep-out took place in February on the night of the winter full moon when temperatures reached zero degrees F. Wearing only woolen or cotton shawls, the monks promptly fell asleep on the rocky ledge, They did not huddle together and the video shows no evidence of shivering. They slept until dawn then walked back to their monastery.

Overcoming obstacles

Working in isolated monasteries in the foothills of the Himalayas proved extremely difficult. Some religious leaders keep their meditative procedures a closely guarded secret. Medical measuring devices require electrical power and wall outlets are not always available. In addition, trying to meditate while strangers attempt to measure your rectal temperature is not something most monks are happy to do.

To avoid these problems, Instructor in Psychology Sara Lazar, a Benson colleague, used functional magnetic resonance imaging to scan the brains of meditators at Massachusetts General Hospital in Boston. The subjects were males, aged 22-45, who had practiced a form of advanced mediation called Kundalini daily for at least four years. In these experiments, the obstacles of cold and isolation were replaced by the difficulties of trying to meditate in a cramped, noisy machine. However, the results, published in the May 15, 2000, issue of the journal NeuroReport, turned out to be significant.

"Lazar found a marked decrease in blood flow to the entire brain," Benson explains. "At the same time, certain areas of the brain became more active, specifically those that control attention and autonomic functions like blood pressure and metabolism. In short, she showed the value of using this method to record changes in the brain's activity during meditation."

The biggest obstruction in further studies, whether in India or Boston, has always been money. Research proceeded slowly and intermittently until February 2001, when Benson's team received a $1.25 million grant from Loel Guinness, via the beer magnate's Kalpa Foundation, established to study extraordinary human capacities.

The funds enabled researchers to bring three monks experienced in g Tum-mo to a Guinness estate in Normandy, France, last July. The monks then practiced for 100 days to reach their full meditative capacity. An eye infection sidelined one of the monks, but the other two proved able to dry frigid, wet sheets while wearing sensors that recorded changes in heat production and metabolism.

Although the team obtained valuable data, Benson concludes that "the room was not cold enough to do the tests properly." His team will try again this coming winter with six monks. They will start practice in late summer and should be ready during the coldest part of winter.

Benson feels sure these attempts to understand advanced mediation will lead to better treatments for stress-related illnesses. "My hope," he says, "is that self-care will stand equal with medical drugs, surgery, and other therapies that are now used to alleviate mental and physical suffering. Along with nutrition and exercise, mind/body approaches can be part of self-care practices that could save millions of dollars annually in medical costs."

Advanced Meditation Techniques

Meditation is not a "relaxation exercise", not confined to some eastern religion, and not some dull vegetating on the couch. Meditation is the mystical process of experiencing God directly (as opposed to merely believing in God). Meditation is not something that is "done", it is the practice of un-doing or non-doing. Even though Meditation is beneficial on many levels, it is not about those

benefits – there is literally *nothing* to expect from it.
The average human is estimated to have hundreds of thousands of thoughts each day. What is amazing is that most of these thoughts (80-99%) are repetitions from the day before. This means we rarely think anything new. The "TV in our mind" just keeps rambling on and much of what it says is not relevant. Meditation is context in which the mind is allowed to relax. Please note that my wording here is very deliberate. I did not say, "Meditation relaxes the mind".

As you have experienced, the mind is comparable to a TV-set that runs on forever. This constant replay of mostly negative and thoroughly un-interesting scenarios covers up deeper, more subtle and creative parts of the Self. Quieting the mind is therefore a gateway to the famous "90% unused potential". However, I do not teach people to try and "stop" their thinking. That is just a further thought, another part of the TV-program. In my extensive and customized coaching work, I teach forms of Meditation specific to the person. Some things about Meditation can be generalized and apply to anyone – you will learn about the generalities in this section. Other things need to be addressed on an individual basis.

One generality that many aspiring spiritual travelers are not aware of is that "the mind" is mostly empty. "What?" you ask. "Is it not the goal of Meditation to empty the mind? And here you are saying it's already empty?" Well, yes. It is mostly empty. Those ignorant of this engage in a fruitless battle to "quiet the mind". We only perceive it as loud and full because we are keenly focused on the 1% of the mind that is active. To help you understand this, imagine sitting in a huge empty stadium. Enjoy the silence for a moment. Then, notice that on the far side of the stadium there is a TV-set in one of the chairs. That TV-set is just babbling away. And just let it. It has nothing to do with you. It just does what it does. The mind's job is to record what it perceives and play it back over and over. Where a soul becomes trapped is when it moves up closer to that TV-set and becomes enamored and hypnotized by it. Soon the soul *assumes* that this is "where the action is". Then it assumes that itself is the babbling mind. Meditation naturally de-identifies you from the TV-set so that you begin perceiving the wider and more expanded states again. There are trillions of fascinating worlds out there if you will just release your fascination with the dumb TV-babbler for a moment.

This analogy actually helps you calm the mind, not by trying to get rid of it but by reducing its relevance. You are not forced to keep staring at it, trying to change it, trying to clear it, or focusing on it. Just leave it alone and it will leave you alone. This realization re-frames the entire Meditation experience from: "I have to calm the mind," to: "I can notice that most of the mind is already calm."

After this paragraph please close your eyes to meditate; noticing there is a mind (stream of thoughts) plus a witness of mind. Observe the TV-set (our metaphor for mind) without getting involved, without trying to do anything, and without trying to turn it off. It's the trying to turn it off that gives it undue importance, you see. In this mode of observation you are no longer the mind but its witness, observing the circus, watching thoughts pass by without reacting. Just be and look. Most of you consider it "normal" to be externally focused while the internal world is of little meaning or interest. Hence the suggestion to focus internally for an hour may seem like a good opportunity to fall asleep. Do your best to remain lucid while meditating. Meditating is not dozing. In Meditation, the difference between internal and external need not be emphasized at all. Meditation means to take a closer look at what-is here-now, and an even closer look, and even closer... It is prolonged observation and awareness, not analysis. Analysis observes and draws conclusions and opinions. Meditation merely witnesses. From this mode of motionless stillness you may later venture out and explore your inner universe of thoughts, feelings, beliefs, identities, and the outer universe of objects, plants, animals, and people. At some point you will have become so silent that you are at a place where you can change your inner blueprint. Playing around with surface-thoughts does not change your inner blueprint, but being aware of deeper layers of thought, which do arise in Meditation, allows you to change it all.

Remember those old overhead projectors we used last century? You put a slide of a picture on it, and it would be projected onto a white wall. Under normal circumstances, to change your reality, you would only have to change one slide, one thought and replace it with another slide, another thought. With this internal change a new external reality is projected onto the wall. The problem is that mind has accumulated hundreds of thousands of slides *all piled up on top of each other*. So removing one negative thought and replacing it with one positive thought may change a little but there is still a lot of chaos and blackness on the overhead projector. The purpose of Meditation is to clear all the slides from the projector. From that zero-state it is so much easier to create something new…or not create anything at all, but to just enjoy your native state of effortless bliss. When all slides are removed, the light of Consciousness shines bright. Change is not only a matter of focusing on the "outside world" and "doing" something there. Much of that doing is nothing more than an after-effect of the thousands of thoughts piled up on each other. It is reactive action. Fundamental and deep change happens within.

The simplest form of Meditation is to **just sit** and allow awareness to rest here-now, with what really-is, without responding to the thousands of "slides". This instantly puts you above mass-consciousness that is locked into a frantic rat-race of unawareness. Meditation is the practice of attention, wakefulness, awareness, mindfulness, and concentration. Some techniques require you to concentrate attention, some to open attention, some to become aware of things you had not been aware of before. Others require you to imagine or release something. It is therefore no surprise that you will not find any Meditators who are scattered, nervous, out of control, overly emotional, forgetful, or weak-willed. Training your attention is a good life-skill: Learning new skills requires attention. Goal-Achievement requires Attention. Communication requires Attention. Winning sports matches requires Attention. Succeeding at anything at all requires Attention! Consciousness cuts deeper than the hardest diamond.

Some Meditations involve becoming aware of the body parts. Gentle and Loving Attention, combined with soft and deep breathing, can heal aches and pains. This type of body-awareness generates well-being. If you will, place your awareness in each part of the body, breathing with it and relaxing it mentally. Let that be your 10-minute Meditation practice for a day.

Other techniques magnify Imagination, opening the creative receptor-channels. Go to a place you would love being and experience it in sight, sound, smell, taste, and touch. Let this be your 10 minute Meditation for another day. By now you have learned of three different meditation techniques that all have very distinct qualities that you can experience. Do not read any further until you have experienced or re-experienced all three. Words mean nothing, experience is everything.

Meditation brings order and clarity into your thought-process and perception. Meditation allows you to access hitherto unknown layers of the subconscious. Meditation facilitates states of lucid dreaming. It improves life quality.

Everyone meditates, they just don't call it that. You don't have to be in a cross-legged sitting position to be meditating. Sports, sex, reading, watching movies, taking walks, massages, spas, and swimming are all very light forms of Meditation. The attitude with which you experience these activities can add or subtract from the meditative state. As a golf-player walks through an endless expanse of fresh green, he alternates between focusing attention and opening it. Walking in fresh air increases one's oxygen intake and produces what is known as the "alpha-state". Some listen to music or watch movies and lose themselves in them so much they forget everything around them, including time and space. So much so that sometimes they won't hear the telephone ring.

Meditation is practical and mystical. Expanding Consciousness is to notice, discover, perceive, feel, hear, or see something you have not noticed, discovered, perceived, felt, heard, or seen up to now. We hear many say that the aim of Meditation is Enlightenment. Enlightenment is described as a higher state of Consciousness, as a state beyond the thinking mind, as an Illumination of Self or the Universe, and as the Ultimate Goal or Purpose of life. It certainly has something to do with becoming Lighter, hence En-light-enment. "Light" here both in the sense of brighter and more radiant as well as of less weight or heaviness. In some languages there is no difference between the word Enlightenment and the word Relief. Relief from what? Relief from Suffering. The more Light a human becomes, the less general suffering there is. The more illusion and delusion there is, the greater the suffering.

I like to say, *"If you want a good life, go to a psychiatric hospital, study the people there, and just do the opposite of what they are doing. Then you'll lead a healthy and successful life!"* Audiences take this as some kind of a joke, but I actually mean it. Just look at what those who suffer the most are saying and doing, and do the opposite of that. For example, while researching the diet of women in psychiatric wards, scientists found that an above-average number of them were habitual users of alcohol, nicotine, sweets, and caffeine. What follows from that? Don't mix alcohol, cigarettes, sweets, and coffee. Why? I don't know. I just know that by modeling successful people I become successful and by modeling unsuccessful people I become unsuccessful. Studying how people who suffer and how people who are happy live and behave teaches you everything you need to know about everything. The same goes for Enlightenment. What do enlightened sages and saints do? They meditate and pray. Both en-light-enment and relief are about shining the light of Awareness into the Unknown, into Darkness, bringing previously subconscious material into plain sight. The more light you shine on abandoned and frozen parts of yourself, the more those parts melt and dissipate. Your subconscious patterns can control you if you are not aware of them. The mere act of Awareness makes what was below your threshold of awareness, come up. Your attention, observation, or perception is like a Sunshine which explores the dark cellars of the soul and shows you connections and concepts you have forgotten. Things that conventional Therapy might take many months to solve can be solved in Meditation within only a few hours. Of course, Meditation also "warms up" parts of yourself you may not want to see. These may manifest as emotional pains. But keep the Sun shining on those items for a little longer and they too burn in the fire of your love. Everything that your Awareness observes without resistance eventually disappears. Why is that? Because Awareness is Infinite/Unchanging and Thoughts/Feelings are finite/changing. Whatever is "more real" wins in the end. A child that is crying wants attention. The same principle applies to an "issue" that is "crying". It wants loving and soft attention. Offer that attention and any issue can be solved.

The following meditations techniques are for advanced explorers of consciousness. Used properly they are more precious than gold. They are designed to be simple, user friendly, and immediately applicable, stripped from all excess baggage.

1. Peripheral Vision
Purpose: A state of calm and presence

As you sit, focus on something in front of you, a bit higher than eye level. As you gently relax focus (while still remaining aware of that point in front/above), become aware of the things in your periphery…things to the left, the right, and behind you. In other words, calmly be aware of your entire surroundings and especially what is at the edge of your vision to the left and right, while still having a calm view to the front of you.

Done correctly this increases your sense of presence and calm within a minute or two. Rest in this state for as long as you like.

2. Observation Without Fixation
Purpose: To explore the tendency of the mind to fixate on things rather than be receptive.

As you sit in a movie theater, become aware of other things outside of the focal point of your attention, things other than the movie screen. The curtains beside the screen. The people sitting in front of you, beside you, and behind you. Places outside of the theater or cinema. As you return your attention back to the movie, do so more softly, with more of an open and receptive eye, without effort or staring.

As another person is telling you something, notice where your attention is. Are you really listening, or is your attention fixed on your mind, preparing what you are going say? Or are you too much fixed on the person? Expand awareness: Without shifting your eyes from the person, become aware of the person's face. Then become aware of other objects in your surroundings. And become aware of other people and things outside of your surroundings. As you return your full attention to the person, do so softly.

There are many ways to use attention, you do not have to use it in the same automatic way all the time. If the person is telling you a story that is boring to you, you are not forced to fix on it. You can be with the person, but your attention need not resist it. As the person is telling you a story that is nice, you need not have your attention on yourself. BEING WITH the person will create an improved sense of communication and contact.

As you view an unpleasant emotion within your body, relax with it. Become aware of it. Then, rather than remaining narrowly focused, notice the empty space around the emotion. And the empty space around your body. And the empty space in the room. And all the space in the Universe. Notice how having de-fixed your attention calms down the mis-emotion.

As you view an unpleasant thought, become aware of other thoughts you could also be thinking now while remaining aware of your unpleasant focal point. Add various other objects and thoughts to your mind. This alone will desensitize the unpleasant thought. Now shift between the unpleasant and more neutral or pleasant thoughts...shift back and forth a few times. This releases fixed attention even more. Finally, release all of it and bring your attention back to your present surroundings.

These are only examples of exploring the behavior and qualities of attention and the consequences of fixation vs. opening. There is much more to learn on this.

3. Time Out
The most basic form of Meditation is not even formally "Meditation". It consists of taking small time-outs throughout the day for contemplation, assessment of the day, relaxation, breathing, or

anything else.

Simply allowing for a few time-outs will boost the quality of your life because you learn to "stop the world", no longer reacting to the expectations and pressures of society or the survival-driven mind. During that time attention is under your command...and that's a rarity. Without time-outs, in between segments of the day, you can neither define your intentions for the next segment of the day, nor can you define if you even want to enter the next segment. Without time-outs you are driven by mechanical routine behavior. But in silence and non-doing; in restfulness, the true-self, beyond the surface-layer chatter of the world and superficial thinking, resurfaces. Good non-doing is the basis of good doing.

4. Meditation on Beauty

Focusing your attention on Beauty increases your level of energy. It does not make much of a difference whether you focus on a mental image of beauty, a picture of beauty on a website or in a magazine, or something beautiful in your physical surroundings.

Observing something beautiful often does more for you than searching for some truth in books, trying to achieve some goal, or trying to heal some issue. People who have, for example, been trying to achieve a goal for a long time without success, are well advised to take a break from their struggle and search and direct their attention to something about which not a bunch of resistance and desire has accumulated. This is how directing your attention to something supposedly "unrelated" to your goal can help you achieve it. Success is a matter of ENERGY, and often focusing on Beauty generates more energy than anything else.

This can be applied in many ways, but the "focus on beauty" should not be applied in order to gain something, not as a strategy, but for the sake of enjoyment itself. Notice and breathe in beauty out in Nature. Notice beauty as you browse various websites and if you want, collect beautiful pictures on the hard drive of your computer. When you see something beautiful pay special attention to it, acknowledge it.

Begin to notice how looking at certain things or listening to certain things, uplifts you, while other images and sounds tend to drag you down. Choose wisely what you give your attention to.

5. Relax Even More Deeply
Relax deeply, deeper than the physical, deeper than the mental.

As you sit there, stop…

…wanting to do something
…wanting to think something
…wanting to change something
…wanting to get rid of something
…wanting to acquire something
…wanting to know something
…wanting to achieve something

and sit. And perceive. And be. Forget everything you know, forget everything you are. Just for now. And be.

How do you feel now?

6. The Inner Coach
The inner coach knows more than any external source. The inner coach responds to what is uniquely appropriate for you and nobody else.

Before addressing your inner coach, become aware that looking for answers anywhere other than yourself is a degradation of your inner divine knowing. Realize that, as a part of Infinity, you too have access to an infinite range of wisdom and information. Once that is accepted, address your own inner coach. Become silent. Ask questions. Vocalize or write down what answers come to mind. Get answers from yourself before consulting any teacher, book, program, or workshop.

7. Non-Duality

Infinity is ONE, not two. Duality is an Illusion. An example: There is really no such thing as "hot and cold". There is only ONE variable, measured on ONE thermometer...either warm or less warm. Otherwise there would be two thermometers. The same goes for up-down, left-right, love-hate, war-peace etc. These are artificial constructs of the mind that do not really exist. What is left or right in Infinity? So rather than thinking in terms of Duality you might want to think in terms of *levels or scales*. I will not say any more on this here to give you the opportunity to CONTEMPLATE this idea and its implications yourself.

8. Converting Fantasy into Memory

One reason some people's visions do not manifest as reality is because they label it "imagination only," "fantasy only," "some future event"... One way to bypass this filter is to focus or visualize a desire you would like to manifest but to pretend that it is a *memory*, that it has already happened, rather than something you want to happen. If you can coax yourself into pretending it already happened, the likelihood of it actually happening increases. At the very least you will experience an elevation of your inner state.

One way to do this (among others) is to remember something you were really doing yesterday. Remember yesterday, then insert the desired reality into yesterday, "remembering" how that too "happened". You mix reality and imagination so that the body-mind has difficulty making the distinction. Then, let go of the memory, let go of what you held in mind, and go about your day. Since it has "already happened" there is no point in dwelling on it.

9. The Meaning of Life

What is the meaning of life?

Life has the meaning you give it. The creative mind creates importance and meaning.

As a meditation, sit relaxed and look around yourself. Observe the various things in your surroundings as having no meaning at all. If you want, you can whisper to yourself that object X has no meaning. Neither does object Y. Then observe your thoughts and do the same.

This meditation will calm the mind and allow for the more meaningful (spirit) to come forth because secondary meanings have been released.

Another meditation involves noticing something you assign negative or positive meaning to and recognizing or telling yourself: "This meaning was created by me." You see a garbage can and automatically label it as "ugly". In this instance, stop yourself and recognize: "This meaning was created by me." Let go of that meaning and simply view the object from a label-free perspective; the perspective infinite awareness would have. Or you see a beautiful person of the preferred sex and notice your inner reactiveness. You stop yourself and recognize: "This meaning was created by me." Then, let go of the meaning and simply view the person from a label-free perspective; the perspective infinite awareness would have.

Do not turn this meditation into a ritual or training. Throughout your life, simply become aware of how meaning is created *by you*. If too much importance is assigned to external realities (rather than Spirit/Infinity), one's attention becomes overwhelmed and sucked into illusions. Assigning too much importance to that which is perceived as positive, or assigning too much importance to that which is perceived as negative, preoccupies the mind in resistance-desire mechanisms that waste a lot of energy.

When navigating down a stream in a boat, you neither want to assign too much importance to the alligator (otherwise you will start focusing and steering in the alligators direction or navigating awkwardly), nor to the mermaid (otherwise you will start navigating awkwardly and miss the rest of the scenario; miss the big picture).
Spiritual-practice's main focus is the big picture rather than the detail. The general ambiance rather than the things one supposedly needs to attain or avoid. The context rather than the content of reality.

10. You Could, but Would You?
Mentally focus on something you would like to let go of. Then imagine someone pointing the barrel of a gun at your head. Imagine this person will shoot you if you do not let go of that specific item.

This simple visualization shows that you *could* let go of anything. The only question that then remains is: Would you? If a gun were pointed at you, you probably would. Using this meditation on things you supposedly have "difficulty" letting go of, can be quite interesting.

11. How to Visualize Properly
The highest form of creative visualization and using imagination as a tool for spiritual growth is not to visualize in order to "manifest something", or "get something", or "heal something", but for the sake of the sheer joy of visualizing itself. To visualize beauty raises one's level of energy, and much more so if it is not attached to any expected outcome but simply enjoyed. So one does not use this type of visualization so that "something happens later", but so that something is happening right now! In creative visualization one enters three-dimensional realities that are pleasant, beautiful, and vivid. While

such a session may begin with willed effort, the scenario may take on a life of its own as one "allows" the images and stories to develop. In colloquial terms this is called "Daydreaming", but it does indeed heighten one's senses in all respects, not only on an imaginary level.

11. Sound and Intention

How much your intentions influence reality depends on the state of energy in which you voice them. In a normal state it is not enough to just voice an intention. The intention would have to be followed by appropriate action. In higher states of consciousness it is however possible to say something and have it come true 1-3 days thereafter. One (of many) ways to temporarily experience a higher state of energy is by singing/voicing/chanting. In this specific Meditation you begin by chanting/voicing the sound aaaaaaaaaaaaaaaaaaaaaaaaaaaaaaaaaaaaaaaaaa aa for a few minutes. You take a soft, slow, and deep breath in, and sing "aaaaaa" (the "a" is pronounced as in car) for as long as is comfortable. You repeat this for a few minutes, until your mind becomes fairly calm and you feel a heightened sense of perception.

Then, you voice your Intention in-between the "aaaas". So it's:

aaaa...
Intention
aaaa...
Intention
aaaa...

This is done until you feel the reality of your Intention or Gratitude for it, throughout your body and being.

In order for this to yield positive results, the entire Meditation + the Intention should be done in the name of the "most high", in the name of "the highest good", or for "the benefit of all". Before choosing your intention make sure it is for your highest good. Make sure to voice it in present-tense or past-tense (as if it's already happened).

12. Just Be
Sit and Be.

Notice that hearing happens naturally, no effort, goal, intention, or self required.

Notice that seeing happens naturally, no effort, goal, intention, or self required.
Notice that breathing happens naturally, no effort, goal, intention, or self required.
Notice that thinking happens naturally, no effort, goal, intention, or self required.
Notice that everything happens naturally, no effort, goal, intention, or self required.
Be with what is as it is. Notice the elation.

13. Not Knowing
Look at some object, event, person, or thought and think or whisper to yourself:
"I do not know anything about this." And look at it.

Proceed to do this with various things, objects, events, and thoughts until you feel humility and a deeper perception of things (rather than the surface-mind perception of them) re-emerges.

14. Certainty
That which you are 100% certain of will manifest as reality.

1. Think of something you are absolutely certain of (such as "The sky is blue," or "I am sitting here.") Notice what certainty feels like.

2. Now think of something you would like to attract into your reality. As best you can, project the same feeling of certainty (that you just practiced) onto that reality.

Alternate between the two until you feel no difference between them. When you are done, let go of the whole thing for now.

15. Reality Diffusion

In your mind's eye, bring a problem-issue into focus. Look at that problem issue, while at the same time remaining aware of many other realities. This means you are looking at the issue and at the same time at other things. The issue is no longer the exclusive point of focus but is viewed along with many other things…anything…tennis rackets, presidents, childhood memories, billboard ads, cartoons, fantasies, etc. It takes about 3 to 5 minutes of this to diffuse negative thought-forms and emotions.

Self-Therapeutic Releasing-Meditation

The first meditation was to just observe your train of

thoughts; to just *be* *perception* void of any resistance, avoidance, labeling, and reaction. Once you can just let a single thought or all thoughts be, without having to do anything with it/them, you will notice it dissipates and never bothers you again. This is not because the thought will never again come up, but because it no longer means anything to you, so you will not as strongly notice it when it does come up again. It is then just another thought, one of millions. There is no more "charge" attached to it. What you resist will persist. Push creates Counter-Push. If there is a problem in your life, then "Stare the Demon in the eye" until the Demon disappears. However, I do not recommend you use this particular method of Meditation only for negative thoughts, but for all thoughts…neutral, positive, pointless, important, and unimportant, so that at least during your Meditation you are serene; you are pure Awareness.

A self-therapeutic aspect of Meditation-practice lies in soft confrontation. Say a dog left a pile of poo on your living room floor. Both you and your partner have a strong aversion to that. Your partner's aversion is so high that he leaves the house instantly. But that doesn't solve the issue. Chances are that somewhere out there, he will discover another pile of poo and will have to once again escape in horror. He lives his life by going "*away from*" rather than "*toward*", reactive instead of proactive. So you are alone in the house with the dog shit. If your aversion is high, you will not be willing to go clean it up. If the aversion is extreme, you won't even look at it or even acknowledge it is there. This is called psychological denial. So you leave it lying in the living room. Some try to practice "positive thinking" which would mean to put a beautiful carpet over the pile of shit and say "You see? All is well. It's gone." That works for awhile, but the problem is still not actually cleaned up. A few hours or days later the smell penetrates the carpet or leaves an ugly stain. Even worse, all sorts of bugs and flies are attracted by the smell and occupy your living space. Putting out that carpet of positive thinking would have worked much better if the pile had been removed first. But we waste our energy fighting the bugs instead of removing what attracts them. Ignoring the pile does not work unless you move into another House. Of course, positive thinking can accomplish that you find another place to go to. But wouldn't it have been easier to just clean the floor? It would have been ten minutes of disgust instead of many weeks of hardship.

The art of self-therapeutic meditational-releasing is no to analyze the dog poo but to get close enough to it so that you can handle it. You cannot control something you run away from. What you cannot take into your hands, you cannot let go of. So if for example I were to ask you to "release your resistance" toward some traumatic event, the purpose of that would be for you to gain some *handle* over it, not to approve of it happening again. So finally you take a deep breath of Courage and confront the issue. You approach the pile of poo, pick it up, and throw it away. Then you wipe away the rest from the floor. Yuck. But the issue is solved. You did not analyze it, talk about it, review it, like you might have done in conventional therapy, but you went straight to the center of the problem, picked it up, and threw it away. Releasing-Meditation involves doing this with a wide variety of energies, thoughts, and emotions. Meditation is an invitation to go "straight to the center" of various issues by focusing your attention to "where the sensation is the most intense". The way through is the way out. If you understand this you can get rid of all sorts of phobias, problems, and pains with Meditation alone. "Taking your meds" then gains an entirely new meaning. Of course the words "medicine" and "meditation" are related in the word "med" which means middle, means, medium, agent. Med-itation thus provides a mid-point between the physical and spiritual universe.

If "full immersion" type of Meditations become painful, instead of breaking off, simply release resistance. It's the resistance/labeling itself that is *causing* the pain. If you succumb to impatience, dullness, boredom, or avoidance you will not leave your Releasing-Meditation with more energy. Always complete your Releasing-Meditation with relief, with less pressure, fear, pain, ignorance, or whatever it was that was bothersome. Helpful energies: Appreciation or Interest, Neutrality, Gratitude, Gentleness, Tolerance, Love, Understanding, and Acceptance.

Here is a step-by-step on *Releasing*:

1. Define *one* topic you would like to dissolve or therapeutically work on. Every issue exists as mental/emotional energy. Define how much "charge" there is on the issue on a scale from 1 to 10. Measuring your progress makes Releasing more real for the mind. So if the intensity of your issue is at an 8 at the beginning of the Session and

down to 5 at the end of it, you know that with your mind alone you allowed change to happen. In your next Session you again check where the issue is and eventually try to get it down to 3,2,1 and 0.

2. Close your eyes and put your Awareness on the subject until you feel Emotion. Most of the time you will feel it immediately. Every issue and every "objective" in reality exists as an energy-field in or around your body. Without that energy-field you would not be attracting it. Put differently: Deliberately re-create the issue emotionally or mentally. Include and Welcome all thoughts, memories, sensations, and feelings that spontaneously come up (If "nothing" comes up, that is *something* too). Only when the issue is really present, go to step three. This may take between 10 and 60 seconds. Do not allow this step to take longer than 60 seconds, otherwise you get lost in a stream of thought or analysis. Feeling-whatever-is-there is easy. Just go with whatever is there.

3. Now gently observe the issue while softly letting go of reactions, labeling, and resistance, or until you can look at it with soft and fairly neutral interest. Regarding the energy-field or thought-form you are looking at: *How big is it? Which shape might it*

have? Where in our around the body is it located? Does it have color, shape, weight, or smell? If attention tries to drift of or get lost, gently return to the issue. It might change while you watch it, but keep aware no matter what. This step takes between 30 seconds and 3 Minutes. You should not go beyond 3 Minutes with it. If you feel you need longer, then you can repeat the process later.

4. Now "go into" the energy-field. Become ONE with it. Go to the center of it. Go to the place of the most intense sensation. Whatever shape or form it exists as, go into that. If it is a headache, melt your attention with that. if it is a Belief you are holding, go into that. If it is a fear or desire, identify with that, experience yourself AS that. You are no longer observing it from the outside, you are going into it. And then remain in that energy-field, release any remaining resistance, until the feeling *disappears entirely* or has turned into something pleasant.

Other Favorite Meditations

Copy Thoughts

Close your eyes, observe thoughts and duplicate

every thought that arises. Right after you notice a thought, deliberately think it again. So if you notice yourself remembering the traffic you came home in, deliberately remember that again. If the thought, "I don't have any thoughts now" comes up, then again tell yourself: "I don't have any thoughts now." By mimicking your mind you gain some deliberate control over its creations and the stream of thoughts slow down.

Time Limits

Meditate on Time and Time Spans for a few minutes or more. Think about various spans of time throughout your life. Notice the beginning of a time span and the end of a time span. For example, Relationships with people or Jobs are usually limited in time. Ponder. As objects are limited in space, events are limited in time. Then contemplate: Which things are less limited in time or more enduring? And then contemplate: Which things are unlimited in time or forever?

Space Limits

Meditate on objects in your surroundings, objects outside of your surroundings, and objects in the Universe. Notice how every object is limited in space. Some may be very big but they are still limited. Notice the empty space between objects. Contemplate: What is not limited in space? And: Who is noticing what is limited and unlimited?

Thought Limits

Meditate over thoughts as objects or shapes. Look inside and notice how thoughts have different shapes, sizes, weights, and limits. Not all thoughts look or are the same. Become more keenly aware of the differences. Then, after a few minutes or more, notice the empty space between thoughts. Notice how thoughts and/or feelings are limited in time and space. And ask: What is not a thought? And: Who is noticing what is and is not a thought?

 Some Meditations are for putting attention back into the control of your inner will. Just in case you haven't noticed yet: Reality is what you invest enough attention into. Reality is maintained through attention and assigning importance. The only exception to this is the Absolute reality (Awareness,

Infinity, God) which exists no matter whether you believe/focus on it or not. The one who can control his/her attention has a greater influence on what s/he experiences.

Recently I was conducting a seminar in a Hotel. On the second day of the Course another group moved into the room beside ours. Either the walls were pretty thin or the people next door were pretty loud, but we could hear each of their words. That is, I couldn't hear their words, nor did it disturb me because I had no resistance. Since I had no resistance I was not really paying attention to it. My attention was with the group. But I noticed there were some who were really bothered by the voices from the other room. And when they mentioned they could not meditate because of them, I started paying attention to them and only then could I hear the words. It still did not bother me. So I included the noise from the other room into the next group-Meditation and taught the students to fully embrace that noise. After the Meditation, nobody paid attention to the voices anymore. A few hours later the group re-located to another room in another part of the Hotel. And that was no coincidence.

Single-Pointedness

Focus your attention on something, anything, some object or thought. Try to keep it there. And try to keep it there some more. At least three minutes. How about 5 minutes? How about one hour? My record was 7 hours of focusing on one point. I was 14 years old back then and had my first experience with what they call the state of "Enlightenment". Every time my attention started drifting away I gently put it back to that one point. In this instance it was not a physical object but the thought of a white star which I kept focusing on. Why did I experience Cosmic Consciousness in this instance? Because the focus had stopped all thought. And when all thought is stopped the world-self disappears and the cosmic-self shines forth.

Lose Yourself

Here's another Meditation: Try to lose yourself in something, completely. For example, sometimes we lose ourselves in a book, a movie, a landscape, a work of art – so much so that we forget everything around us, including time and space. This produces a pleasant state of body/mind. Actually taking vacation or watching a two hour movie is not required to produce this state. It can be produced in 15 minutes with mundane and even "boring" objects. No outside stimuli required. Simply choose some random object in your surroundings. Put your attention to that object. Explore and examine it with interest, fascination, and curiosity. Notice things about that you had not noticed up to now. Look at it until details reveal themselves. Do not fix on one point but glide over, around or even inside it. Continue until you forget everything around you, including yourself (and any impatience that goes along with that).

After you have been immersed for 3 to 10 minutes, feel free to continue with another object. Even take a walk outside and immerse yourself into things you have never really looked at. You do realize you have never actually **looked** at reality, yes? The mind is superficial and narcissistic. It does not care about what reality looks like, it cannot focus on anything, it is only concerned with thoughts regarding its own Ego-Self. So feel free to practice this particular exercise for hours. It's a real Ego-Dissolver.

If you enjoyed this Meditation in wish to expand on it, start with neutral objects and then continue it with objects that interest you or which you think are desirable or beautiful. Finally, go within and start using the "Attention Immersion" technique on inner issues you wish to dissolve and other inner issues you wish to create. Focusing in this way on stuff you want to dissolve…dissolves them. Focusing in this way on stuff you want to create…creates them.

All That Is

Create a mental bubble or space in which you put everything that exists. Every thought that is there, or comes up, or that you have been preoccupied with, all fantasies, all information, simply all-that-is. All-that-is may include the President of your country, your boyfriend, a Continent, Planets, your apartment, books you have, or anything else that spontaneously comes to mind when you think of "all that is". Once you get a sense of everything being within that space or bubble, allow yourself to let go of all of that, for the whole bubble to dissolve or disappear. Once you have done that and just relaxed and released, notice what is still left.

Whatever is still left, put it into that all-encompassing bubble or space. Then, once again, let go of everything, release everything-that-is. And then, once you have done that, look at what is still left. What are you still perceiving? And expand your attention to include all of that. Whatever is left…body sensations, the universe, a blue bottle, a memory from childhood, "nothing", an itchy nose…just include all of it. And once again let go of it all, allow it to disappear. Look at what is still left after you have let go of everything. If it's "nothing", or "bliss", or "the witness", or "blackness", or "whiteness", or "being", or whatever, that is still something. So include it into that near-Infinite bubble. (If, at any time, you feel discomfort, simply include it into the all-that-is space. Break off only if the discomfort becomes overwhelming. Normally you will not feel any discomfort doing this but will get more and more relaxed/awake.) Continue with the same process until you feel very high.

Aware of Awareness Itself

What are you aware of?
And, taking one step back…*who or what is aware?*
How are you aware? What is it that is aware?

One of my favorite Meditation-Techniques is to become **aware of awareness itself**. The technique quite instantly removes attention from the world of **form** and places it to the **formless** world whence everything originates. The Meditation does have a tendency to relax and expand the mind. The default state of the mind seems to be to have one's attention on *something, anything,* but rarely on attention *itself.* So this is a putting attention on attention rather than on something external. One of the first things you notice when doing that is that "who you really are" is rather vast and unconfined because it's undefined. You may also notice that the field that is aware-of-awareness is an even vaster, more impersonal field than awareness itself. You also notice that it is here that ideas of time, space, and causality have no meaning. There is certainly more to discover in this rare meditative mode of consciousness, but it's best you discover it for yourself rather than being told by me.

The deeper version of this practice is to sit down, close your eyes, and notice what comes into awareness, then **to ask yourself who or what it is that is aware**, remaining more mindful of the one-aware rather than *what* one is aware *of* throughout.

It does not have to be done sitting and with eyes closed of course. You could set the deliberate intention to remain a little aware of awareness or the-one-who-is-aware throughout the whole day, then go about your daily activities while reminding yourself of the awareness-of-awareness now and then.

One of my favorite quotes says, *"Meditation is not a means to an end, it is the means and the end."* That means you are not doing this so you can achieve a particular goal or state. Instead, the awareness-of-awareness **is** the state that is already achieved with this simple shift. It is my view that if this is taken deeper, you can actually experience hints of the state the ancients traditionally describe as "spiritual enlightenment" or "cosmic consciousness".

This technique is like the eye turning on itself. The eye sees many things but it does not see itself because it **is** itself and views from the viewpoint of itself. The eye is that which is aware, but there is also a faculty or an aspect-of-you that can become aware of the eye itself. And then there is an even more superordinate faculty that is aware of the one that is aware of the eye….and so on, like in concentric circles that radiate out ever more expansively.

If you are interested in trying this Meditation-Technique (there is also a guided version of it in the Infinity Course) and it appears too abstract or difficult to you, then an intermediate step would be to simply notice what you are aware of, first. This is an intermediate step I sometimes implement in live-coachings when guiding a student into this state. So you would, for example, walk around and simply note the things you are aware of. "I am aware of the sound of this train. Now I am aware of my right foot itching." This may later turn into shorthand of simply noting "train sound", "foot itch", "thought about schedule", "voice speaking" etc. **This exercise alone can produce extraordinary states and insights** you have never experienced before and is, for the most part, easier to do than being aware of awareness itself. Then, as you become practiced at noticing what you are aware of, you can gently start shifting to inquiring **who** is aware of those things. One level higher still does not ask "who" is aware of them, but **"what"**, because it's really more of a what than a who. "What am I?" is perhaps a more accurate question than "Who am I?" because this vast and incredibly powerful field of energy is "me" in a sense, but it's also without the typical positions, fixed viewpoints, beliefs, and conditionalities of the Ego-Self. Many enlightened sages have in fact recommended the Meditation-practice of inquiring "Who am I?" but in my experience the question "What is aware?" may be a more accurate one.

Expand the Silence

There were three drunk men behind me in the airplane. You could tell that these men were uncomfortable with either flying or with each other because they were chatting away incessantly the entire flight of many hours. The more beer they drank, the more they talked. Every time just a hint of silence arose, one of them would desperately look for the next topic to cling to or the next joke to crack. Their laughs felt forced and their inebriation gave them an aggressive edge rather than calming them down. After a couple hours of their non-stop chatter, I finally re-seated myself so that I might find some silence and quality-thoughts.

The episode got me thinking about alcohol's relation to states of consciousness. Alcohol is so popular because it quiets the mind, helping people who would otherwise feel awkward or self-conscious, to socially interact with each other. It loosens the tongue, letting people to speak freely. When the mind is quiet and communication no longer withheld, people have more fun.

When you allow yourself to relax into silence with another, without judgments and filters, or when you stop withholding communication and what you *really* think, you can experience highly improved states of consciousness without a drop of alcohol. From my perspective, the inebriated state is a poor substitute for a state of true presence. In fact, habituation to alcohol cripples your ability to find these light-states naturally.

In my last two seminars I practiced this state of presence by having students sit in silence with each other. I've also asked them to stop withholding their true feelings and thoughts. In the combination of both, well-being and hilarity ensue. When you allow for more silence, you emulate the nature of the universe and the nature of awareness. This is why things improve when your silence expands. You can allow for more silence between you and other people. Once you break through the barriers of boredom or needing distraction (TV, Phone, Food, and Radio are among the most common) and "needing to say something", and can just sit in silence with another, you begin feeling both yourself and the other at a deeper level. Phases of prolonged silence throughout the day will greatly expand your sense of aliveness. It will make things appear more vivid, interesting, and real. The need for alcohol or any other external relaxant begins to disappear.

You can allow for more silence with yourself. I usually do most of my long, cross-country car rides without radio. Being of a meditative mind-set, too much radio actually annoys me. You see, I do not feel the need to cover up my thoughts and emotions with the car-radio because my thoughts and emotions actually feel good. When you are at peace inside, no distractions are needed. The constant need for distraction indicates a subtle running away from your true inner state. What if you were to turn off the radio or TV or smartphone now and then? Could you handle the silence? Could you allow your true inner state to arise? You might not like what you see at first. The silence might make you feel uncomfortable. But as you stick to it and allow the silence to expand, it will lead you back to your true and natural state of well-being that you so much miss without even knowing it.

The Marines Meditation Training

When the outermost limits of physical proficiency, knowledge, and skill are reached the only way upwards is to turn to spiritual reality – such as in meditation, contemplation, prayer, and the art of conscious intention.

Even the Marines – who pride themselves on taking physical training and skill to its outermost limits – are finally discovering that the only way up is a journey into spirit realms. Some quotes from the article "Marines Expanding the use of Meditation Training":

There were weapons qualifications. Grueling physical workouts. High-stress squad counterinsurgency drills, held in an elaborate ersatz village designed to mirror the sights, sounds and smells of a remote mountain settlement in Afghanistan. There also were weekly meditation classes — including one in which Sgt. Hampton and his squad mates were asked to sit motionless in a chair and focus on the point of contact between their feet and the floor. "A lot of people thought it would be a waste of time," he said. "Why are we sitting around a classroom doing their weird meditative stuff?" "But over time, I felt more relaxed. I slept better. Physically, I noticed that I wasn't tense all the time. It helps you think more clearly and decisively in stressful situations. There was a benefit."...

A study of those Marines subsequently published in the research journal Emotions found that they slept better, had improved athletic performance and scored higher on emotional and cognitive evaluations than Marines who did not participate in the program, which centers on training the mind to focus on the current moment and to be aware of one's physical state.

As Business people, politicians, and now military start using Meditation you realize that the overall consciousness of the planet is riding. Meditation is indeed performance enhancing, and without it I could not deliver the good results I have been having with a wide variety of people over the last 20 years. Meditation enhances performance because it produces Awareness and Awareness itself is the basis of everything.

Cosmic Consciousness

My body became immovably rooted; breath was drawn out of my lungs as if by some huge magnet. Soul and mind instantly lost their physical bondage, and streamed out like a fluid piercing light from my every pore. The flesh was as though dead, yet in my intense awareness, I knew that never before had I been fully alive. My sense of identity was no longer narrowly confined to a body, but embraced the circumambient atoms. People on distant streets seemed to be moving gently over my own remote periphery. The roots of plants and trees appeared through a dim transparency of the soil; I discerned the inward flow of their sap.

The whole vicinity lay bare before me. My ordinary frontal vision was now changed to a vast spherical sight, simultaneously all-perceptive. Through the back of my head I saw men strolling far down Rai Ghat Road, and noticed also a white cow who was leisurely approaching. When she reached the space in front of the open ashram gate, I observed her with my two physical eyes. As she passed by, behind the brick wall, I saw her clearly still.

All objects within my panoramic gaze trembled and vibrated like quick motion pictures. My body, Masters, the pillared courtyard, the furniture and floor, the trees and sunshine, occasionally became violently agitated, until all melted into a luminescent sea; even as sugar crystals, thrown into a glass of water, dissolve after being shaken. The unifying light alternated with materializations of form, the metamorphoses revealing the law of cause and effect in creation.

An oceanic joy broke upon calm endless shores of my soul. The Spirit of God, I realized, is exhaustless Bliss; His body is countless tissues of light. A swelling glory within me began to envelop towns, continents, the earth, solar and stellar systems, tenuous nebulae, and floating universes. The entire cosmos, gently luminous, like a city seen afar at night, glimmered within the infinitude of my being. The sharply etched global outlines faded somewhat at the farthest edges; there I could see a mellow radiance, ever-undiminished. It was indescribably subtle; the planetary pictures were formed of a grosser light.

The divine dispersion of rays poured from an Eternal Source, blazing into galaxies, transfigured with ineffable auras. Again and again I saw the creative beams condense into constellations, then resolve into sheets of transparent flame. By rhythmic reversion, sextillion worlds passed into diaphanous luster; fire became firmament. I cognized the center of the empyrean as a point of intuitive perception in my heart. Irradiating splendor issued from my nucleus to every part of the universal structure. Blissful amrita, the nectar of immortality, pulsed through me with quicksilver-like fluidity.

– Paramhansa Yogananda, "Autobiography of a Yogi",

Deep Silence of Mind

Meditation is taught because a deep silence of mind is the basis of many different states of well-being. But even if you do not meditate there are some facts derived from Meditation that will calm even the mind of the non-meditator. These are:

- You know nothing. You need presume no reliable knowledge of anything at all. The "know-nothing" state is an attitude you can enter, from which the mind naturally calms into a space of spontaneity. Many times one is able to help people effectively because you know nothing about their issues and do not share their History and Beliefs. If I know nothing, I can allow Intuition to guide things. Or I can say, "I have no clue what any of this means, dear Higher Self, please reveal what it means to me." This kind of surrender and letting go has a calming effect (if it is not misused to give up self-reliance).

- Resist nothing. Another way to say this is: "Say Yes to Everything". No, I don't mean externally and verbally. I mean inwardly. Inside, embrace and welcome anything and everything that happens here/now. Even if you are saying "No" to someone externally/verbally, say "Yes" to them inside. You see, most people say "Yes" outside while they really mean "No" inside. I am recommending you say "Yes" inside, no matter what. As you embrace everything that happens, you live from the implication that the Universe and whatever it provides is perfect. And for you it will turn perfect. Every time you realize you lost Awareness, you are back to Awareness. To resist nothing does not mean to no see nothing as good or bad, but to welcome the positive as your soul's joy and the negative as a stepping stone on the path of life.

- Realize that the content of mind is just not that important. The mind is like a TV-set that just babbles on whatever it was told throughout life. It's a phantasmagoria. It's a recording-device. If you don't believe that it's not-you, try this: Right after waking up, in that very split second, ask what your name is. Or have someone ask you. You will notice a completely blank mind, without a clue of what your name. Only then does the mind begin to switch on, creating all types of definitions of who you are. You are not your memories either. In lower and higher states of consciousness, a human experiences memory gaps and memory loss...proving that one's "memory" is only valid in a limited strata. Your entire thinking-apparatus is impersonal, like hair growing. Do not give it more importance than that, and it will calm down naturally. You juice it by thinking it's "you" and it's "important". If you stop flooding it with stimuli and importance, it calms down.

- Heed the recommendations of the London Subway system that keeps saying "Mind the Gap", to draw attention to the empty space between the subway train and the platform. That is actually a great Mantra because Mind is indeed a Gap. If you look carefully you will notice that Mind is mostly silent, except when you pay attention to it. It may be more silent if you don't try to silence it in the first place. Some of these Meditation-Manuals are actually achieving the opposite of silencing the mind.

- Concentration calms the mind. You cannot control all thoughts all at the time. But you can concentrate on something, by which all mind-noise recedes. If you are laden with problems, check if you lack concentration…concentration for your work, for friends, for projects, for whatever. It's silent when something fascinates you – such as beauty. Beauty can make the mind go still for awhile.

Here's an exercise: Take a walk through town or the countryside. Notice something. Keep your awareness there for half a minute or a minute, feeling and perceiving that thing, place, object, person, space, idea, or plant. Then move on to the next thing, place, object, person, space, plant, and/or idea. Continue for hours and start experiencing deep silence of mind. You will feel very, very high afterwards.

\
Sensory Deprivation

Hyperactive minds perceive most of reality through their visual senses. They are over-focused on what is being seen and tend to disregard what is being heard, felt, smelled, and tasted. Then there is "the sixth sense" which lies even more dormant. The "sixth sense" is to get things intuitively. Focusing on any of these other senses can heighten your perception and aliveness for the sole reason that they are usually filtered out by our extreme emphasis on visual input. But as you expand awareness, you want to quit judging things by their looks only. Looks are *one* way of perceiving, but if you rely on outer appearances only, you can easily be deceived. If you also pay attention to how something or someone sounds, smells. and what you feel and sense about it/him/her, the chances of you being deceived are much lower. Being cut off from one's senses is one of the less happy side-effects of our rapid modern life in front of computer screens. The computer, being an imitation of the mind (and Twitter itself being the *ultimate* physical copy of how the chattery mind works), is all set-up around and based on seeing. You smell nothing, taste nothing, touch nothing, and only rarely hear and sense. Too much computer sitting can condition you to experience the world more flatly...without those other beautiful senses the Universe has given you from birth. Eating while at the same time watching a movie does not help you develop your sense of taste but keeps you firmly focused in the visual world of the mind. To all the screen-people out there: When is the last time you smelled pine trees, saltwater, or flowers?

One method to rapidly expand your aliveness is through sensory deprivation. I spend at least one day a year completely blindfolded all day. On that day I negotiate my way around by sound and touch. Suddenly the auditory sense becomes very acute. After a few hours I begin hearing things I haven't heard in years. Things we don't pay attention to, we don't hear. That's why you usually hear the creaks your house makes only at night – because in the daytime you are visually focused and not paying attention to them. The blindfolding has a relaxing effect because it reduces half of the overall data input. The mind thinks in images, so all this visual input will keep someone in thinking-ness all the time. The silence of mind experienced when blindfolded a day will create higher states of Awareness.

Smell and Taste are among the most disregarded senses. When was the last time you took time to smell something? To smell a flower, to smell a leather wallet, to smell perfume? People are forever looking for higher states not suspecting that conscious smelling can quickly transport them into the Infinite Here and Now. See if you can go around your place and consciously smell objects for 10 Minutes. Don't rush this. Take your time to actually smell, spending more than 30 seconds with each object. Do the same for taste. See if you can actually eat without doing something else. Or, if you are a smoker, see if you can smoke without doing something else. For all you tobacco addicts out there, this is a chance to re-learn how to actually *enjoy* smoking (which reduces the negative effects of it). When was the last time you saw someone smoke and do nothing else? Maybe never. That is an indicator of the attention-deficit-society we live in. And the main cause of unhappiness.

To get more aligned with one sense, deprive yourself of the others. If you want to regain your sense of touch, go around consciously touching things. Or blindfold yourself and plug cotton into your ear. Not hearing or seeing it is touch you must rely on. See if you can consciously touch your spouse instead of the automatic-caress so frequently seen.

To get in touch with your "sixth sense" you may want to deprive yourself of all other senses. This can be done in a sensory deprivation tank (floatation tank). Or, when trying to determine what something is, see if you can listen to that "inner voice" instead of what your eyes are telling you. Intuition knows more than the senses are showing because it is the sense of the soul that has more information available.

How to Stop Thinking

This is a excerpt by Osho on "stopping thinking" as it relates to Meditation:

THINKING cannot be stopped. Not that it does not stop, but it cannot be stopped. It stops of its own accord. This distinction has to be understood, otherwise you can go mad chasing your mind. No-mind does not arise by stopping thinking. When the thinking is no more, no-mind is. The very effort to stop will create more anxiety, it will create conflict, it will make you split. You will be in a constant turmoil within. This is not going to help. And even if you succeed in stopping it forcibly for a few moments, it is not an achievement at all — because those few moments will be almost dead, they will not be alive. You may feel a sort of stillness, but not silence, because a forced stillness is not silence. Underneath it, deep in the unconscious, the repressed mind goes on working. So, there is no way to stop the mind. But the mind stops — that is certain. It stops of its own accord. So what to do? — your question is relevant. Watch — don't try to stop. There is no need to do any action against the mind. In the first place, who will do it? It will be mind fighting mind itself. You will divide your mind into two; one that is trying to boss over — the top-dog — trying to kill the other part of itself, which is absurd. It is a foolish game. It can drive you crazy. Don't try to stop the mind or the thinking — just watch it, allow it. Allow it total freedom. Let it run as fast as it wants. You don't try in any way to control it. You just be a witness. It is beautiful! Mind is one of the most beautiful mechanisms. Science has not yet been able to create anything parallel to mind. Mind still remains the masterpiece — so complicated, so tremendously powerful, with so many potentialities. Watch it! Enjoy it! And don't watch like an enemy, because if you look at the mind like an enemy, you cannot watch. You are already prejudiced; you are already against. You have already decided that something is wrong with the mind — you have already concluded.

And whenever you look at somebody as an enemy you never look deep, you never look into the eyes. You avoid! Watching the mind means: look at it with deep love, with deep respect, reverence — it is God's gift to you! Nothing is wrong in mind itself. Nothing is wrong in thinking itself. It is a beautiful process as other processes are. Clouds moving in the sky are beautiful — why not thoughts moving into the inner sky? Flowers coming to the trees are beautiful — why not thoughts flowering into your being. The river running to the ocean is beautiful — why not this stream of thoughts running somewhere to an unknown destiny? Is it not beautiful? Look with deep reverence. Don't be a fighter — be a lover. Watch! — the subtle nuances of the mind; the sudden turns, the beautiful turns; the sudden jumps and leaps; the games that mind goes on playing; the dreams that it weaves — the imagination, the memory; the thousand and one projections that it creates. Watch! Standing there, aloof, distant, not involved, by and by you will start feeling...

The deeper your watchfulness becomes, the deeper your awareness becomes, and gaps start arising, intervals. One thought goes and another has not come, and there is a gap. One cloud has passed, another is coming and there is a gap. In those gaps, for the first time you will have glimpses of no-mind, you will have the taste of no-mind. Call it taste of Zen, or Tao, or Yoga. In those small intervals, suddenly the sky is clear and the sun is shining. Suddenly the world is full of mystery because all barriers are dropped. The screen on your eyes is no more there. You see clearly, you see penetratingly. The whole existence becomes transparent. In the beginning, these will be just rare moments, few and *far in between. But they will give you glimpses of what samadhi is. Small pools of silence — they will come and they will disappear. But now you know that you are on the right track — you start watching again. When a thought passes, you watch it; when an interval passes, you watch it. Clouds are also beautiful; sunshine also is beautiful. Now you are not a chooser. Now you don't have a fixed mind: you don't say, "I would like only the intervals." That is stupid — because once you become attached to wanting only the intervals, you have decided again against thinking. And then those intervals will disappear. They happen only when you are very distant, aloof. They happen, they cannot be brought. They happen, you cannot force them to happen. They are spontaneous happenings. Go on watching. Let thoughts come and go — wherever they want to go. Nothing is wrong! Don't try to manipulate and don't try to direct.*

Let thoughts move in total freedom. And then bigger intervals will be coming. You will be blessed with small satoris. Sometimes minutes will pass and no thought will be there; there will be no traffic — a total silence, undisturbed. When the bigger gaps come, you will not only have clarity to see into the world — with the bigger gaps you will have a new clarity arising — you will be able to see into the inner world. With the first gaps you will see into the world: trees will be more green than they look right now.

You will be surrounded by an infinite music — the music of the spheres. You will be suddenly in the presence of God — ineffable, mysterious. Touching you although you cannot grasp it. Within your reach and yet beyond. With the bigger gaps, the same will happen inside. God will not only be outside, you will be suddenly surprised — He is inside also. He is not only in the seen; He is in the seer also — within and without. By and by... But don't get attached to that either. Attachment is the food for the mind to continue.

Non-attached witnessing is the way to stop it without any effort to stop it. And when you start enjoying those blissful moments, your capacity to retain them for longer periods arises. Finally, eventually, one day, you become master. Then when you want to think, you think; if thought is needed, you use it; if thought is not needed, you allow it to rest. Not that mind is simply no more there: mind is there, but you can use it or not use it. Now it is your decision. Just like legs: if you want to run you use them; if you don't want to run you simply rest — legs are there. In the same way, mind is always there. When I am talking to you I am using the mind — there is no other way to talk. When I am answering your question I am using the mind — there is no other way. I have to respond and relate, and mind is a beautiful mechanism. When I am not talking to you and I am alone, there is no mind — because it is a medium to relate through. Sitting alone it is not needed. You have not given it a rest; hence, the mind becomes mediocre. Continuously used, tired, it goes on and on and on. Day it works; night it works.

In the day you think; in the night you dream. Day in, day out, it goes on working. If you live for seventy or eighty years it will be continuously working. Look at the delicacy and the endurability of the mind — so delicate! In a small head all the libraries of the world can be contained; all that has ever been written can be contained in one single mind. Tremendous is the capacity of the mind — and in such a small space! and not making much noise.

If scientists someday become capable of creating a parallel computer to mind… computers are there, but they are not yet minds. They are still mechanisms, they have no organic unity; they don't have any center yet. If some day it becomes possible… and it is possible that scientists may someday be able to create minds — then you will know how much space that computer will take, and how much noise it will make. Mind is making almost no noise; goes on working silently. And such a servant! — for seventy, eighty years.

And then, too, when you are dying your body may be old but your mind remains young. Its capacity remains yet the same. Sometimes, if you have used it rightly, it even increases with your age! — because the more you know, the more you understand, the more you have experienced and lived, the more capable your mind becomes. When you die, everything in your body is ready to die — except the mind. That's why in the East we say mind leaves the body and enters another womb, because it is not yet ready to die. The rebirth is of the mind.

Once you have attained the state of samadhi, no-mind, then there will be no rebirth. Then you will simply die. And with your dying, everything will be dissolved — your body, your mind... only your witnessing soul will remain. That is beyond time and space. Then you become one with existence; then you are no more separate from it. The separation comes from the mind. But there is no way to stop it forcibly — don't be violent. Move lovingly, with a deep reverence — and it will start happening of its own accord. You just watch. And don't be in a hurry.

The modern mind is in much hurry. It wants instant methods for stopping the mind. Hence, drugs have appeal. Mm? — you can force the mind to stop by using chemicals, drugs, but again you are being violent with the mechanism. It is not good. It is destructive. In this way you are not going to become a master. You may be able to stop the mind through the drugs, but then drugs will become your master — you are not going to become the master. You have simply changed your bosses, and you have changed for the worse. Now the drugs will hold power over you, they will possess you; without them you will be nowhere. Meditation is not an effort against the mind. It is a way of understanding the

mind. It is a very loving way of witnessing the mind — but, of course, one has to be very patient. This mind that you are carrying in your head has arisen over centuries, millennia. Your small mind carries the whole experience of humanity — and not only of humanity: of animals, of birds, of plants, of rocks. You have passed through all those experiences.

All that has happened up to now has happened in you also. In a very small nutshell, you carry the whole experience of existence. That's what your mind is. In fact, to say it is yours is not right: it is collective; it belongs to us all. Modern psychology has been approaching it, particularly Jungian analysis has been approaching it, and they have started feeling something like a collective unconscious. Your mind is not yours — it belongs to us all. Our bodies are very separate; our minds are not so separate.

Our bodies are clear-cutly separate; our minds overlap — and our souls are one. Bodies separate, minds overlapping, and souls are one. I don't have a different soul and you don't have a different soul. At the very center of existence we meet and are one. That's what God is: the meeting-point of all. Between the God and the world — 'the world'
means the bodies — is mind. Mind is a bridge: a bridge between the body and the soul, between the world and God. Don't try to destroy it! Many have tried to destroy it through Yoga. That is a misuse of Yoga. Many have tried to destroy it through body posture, breathing — that too brings subtle chemical changes inside. For example: if you stand on your head in shirshasan — in the headstand — you can destroy the mind very easily. Because when the blood rushes too much, like a flood, into the head — when you stand on your head that's what you are trying to do…. The mind mechanism is very delicate; you are flooding it with blood. The delicate tissues will die. That's why you never come across a very intelligent yogi — no.

Yogis are, more or less, stupid. Their bodies are healthy — that's true — strong, but their minds are just dead. You will not see the glimmer of intelligence. You will see a very robust body, animal-like, but somehow the human has disappeared. Standing on your head, you are forcing your blood into the head through gravitation. The head needs blood, but in a very, very small quantity; and very slowly, not flood-like. Against gravitation, very little blood reaches to the head. And that, too, in a very silent way.

If too much blood is reaching into the head it is destructive. Yoga has been used to kill the mind; breathing can be used to kill the mind. There are rhythms of breath, subtle vibrations of breath, which can be very, very drastic to the delicate mind. The mind can be destroyed through them. These are old tricks. Now the latest tricks are supplied by science: LSD, marijuana, and others. More and more sophisticated drugs will be available sooner or later. I am not in favour of stopping the mind. I am in favour of watching it. It stops of its own accord — and then it is beautiful When something happens without any violence it has a beauty of its own, it has a natural growth. You can force a flower and open it by force; you can pull the petals of a bud and open it by force — but you have destroyed the beauty of the flower. Now it is almost dead. It cannot stand your violence. The petals will be hanging loose, limp, dying. When the bud opens by its own energy, when it opens of its own accord, then those petals are alive.

The mind is your flowering — don't force it in any way. I am against all force and against all violence, and particularly violence that is directed towards yourself. Just watch — in deep prayer, love,

reverence. And see what happens! Miracles happen of their own accord. There is no need to pull and push. You ask: How to stop thinking? I say: Just watch, be alert. And drop this idea of stopping, otherwise it will stop the natural transformation of the mind. Drop this idea of stopping! Who are you to stop? At the most, enjoy. And nothing is wrong — even if immoral thoughts, so-called immoral thoughts, pass through your mind, let them pass; nothing is wrong. You remain detached. No harm is being done. It is just fiction; you are seeing an inner movie. Allow it its own way and it will lead you, by and by, to the state of no-mind. Watching ultimately culminates in no-mind. No-mind is not against mind: no-mind is beyond mind. No-mind does not come by killing and destroying the mind: no-mind comes when you have understood the mind so totally that thinking is no longer needed — your understanding has replaced it.

The Benefits of White Noise

White noise (or similar so-called pink, blue, gray, & violet noises), are wonderful relaxants that have a tendency to calm the mind. That's why when you pass by a waterfall it is a good opportunity to sit down for some Meditation. I lived near a waterfall for many years and would spend many blissful hours sitting on a rock right between two streams of waterfall. Some other sources of white noise or similar mind-soothing sounds:

- Rain
- A vacuum cleaner
- A hairdryer
- A ventilator or air conditioning
- Waves of an ocean or waves at a beach
- A water sprinkler
- Crickets
- Tibetan bowls
- Wind chimes
- A shower
- Inside an airplane
- Atmospheric background noise of an airport
- Atmospheric background noise of peaceful crowds
- Soft and repetitive machinery

If you wish to give your mind some rest and have it go on "empty", simply put on some White Noise and zone out for awhile. It meditates you.

10 Meditations for Higher Consciousness

The purpose of these Meditations is to experience states of pure consciousness prior to mind and concept. Descriptions are kept minimal so that you can develop your own explorations.

1. Meditate on Things as Nameless

Spend some time viewing different objects, situations, concepts, places, and spaces as nameless and without label or meaning. If you notice yourself automatically ascribing a name to something, take that label back and view it in the pre-mind state you had as a child, before you were told what things are. You may also view memories and internal objects from the perspective of "not knowing what it means".

2. View Things for the Very First Time

What if you had never seen an image, never heard a sound, never touched anything or been touched, never smelled or tasted anything? What is your state prior to sensual experience? What if you were about to make those experiences but hadn't yet? What if you were experiencing everything for the first time? Sit in this attitude for a while.

3. A Drop of Water Surrounded by Infinite Space

Imagine yourself a drop of water surrounded by infinite space. You can have your eyes opened or closed. You may imagine yourself smaller and smaller, perhaps even atom sized and surrounded by Infinity. Feel. Experience.

4. Empty Spaces

Meditate on the empty space surrounding objects. Surrounding bodies. Surrounding feelings. Surrounding thoughts. Keep your awareness on the emptiness that both surrounds and permeates all things. You are peripherally aware of objects and feelings, but even more aware of the emptiness outside and inside of the objects and feelings. You may do this with eyes opened or closed.

5. Remove Everything and Notice What's Left

Remove everything from the universe and see what's left. You might imagine a huge bubble that contains all-that-is. Then you might burst that bubble, allowing all things to disappear. Then notice what's left. Whatever is left, allow it to be included into that bubble. Then allow that too, to disappear. Continue with this until nothing is left. Include anything at all: any idea, concept, memory, thought, object, space, place, sensation, etc. Even "nothing" being something, includes that too. See where it takes you.

6. Aware of Awareness

What are you aware of? What is aware of awareness? And what is aware of that? Meditate in this manner for a while.

7. Perspective

Meditate on the body and mind as sitting in another room. Then further away, perhaps on a field, then in another city, then another country, then another planet, then another galaxy, then another universe, then infinitely far away.

8. Motion

Notice something that is moving. Contemplate where it might have come from and where it might be going. Remain aware of motion and non-motion for some time.

9. Similar and Different

Notice something in the here and now. Notice how it's similar to something in the past. Then notice how it's different to something in the past. Continue until you feel a heightened sense of aliveness.

10. Observe

Go to a public place. Simply sit and observe for hours.

9
Hyper-lucid Dreaming

Lucid Dreaming is the advanced state of consciousness where you are aware that you are dreaming while you are dreaming. "Hyper-lucid Dreaming" is an even more advanced state of energy in which you experience states beyond your wildest dreams. For your orientation and education, here is a scale of Awareness as it pertains to night dreams:

Scale of Lucidity

1- Oblivion
Every human dreams every night, but at this stage we are entirely unaware of it. After waking up you don't even know that you dreamed. You pay no attention to it and have no real interest in your dreams. This stage can be accompanied by stress and exhaustion in daily life, so that the night is used for regeneration during which awareness is mostly shut off.

2- Unawareness
You know that you dreamed but only after waking up. During sleep you are oblivious to your dreams

-as-dreams. The dreams are usually muddled and unclear, so you derive no insight or benefit from them after awakening. If there were nightmares you feel like a victim of it rather than in a position to deal with or transform it.

3- Semi Aware

Dreams are somewhat clearer and more vivid or memorable, especially after awakening. While dreaming you notice something strange is happening but you do not question it enough to become lucid. There are various hints that it's a dream, but you never quite reach that point of realization. Instead you take the dream as something that is "really happening". You are fully unaware that there is another life in which you are in bed and sleeping.

4- Semi Lucid

The dream is clear and vivid. At this stage you are usually aware enough to face a nightmare and transform it or make it better. Normal dreams are experienced with more interest and a kind of wakefulness, as if your sleeping-self is not entirely asleep. You notice the typical hints that show you that you are dreaming. Sometimes you question things or even notice that you are lucid, but you don't become fully lucid. Instead you shift between Unaware, Semi Aware, and Semi Lucid. But these short glimpses of lucidity are enough to inspire you on the subject of Lucid Dreaming. They are short moments of realization that ask, "Wow...I am dreaming, aren't I?" and, "Is this a dream?" Because the state is not stable these questions are sometimes quickly forgotten as you fall back into unawareness. This "falling back into unawareness" comes from a kind of tiredness or exhaustion with life. The less resistance you build up throughout the day, the easier it will be to maintain dream awareness. Sometimes the subconscious plays tricks on you at this level so you go back to unawareness. For example, you might experience a "false awakening" – that is dreaming that you have awoken and are no longer dreaming. Frequent instances of semi-lucidity will produce full lucidity.

5- Lucid

You notice the dream as a dream. You know that there are two worlds…one is the dreamscape and the other is what you consider "real life" lying in bed and sleeping. You realize that all of these events and dreamscapes are actually taking place "within you" and not "out there". The realization of lucidity parallels the spiritual self-realization of waking life where you realize that it's "all happening within". For beginners, the state of lucidity might be accompanied by a moment of awe or great happiness. Others report that they just acknowledge it as a matter-of-fact. Compared to higher levels, this state is fairly passive. That means you know you are dreaming but don't do anything with this knowledge. Instead, you enjoy the scenery passing by.

6- High Lucid

In this state the dream scenario is even more intense, as if it were "more real" than your waking life (and in a sense it is). You are also aware that you can influence the dream, where to travel to, what to change, and what might be worthwhile. You are lucid enough to recognize this as an opportunity to transform energy-patterns which will also have an effect on waking life. You are aware of the meaning of various dream symbols and can receive direct communication from your soul/higher self. This level of lucid dreaming is highly enjoyable and fulfilling. At this stage you can use your dream for research, for creative exploration, and for healing purposes.

7- Hyper-lucid

Your dream experience and perception (seeing, hearing, feeling, & touching) become crystal clear. A sense of Elation, Bliss, and Ecstasy course through you as the physical and spiritual Dimensions overlap. This feeling of intense happiness usually spills over into waking life. At this stage you find gates to other Dimensions and parallel lives. If you choose not to enter those gates, you can also explore your life's purpose and the status of your mission (see Lives of the Soul). This state can be more exhilarating than anything you have ever experienced anywhere...in waking or dream life. That's why the Hyper-Lucid-Dreaming was created: So that every human being who would like to do so, can experience this state.

Lucid Dreaming Intro

Definition: Semi-lucid dreams are more vivid, symbolically, and directly significant and more rememerable after waking up. Lucid dreaming means knowing that you are dreaming while you are dreaming, which implies knowing about another reality (your waking reality) while asleep. Hyper-Lucid Dreaming means being able to use your dreams creatively in deliberately travelling to other dimensions, parallel realities, and learning skills while your body is asleep, accessing hidden knowledge, and yes, even influencing your waking life from a higher vantage point.

Usefulness: Becoming lucid in your sleeping state as in, "Ah, this is a dream! I am creating this! This is taking place in my psyche!" reflects becoming lucid in your waking state as in, "Ah, this is a dream! I am creating this! This is taking place in my psyche!" Both types of awakenings have the same effect on your self-confidence and appreciation of life. Dreaming…be it at night or in the daytime (daydreaming) are both essential for enjoyment of life and creatorhood over life.

Method: Becoming more interested in your nightdreams and remembering more of them after waking will eventually lead to lucid dreaming. <u>Becoming more aware of your dreams will eventually lead to becoming more aware within your dreams</u>. It's as simple as that. Attention to dreams will create awareness of dreams which will create lucid dreams. As in everything else, it is a matter of attention and the free attention you have at your disposal to focus on the subject of dreams and your own dreams in particular.

Related Phenomena: Scientist have clinically tested and repeatedly demonstrated the following phenomena in connection with Lucid Dreaming: Mutual Dreaming (Telepathy), Remote Viewing (Extra Sensory Perception), Increase of Athletic Performance through exercising in a dreamscape, and various states of bliss associated with spiritual enlightenment, Spill-overs from dreamworld to waking life, acquisition of useful knowledge formerly unknown (including new inventions), OBE (out of body experiences), healing experiences, and countless other things. It is not expected for you to do the same, but merely to gain a bit more interest in dreaming in general.

Difficulty: The difficulty in achieving lucidity is in the paradox that "falling asleep" traditionally means "losing awareness", whereas lucid dreaming asks you to maintain awareness while falling asleep (while losing awareness) or regain awareness during sleep (during unawareness). It is due to this difficulty that most people don't even believe such a thing as lucid dreaming even exists. The author of this writing can tell you from his own experience that it not only exists but holds some of the most profound experiences available to mankind. Our supporting tool "Lucid Dream Creator" was developed to overcome this threshold.

"THE EYES SEE THINGS MORE CLEARLY WHEN DREAMING, THAN THE IMAGINATION WHEN WAKING." – LEONARDO DA VINCI

The Hypnagogic Threshold

You can become lucid during a dream or you can fall asleep "into" a lucid dream. To use the latter method you must overcome the so-called "Hypnagogic Threshhold", which is both a block and a lever to lucidity. If you have ever watched what happens while falling asleep, you will notice that as the body gets tired the mind produces all kinds of thoughts and images that seem completely random and unconscious. The body produces chemicals that make you sleepy and the mind produces "hypnagogic images". This is needed so that we can fall asleep (and dream), but it can also become an obstruction to being lucid because it seduces us into a state of unconsciousness. We were just noticing those thought-flashes and the next thing we know we wake up the next morning! Lucid Dreamers seek a middle path: We allow that lulling, uncontrollable, and sleep-inducing processing to happen, but we do not allow it to completely overrun us. A part of you stays aware and observing at all times. It is only when the aware observer disappears that the hypnagogic and automatic takes over. Remaining conscious is sometimes not that easy. "Going unconscious" is felt by most as relaxation and release. "I just want to stop trying, I just want to sleep," most people say. This is why having some energy left after a long day is crucial to lucid dreaming, and a stress-laden and turbulent life is not really conducive to this mystical art.

As you fall asleep your brain frequency goes from beta (awake), to alpha (relaxed), to theta (asleep), and maybe to delta (deep sleep). Delta is usually too low to have lucid dreams or any dream recall at all. On the other hand, remaining awake in delta state will produce what is called an "out of body experience" (OBE). Lucid Dreaming usually happens in a theta state. If you can maintain lucidity all the way down to the delta state, you get to the "super lucid" states.

Going unconscious begins by not being aware of when you became unaware. Awareness of the fact that you have lost awareness = having regained awareness. If you become too aware during the hypnagogic phase, you do not fall asleep. If you become too unaware during the hypnagogic phase, you do not lucid dream. Your goal is to find that mid-point gateway to another dimension. Sometimes remaining aware during this phase can be somewhat unpleasant because the mind is processing all kinds of subconscious garbage that we normally do not notice. But as you move through that garbage without going unconscious, you can come out on the other side into great lucidity.

One of the first things that happens in the hypnagogic phase is that your senses invert. You're seeing, hearing, feeling, tasting, and smelling have an equivalent in the hypnagogic realm and another equivalent in dreamscape. You can see with your waking-life self, you can see with the hypnagogic-self (the subconscious), and you can see with the dream-self. The hypnagogic state is chaotic, unstructured, and vague. It is similar to a level 1 or 2 dream. Lucidity on the other hand is clear, bright, and pleasant. Do not mistake one with the other. So as your senses invert you begin to replicate waking-life experiences into this non-physical realm. The "flashes" or scraps of thought are the beginning of the inversion of your visual sense. First there is a black "screen", and then visual impressions come up. The more you fall asleep, the more this process moves to automatic. What begins as foggy and vague scraps becomes more intense, big, and real as you sink deeper. Most people don't actually stay awake this long, but if you do remain aware, you will witness these very interesting phenomena. If before going to bed you watched a movie or played a video game, it is possible that this is included in those images (yes, movies and video games leave their impression on the subconscious). The more real the images appear to be, the more your senses have inverted, the closer you are getting to dreamstate. If you are still awake at this point, you have a huge chance of lucid dreaming. Don't let the images hypnotize you, stay in observer-mode. Do not let the intensity of the imagery scare you into unconsciousness, stay in observer-mode. As you drift even deeper the images increase in depth and dimension. The movements become more flowing and congruent. Maybe a meadow takes shape, and a few minutes later you are in your dream in this meadow. The transition from hypnagogic image to dream is highly fascinating and makes all the effort put into it worthwhile. It is the transition from the physical to the non-physical realm; from earth-life to soul-life.

This same inversion happens with sound. Maybe you remember a time you fell asleep with a song or melody in your head, and while becoming sleepier you noticed how the song suddenly got louder all by itself as if someone had turned up the volume. This is because the more your auditory sense inverts inwards, the more vivid it becomes within. It is extremely fascinating to be able to hear sounds that cannot be heard by other people in waking life. Don't worry, you have not gone crazy, you are just hearing hypnagogic sound. If you remain aware and half-awake, you will notice that things begin with silence of the mind, then move on to singular voices and sounds flaring up, and finally culminating in really loud sounds that we sometimes mistake with physical ones. Sometimes we think we might have heard a neighbor or people outside of our house, but most often these are sounds of the inner world. As with the visual input, this process has the potential to carry us into a lucid dream. What might begin as a whisper can develop into a loud bang or an Orchestra. Some notice how their thinking becomes a sound or how they can create a sound with their thinking (creating songs in your mind is a good LD-Induction technique, by the way). Being startled at loud and sudden noise can cause us to reject the experience, wake up, or go unconscious and lose ourselves in sleep. I am telling you this because you are not used to loud sounds on the verge of sleep (because you have rarely stayed awake long enough to experience them), and not knowing about it will not help you stay in observer-mode. If you start hearing music, voices, plopping sounds, knocking, honking, or explosions, don't startle, but just maintain awareness. Everything belongs. If the sounds are very surprising or loud, you are already at the later stages of hypnagogic awareness and on the verge of fantastic lucidity.

Just keep going. At this stage sounds naturally transform into a dream state, and you will soon find yourself "awake" and aware in a dream.

Your sense of touch and feeling also inverts to the magical world of dreams. Your whole body is part of that inversion process. Inner touching and feeling are experienced just as real as they are in waking life. The feelings are rarely painful but sometimes they are electric. Vibrations, Numbness, Itching, and "electric tickling" are all indicators of the hypnagogic state. As you sink down into sleep and remain aware, these feelings will become the dream. As you relax with these sensations and just go with them, they help you remain somewhat alert. Sometimes the vibratory energy increases to awesome levels as if being electrocuted. The energy is harmless and you can move through it into lucidity. Sometimes your muscles or body parts will jump or make involuntary movements. That is alright, it just indicates a change of frequency. In the most unpleasant case you will experience sleep paralysis. This means your body has actually fallen asleep and you can't move your muscles. If this rare event occurs, do not panic. Slowly regain wakefulness until you can move your body again. In some cases you will also experience the inversion of taste and smell. Some will even "smell music", "see sounds", "hear images", and all other sorts of weirdness.

If you find yourself falling asleep during the hypnagogic phase, don't worry about it. This is "normal"; it's what happens to 99.9% of the population. Simply try to observe the hypnagogic state for progressively longer amounts of time until you reach that threshold to dreamworld.

Learning to Dream

You can learn lucid dreaming just like you learn anything else…languages, dancing, cooking… All learning follows similar principles, the foremost of which is investment of time, money, or attention. A bad workman does not use his tools or he blames his tools. A good workman could take even mediocre tools and, with some loving attention, make much more out of them. Regularity of practice and loving attention to practice is more important than which tools exactly you use. You do not get something for nothing. Invest energy and you get energy back. Habit is created by repetition.

Repetition creates results. That's what learning is all about. Repeat something new for a whole month on a regular basis (every day, every second day, or every third day for example), and you have created a new habit that you will start "missing" if you don't do it.

Having a dream journal in which you write down your dreams not only improves dream memory and access to subconscious information, but also demonstrates that you are really interested in learning it. It helps you to stay focused on lucid dreaming as a skill you are developing. Enthusiasm and high Interest are created by high experiences. Without any high experiences you won't be that motivated to push on. If you have not yet had high experiences, then substitute those high experiences by associating all kinds of grand abilities and experiences with it. You can also keep enthusiasm high by already having invested time, attention, or money. Having invested such has the psychological effect of you needing to justify your investment...with some really vivid lucid dreams!

Gateway to Another World

"OUR REVELS NOW ARE ENDED. THESE OUR ACTORS, AS I FORETOLD YOU, WERE ALL SPIRITS, AND ARE MELTED INTO AIR, INTO THIN AIR. AND LIKE THE BASELESS FABRIC OF THIS VISION, THE CLOUD-CAPPED TOWERS, THE GORGEOUS PALACES, THE SOLEMN TEMPLES, THE GREAT GLOBE ITSELF, YEA, ALL WHICH IT INHERIT, SHALL DISSOLVE. AND LIKE THIS INSUBSTANTIAL PAGEANT FADED, LEAVE NOT A RACK BEHIND. WE ARE SUCH STUFF AS DREAMS ARE MADE OF, AND OUR LITTLE LIFE IS ROUNDED WITH SLEEP."
– William Shakespeare

This writing assumes that you have already had plenty of nice sounding theory on lucid dreaming and are here to instead enjoy specific techniques to master the art. Anything you learn, be it dancing, playing the piano, language, web design, and so forth, requires you to learn a set of attitudes, techniques, and skills. You will find some of the best lucid-dream induction techniques right here on these pages. Because of these techniques you will indeed lucid dream. And once you lucid dream, you will tell others of the endless possibilities. And in this way, you will contribute to the awakening of mankind. We live in exciting times and Lucid Dreaming will be one of the basic lifestyle choices of future generations. Once you have learned LD you will go beyond even that, into Hyper-lucid Dreaming.

Lucid Dream Induction Techniques

In due time, you may use all and any of these techniques, but not more than one each night. The basis of any of these exercises is Awareness.

1. You first become more interested in and AWARE of your dreams in general.

2. 2. You then become more AWARE within your dreams.

The more aware of your night-dreams you become, the more likely it is that you will soon become aware within those dreams and know that you are dreaming. For this purpose many lucid dreamers write a DREAM JOURNAL. In that journal they write down what they dreamed last night and intend to dream next night. This gives their practice some context, but it also increases dream memory and dream awareness. Normally, after waking up, you forget what you dreamed within only a few minutes. With most dreams, by the time you are in the shower or at breakfast you have completely forgotten that you even dreamed. Therefore, one of the best techniques you can use is to run through your entire dream again right after waking up. In the very minutes right after waking up, remember the dream. Which thoughts did you wake up with? What is the sequence of events you had during your night dreams? If you want to capture your dreams, it is best done right after waking up. If you can install that habit into your morning routine, you increase your chances of becoming a lucid dreamer. And, you intensify the habit of re-running your dreams right after awakening if you also write them down in a journal. This is difficult for many because it really requires some focus and patience…the type that says, "Yes, I do take my dream world seriously." By whether someone is willing to do this or not, you can tell whether s/he is really serious about becoming a lucid dreamer or whether s/he is just fantasizing.

1. Focusing While Falling Asleep

The idea is to completely let go and drop into sleep as you usually do but while keeping a part of you awake... This would result in you falling into a lucid dream instead of waking up into one while already sleeping. There are many ways to do this. One is to simply keep reminding yourself to keep a small part of yourself awake while your entire body has fallen asleep. If there has been stress or tension throughout the day, this is easier said than done. When you are on vacation and have had a round of massages, a good swim, and a lot of relaxation throughout the day, this will be much easier. The easiest time for me to do this was after lying in a floatation tank for three hours. I had "fallen asleep" in that tank but kept part of me awake and aware, which resulted in a beautiful and vivid state of lucidity. Another way to do this is to follow a guided imagery audio-program or to imagine some scenery or journey yourself. Doing it yourself can work if you are determined to keep focused. Drifting off can send you straight to sleep. Can you keep visualizing your vivid scenes while falling asleep? If you can maintain conscious visualization, you take something you were doing in waking life over into sleep life, which guarantees a lucid dream experience. Your imagery will take on a life of its own or suddenly become "more real than real" (this is why we prefer lucid dreams to mere visualization), and you will know that you are dreaming. A guided-imagery audio-program from someone else might be better because you will then have a voice coming from your waking-life into your sleeping-life which can trigger a lucid dream. Anything you recognize as coming from that "other life" can awaken you to the two worlds and thereby induce LD. Guided Imagery can give you a seamless transfer into a lucid dream and may indeed the easiest way to achieve this

2. What you do before going to sleep

Most people have their first lucid dream right after learning about the subject. That is, after reading a book about lucid dreaming, reading a website about it, watching a movie about Lucid Dreaming (such as "Vanilla Sky" by Cameron Crowe, featuring Tom Cruise or "Inception" featuring Leonardo DiCaprio) or listening to an audio about LD. It does seem to play a role in what you do before bedtime. If you eat a little, take melatonin, or vitamin B4, drink a little coffee or plum juice to get your digestion going, this will certainly benefit LD because you don't drift off into deep sleep when your body is still active. You can also read books that are not specifically about lucid dreaming but transmit the atmosphere of LD – science-fiction, metaphysics, fantasy, fairy tales, and poetry. One thing I have found to be conducive is to remember what I read or what movie I saw *while falling asleep*. You can use any movie with dreamlike atmospheres and mindscapes. The LD-movie "Vanilla Sky" is interesting because it contains elements that you only notice if you are sufficiently aware while watching the movie. Ninety-percent of all viewers will not notice those parts of the movie, not notice when the protagonist is only dreaming because they are just not awake enough. In this way "Vanilla Sky" mimics what happens during the dream state: Most of us are just not aware enough to notice the hints and signs that is a dream. The LD movie "Inception" is interesting because it shows how there are many layers, and layers, and layers of reality that all follow different laws of space and time. So if you have not seen those two yet, I recommend them as an inspiration for LD. But apart from those, do not miss movies of high aesthetic value and beauty. You want to feed your mind with the nice stuff so that you gravitate toward those areas in your LD.

3. Reality-Testing

Reality-testing is questioning whether you are waking or dreaming throughout your waking life, and frequently, and especially when odd or out-of-place things occur. "Am I dreaming?" "Is this a dream?" "Is this real?" The idea of this technique is that if you get used to reality-testing, you will do the same during your night dream thus increasing the likelihood of becoming aware of the dream-reality you're in, making you lucid. Reality-testing can be supported by hanging up little reminders or cards throughout your living space, in your car, or the office. Such reminders do not only increase your lucidity at night, but remind you that our daily life can be hypnotic and on-automatic, and that we can "snap out of it" for more wakefulness and self-determination in everyday life. While you are reading this, imagine for a moment you would find out that everything you deem real and "my life" is just a dream. Imagine you just had this realization.

Nothing you currently see in your surroundings or living space is ultimate reality but just a dream that a more real and expanded Self is having. And it can all dissolve within seconds. Your real self is not in this scenario but only dreaming this scenario. Your real self, is "elsewhere" or more precisely, you are a small part contained within your real self. That real self is waiting for your return from this dreamworld you think is real. Try to get this sense of life being a dream for a few minutes. Try to feel the sense of wonderment or relief, or whatever you would feel if it were all just a whisp of air. Your dream-self thinks it is real, until you question it. Awakening within a dream is called lucid dreaming. Awakening within "waking life" is called enlightenment. To intensify reality-testing especially notice everyday-life situations that seem odd or unusual. I was sitting on my porch one morning. It was early and no people were in sight. It had rained and the sun was beautifully reflected on wet streets. The scenario had a dreamlike quality about it. So I asked, "Is this a dream?" In that moment something even stranger happened, making the exercise even better. A strange, futuristic looking three-wheel car drove by very slowly and there was some elderly woman sitting in it. How often is it that we see a three-wheeler? I had never seen one sitting on that porch. So again I exclaimed, "I'm dreaming!? This must be a dream!" Looking for and discovering the strange and unusual will help you get into dream-mode.

There are a few typical indicators that you are dreaming while you are dreaming. What, for example, happens when you try to turn the light on or off? This is not possible in a dream because light is non-dual and eternal on this level. Have you ever been in a dark room and afraid that the light wouldn't turn on or that some hand would reach out to prevent you from turning on the light? I think this special type of "Light-switch fear" is a memory of dreamscape where it is not possible to turn on the light. Remembering this can actually make you lucid. If you can't seem to turn on the light, you are probably dreaming. And if you have difficulty reading, counting, and with math and numbers, you are probably dreaming too. Math and words are a faculty of the waking-life mind, not the dream-self. What's 26 minus 18? In dreamscape you will have lots of difficulty figuring that one out. And that again can be an indicator that you are dreaming, a REALITY-TEST that makes you lucid.

Dreamscape is very fluid and oceanic, not stable at all. And when you try to re-read something you just read you will notice that the words escape you. Just because they were there a moment ago does not mean you can fix your gaze on them again and keep them in place. Programming yourself to turn around your own axis and then stopping abruptly will make you lucid because you will notice that your surroundings are still turning after you have stopped. This shows you that the dreamscape is something that is being created by you and your movements in mind and dream-body. The realization: "I am creating all of this," is the beginning of lucidity. Making abrupt movements and stops, you will notice that reality has to re-assemble after you do so.

Another reality-test within a dream or for waking life is to ask, "Where was I just now?" If you can't remember where you were before, you are probably dreaming. If you were just sitting in a cafe in India and ask, "Where was I just now?" and find that before that you were in the Antarctic, you know you are dreaming. But even getting to a stage where you are able to reality-test within a dream does mean that you are already lucid. Reality-testing in a dream then, tends to make you *more* lucid.

One way to intensify the reality-testing technique is to write down ten instances at which to reality-test yourself throughout the day, and to continue this exercise on a daily basis until you remember all ten. So you'd write: 1. When I am showering, 2. When stopping at the gas-station, 3. When someone greets me, etc. Then you will try to reality-test yourself when it happens. So you are at the gas-station and remember your intention and ask yourself, "Am I waking or dreaming?" If you forget to reality-test at any of the stations throughout the day, you have to repeat the whole exercise the next day. And so you keep repeating until you have remembered all ten and perfected your reality-testing recall. The idea behind this technique is that the habit rubs off on your dream-self.

4. Discomfort Techniques

Another approach some use is to add artificial levels of discomfort to one's sleep or pre-sleep to prevent drifting off and to allow a part of oneself to stay awake. While I have never used any of these techniques personally, I know many who have with success. One way is to take in a very uncomfortable body position while falling asleep. This is best done when you are already tired, otherwise you may not be able to fall asleep at all. The idea is that in an uncomfortable lying or sitting position you remain aware of a body part and take this awareness of "the other side of reality" with you to the sleeping side. Another way is to set your alarm clock several times throughout the night so that you keep bringing yourself back to awareness of your waking-self and your intention to lucid dream. An easier version of this would be to simply set it once about two hours before you normally wake up. After the clock rings, do not go back to sleep immediately but do something that helps your wakefulness, such as a breathing technique or a concentration exercise. Then go back to bed and to sleep. Let go, but this time observe.

Observe how you drift back into sleep. Since you already have a good night's sleep behind you, it will be easier to have a part of you remain aware and to sink into a lucid dream.

5. Programming Dreams

Some say that it is easier to become aware that you are dreaming if you programmed the dream before falling asleep. By remembering that it's the dream you programmed, a bridge to the "other side" is made and you become lucid. You can simply program the intention: "I lucid dream tonight," or a specific type of dream – a healing dream, a dream where you practice sports-movements, a telepathic dream, a shared dream, a therapeutic dream, an adventure dream, an exploration dream, or a dimensional-travel dream... If you say, "I intend to use my dream to travel out of body to the planet Mars and explore it as it is in its current state," and you visualize the same while falling asleep, your attention will tend to go in the direction you programmed it to go. And if you become lucid, you can re-affirm your intention during sleep by which you will perceive that place even more clearly. Having clear and specific aims are helpful because they give your dreamwork a context within which to operate. Saying, "I will lucid dream," can be taken as vague by your subconscious. "I intend to fly above earth," or, "I intend to see my hands in my dreams," gives it something to work with. One of the most interesting programming techniques is to ask your dream-self to show you an object, gadget, or potion which will help you lucid dream. Your dream-self knows better than you what is needed. I once intended for my dream to reveal the best lucid dreaming method for me, night after night. Then, on the fourth night of having repeated this intention, I dreamed of a Yankees baseball cap (I am neither a Yankees nor a baseball fan, but apparently my dream-self is!). So I got a Yankees cap and wore it and had my first lucid dream after several months of non-lucidity.

6. Dream Re-Entry

Upon waking up, repeat the dream you had last night, to memorize it. Then, try to go back to sleep with the intention of continuing that same dream. You have memorized the dream, then you simply re-enter the dream by visualizing the scenario of that dream while falling back asleep. The likelihood of having a lucid dream is very high now because you are deliberately going back into the dream you had. The visualization is a substitute for the dream until you sink back into sleep. Another factor in lucidity is that after already having slept, your sleep is now not as deep as it was. This is why people who like to sleep in, in the mornings are more likely to lucid dream. All the light and noise from their surroundings keeps their waking-life-self somewhat alert.

7. Wake-Induced and Dream-Induced Lucid Dreaming

Wake-Induced lucid dreaming is sinking into a lucid dream from waking-reality while falling asleep. Dream-Induced lucid dreaming is waking up within a dream. One way to heighten the probability of dream-induction is to state your Intention to Lucid Dream before going to sleep. No matter whether you experienced the lucid dream or not, re-state the intention after waking up. Keep repeating your statement of intention, and try to build up a high conviction that you are truly lucid dreaming tonight. While falling asleep, deliberately feel and relax your entire body. Having a deeply relaxed body allows your awareness to stay a little alert during sleep (it would otherwise have to use its energy with recovery). While fully relaxing, repeat your statement of intention too. Not like a broken record but as a firm conviction. You then fall asleep. The idea is that your dream-self is aware of the intention and will support you in awakening to your dream.

With Wake-Induced lucid dreams you allow a part of you to stay awake while the rest of you falls asleep. The idea is to stay awake even in the "hypnagogic phase". This phase is where you start going unconscious as many rapidly passing mental images are being processed by your mind. Notice that you are indeed entering the hypnagogic phase, recognize it as such. This will slightly re-awaken you. And if you have enough energy you will be able to slip right into a delightful lucid dream from here. As previously mentioned you can also visualize yourself into a lucid dream. Another method of wake-induced LD is to count yourself into sleep. For instance: "One, I'm dreaming, two, I'm dreaming, three, I'm dreaming, four, I'm dreaming..." This one is especially effective when you are already sleepy and ready to doze off.

8. Remembering Other Dreams During Your Dream

Some dreams and states can only be remembered when you are back in a dream or in that state. Similar is true in waking life. A drunkard may only remember what happened last night once he is back in a drunken state. Outside of that state he may not remember anything. It is easier to remember what happened last spring when spring returns, and the smell of the trees or flowers takes you back to that time. You experience a whole lot more than you are aware of. You don't remember 99% of what you experience due to your rigidity and unawareness. It is therefore smart to try to remember other dream-experiences during your dream. This can cause intense lucidity because you are remembering different energy-frequencies, which implies that your awareness resides above and beyond those realities. Your dream-self has a different time-line, memory-bank, and personal history than your waking-self. Some of this memory bank directly accesses the memories of your soul throughout its many lives and travels through planets, worlds, and dimensions. "Remembering other dreams during your dream" is one of techniques that supports Hyper-Lucid Dreaming.

10. Placing an Intention While It Is Happening

The best time to reinforce lucid dreaming is while it is happening. One of the first things I used to do when I realized I was dreaming was to install my next lucid dream by saying, *"Every time I am dreaming, like I am right now, I will know that I am dreaming, like right now."* This is, of course, much more powerful than affirming something that has not happened yet because you are willing to believe that it is so. The mind tends to have a much easier time believing something that is actually happening.

11. Letting the Mind Sleep

The body may need about 6-8 hours of sleep, but the mind usually only needs 4-6. After having slept for that time the mind is usually awake and refreshed enough to play – to lucid dream. It is therefore the practice of some to set the alarm clock a few hours earlier than normal to wake up, and then use a wake-induced lucid dream.

12. Sensory Immersion

This technique can both intensify the quality of your lucid dreaming as well as induce a lucid dream.

a) Focus all of your senses on something in waking reality while thinking about night dreaming. For example fully enjoy and fully experience the taste, smell, and look of vanilla ice-cream. While experiencing vanilla ice-cream like never before, think about experiencing the same intensity while dreaming.

b) While falling asleep, remember the sensory experience you had during the daytime. Re-experience it in your mind and intend to dream of it later. For example, fully visualize and remember the smell and taste of vanilla ice-cream from earlier. Try to experience it as intensely in your mind as you did in waking life, while also intending to re-experience it a third time in your dream.

c) While dreaming do your best to remember the command you gave yourself when you were awake. In our example that's to eat the vanilla ice-cream once again. The moment you remember that you gave yourself that command, you become lucid.

This technique combines three levels of reality: The "real" one, the one on the mental plane, and the one of the dream-self. I recommend you try this with various things that activate your senses (seeing, hearing, smelling, tasting, and touching).

13. The Mind's Eye

With eyes closed and while falling asleep, try to see your current surroundings and the room you are in. Remain fully aware of the room; see the room while drifting off.

14. Soft Awakening

Harsh and rude awakenings can cause "dream amnesia", a state where you cannot remember what you dreamed. Dream-recall is a pre-level to lucid dreaming, so it is important that you awaken softly and slowly in the morning. Any abrupt awakening will discontinue your line of thought. Your line of thought in the morning is usually connected to what you dreamed at night. If you use an alarm clock you might consider doing away with it and using mental time-programming instead. Or, if you want to use an alarm-clock you might at least get one that is a little softer...whistling birds, piano playing, rush of the ocean. or similar.

15. To Continue Last Night's Dream

To become a vivid lucid dreamer you start paying attention to what you are doing right before sleeping and what you are doing right after waking up. As a lucid dreamer but also as someone who lives consciously, those are your two most important states. Try improving your dream recall by remembering and repeating what you dreamed after you wake up. A trick to induce lucid dreams is to take that memory and play it again while falling asleep. If you can remember last night's dream while falling asleep, the likelihood of lucidity is increases.

16. Talking to Yourself

In this method you talk to yourself while falling asleep. I recommend positive self-talk because in this state your subconscious is highly suggestible.

Once you reach the point that your body is so tired you can't open your mouth, you continue the conversation in your mind. This method serves to overcome the hypnagogic state.

17. If This Were a Dream...

If everything around you were a dream, what would you change? Daydream about what you would change in your surroundings or daily life. Later, while falling asleep, remember this visualization once again. Having done this daydream twice – during the daytime and while falling asleep – the likelihood of you doing it a third time during sleep increases.

18. Shifting Awareness Around

Focus on a point on or in your body or on the whole body. Then focus on a point outside of your body (in your immediate surroundings or far away). Move back and forth between body and elsewhere (car, tree, piece of furniture, foreign country, other planet...whatever you want) while you fall asleep. Not only will this help you to keep awareness, it will also loosen your identification with the physical body. Too strong of an identification with the physical self is actually a block to experiencing your dream-self. People who think they ARE the body will rarely succeed at lucid dreaming.

19. Non-Moving

Just lie there without moving. That's all: Do not move and fall asleep. Of course, if you need to scratch yourself you can do so, but other than that, remain unmoving, as if you did not have a body. Many have reported that after awhile they feel a peculiar vibration throughout and above the body. This is the astral-body or the dream-self (which are the same thing. The difference between astral travel and lucid dreaming is that astral travel is even more detached from the physical self). Since the body is not moving, the urge to move is played out in non-physical reality, which can induce lucid dreaming.

20. Singlepointedness

If you can maintain single-pointedness of attention while falling asleep and even into sleep, you will almost certainly experience a lucid dream, possibly even a hyper-lucid dream. Of course this is easier said than done.

21. Deep Relaxation

Totally relaxing does not necessarily mean getting tired. If you have built up a lot of resistance and stress throughout waking life, you will get tired when you relax. But true relaxation is actually a wakeful state and conducive to lucidity. Applying relaxation techniques such as body-sensing, massage, or floatation tanks is helpful not only for an improved dream-state but for life in general. Note that relaxation is not only possible while awake. You can also center yourself and calm down during a dream. That is the key to turning nightmares into pleasant states. If you can calm down in the face of a nightmare, you have progressed far beyond the "normal" human condition.

22. The Point of No Return

If you can remain aware of the very moment you fall asleep, you are lucid. The paradox is "staying awake and falling asleep" which can be really challenging. Prior to falling asleep you will notice the "hypnagogic state" which is a collection of garbled, rapid, and random thoughts which appear to move more quickly and more independently of you. The hypnagogic state is an indicator that you are on the verge of losing conscious awareness. But if you can remain somewhat aware during this stage, you will become lucid. Everything is a matter of awareness.

23. Beautiful and Strange

If you can think of or visualize places of beauty and strangeness while falling asleep, you change your own energy frequency to a state that is more attuned to lucid dreaming. Also try putting your attention to places you have never been before. To the waking-life-mind lucidity appears beautiful and strange. The idea of this exercise is to "lucid dream" before you lucid dream, that is, to create the state yourself rather than waiting for a lucid dream to deliver results. And as you create the desired state from your own power and initiative, it will be many times magnified in the *actual* lucid dream.

24. Signs You Are Dreaming

You could review this list before falling asleep.

These are signs that you are dreaming. Once you realize you are dreaming, you lucid dream:

- New places

- Living in a new house

- Having moved

- New faces

- Meeting old acquaintances

- Meeting old friends

- Back in school

- Paranormal activity

- Trying to escape

- Danger lurking

- Travel

- Problems moving

- Can't control the body

- Surprising sexual activity

- Being in or out of a relationship

- You look different

- Sudden change of place, pace, or time

- Frustrating tasks that you can't seem to solve

- Special abilities

- Feeling elated

- Anything beautiful and strange

We often lose ourselves in a dream as we would lose ourselves in a good book or movie. Since we are also participating in the dream it is easy to forget that we are dreaming. When attention is immersed, you are dreaming, when it is detached or aware of other things than the focal point, you are more lucid.

25. Someone to Remind You That You Are Dreaming

One of the most obvious but often overlooked methods is to have a person near you who remains awake and gives you nudges now and then to remind you that you are sleeping. The person only ever so slightly wakes you back up to help you stay somewhat lucid and not fall too deep into sleep. This should be in the form of gentle nudges, caressing, or pleasant vocal reminders. You can agree to signal to him/her that you got the message by moving your index finger or whispering "OK". The person helping you does not have to be present most of the time, but having someone around to give you that reminder throughout can work miracles for your lucidity.

These are some of the best techniques for beginners who wish to induce lucid dreams and for former lucid dreamers who wish to regain their ability to lucid dream. Lucid dreaming is a lifestyle and science of the 21st Century. Those of you who have not experienced it yet have never really been awake. You are literally sleeping away half of your life although you could be going on far out journeys beyond your current potential. Waking and Dreaming Life influence each other. To illustrate what exactly lucid dreaming is, consider this picture:

The left loop is spiritual reality. The right loop is physical reality. The side one is on appears more real. So when you are in spiritual reality, physical reality appears vague and dreamlike. When you are in the physical world, like right now, spiritual reality appears vague and dreamlike. The loop is here depicted as a movie-reel because it works similar to movies, except that the physical universe is a three-dimensional movie. Dreams take place in the mid-point of the loop, the intersection between physical and spiritual reality. Dreams are not as subtle as the purely spiritual world and not as dense as the purely physical world. Most of us understand that our actions in waking life influence what we dream. Much of what we dream appears as a form of processing what happened throughout the day. Only very few people know that your actions in a dream can influence what happens to you in waking life. And the best way to influence your actions in a dream is if you are lucid. Lucid dreaming is an endless field of possibilities in an infinite number of Dimensions. These are some of the types of dreams one can experience in a lucid state:

1. The Leisure Dream

These type of dreams are for recreation, relaxation, and enjoyment. Did you know that in ancient Greece and Rome they built special temples dedicated to dreaming dreams in which you could do whatever you liked? Some visit places that are not convenient to visit in waking life...such as other countries and planets. Others use it to experience sexual encounters or celebrate professional successes, possibly as an inspiration to copy the example in waking life. Others use the dream to experience actions that would have inconvenient consequences in waking life, such as getting back at someone.
Some try flying and floating, try tasting the air, smelling colors, and seeing sounds. The more lucid you are the more enjoyable this experience will be.

2. The Creative Dream

This type of dream is to increase the depth of your thinking, your performance, or creativity. Dreamscape offers you access to information, ideas, and solutions that you cannot access in waking life. Why can you not access these? Because your mind only has information it has recorded in daily life and that does not include soul-information. Hundreds of now famous scientists, athletes, and artists have gone on record saying that they got their ideas in dreams. The lucid dream gives you direct access to the archives of Infinity. Some dreams are so energetic that you wake up the next morning feeling high as ever, as if reborn.

3. The Research Dream

This type of dream is used to learn, to explore the functions of consciousness, perception, and reality or, after programming to find a solution to a particular issue of interest. Dreams give you access to the subconscious and semi-conscious. You can look at layers of yourself that you cannot see in waking life.

4. The Healing Dream

This type uses dreams a tool for psychological and physical self-therapy. Because the subconscious can be directly accessed you can heal traumatic incidents, unblock stuckness, and even look into karmic pay-offs you might be running. Some healing dreams run automatically because you are in a higher state (higher states tend to bring up anything standing in their way).

5. The Sports Dream

This dream is for practicing athletic movements. You can practice various processes and movements for sports or change habitual movements that do not benefit you. This dream occurs especially for Sports-Pros who are immersed in sports on a daily basis. According to lucid dreamers' reports, the movements you practice in dream state have a direct and real effect on your movements in daily life. One lucid dreamer for example reported practicing golf strokes over and over again in his dream, and on the next day delivering the best performance of his life.

6. The Creation Dream

This one is to effect events in waking life. What may sound as "magic" to most people has actually been reported by lucid dreamers all along. What you act out in a super-lucid state influences waking reality. A change in the dream state creates a change in your energy (emotional) set points, thus changing your actions and perceptions when awake. A student reported that she felt she had not rehearsed enough for her exams. She took that intention with her into dream state. In her dream she failed her exams, indicating that her emotional set point was not yet up to the task. By becoming lucid she was able to re-dream the scene, this time passing the exam. Her experience on the next day in waking life corresponded to that success.

7. The Paranormal Dream

This is to use the lucid dream for remote viewing, astral, and time travel. This is a lucid dreamer's favorite. The reason paranormal events are easier to experience in this state is because the mind is in a "Theta" or "Delta" state. This means there is no censorship by the mind and time/space are more malleable than in waking life. A more advanced technique is to perceive events at other places or in other times that can be checked and verified after you wake up. Some lucid dreams are actually out-of-body experiences that you are not "fully" experiencing, hence they appear as dreams. I have been able to have a friend put an object in a specific place in the woods for me to "remote view". I intended such for a few consecutive nights and finally perceived which object he had laid out. I then visited the place in waking life to verify my perception. Getting things verified in this manner is very, very important when dealing with spiritual realities..not to "scientifically prove" something to someone else, but for your own confidence in your sanity. Experience has shown that when you try to "prove it to someone else" it weakens the effect your work has. But when you set out to just have fun and try out your skills, 5 times out of 10 you will actually succeed.

8. The Spiritual Dream

This dream is for deeper insight. Spiritual LD allows for states of tremendous well-being, connection to higher sources or vivid confirmation of the things you have only caught glimpses, hints, or intuitions of. There are higher levels of consciousness within the lucid dream experiences, as well as realms beyond LD. It was from a lucid dream that I had ascended to a state of cosmic consciousness, leaving me high for several days in waking life.

These possibilities may trigger some skepticism in you. By no means is this meant to make you believe that it's easy for everyone to achieve such states. Our skepticism is created by a day-to-day flood of false advertisement and marketing promises, especially in new-age circles. The intent behind these write-ups is to deliver material that is not only pleasant to beginners but also for advanced practitioners. That's why some of this material might seem "way out there". Can you imagine how boring it is for advanced lucid dreamers to keep reading the same old basics? So this is not only for beginners.

Co-Dreaming

Co-Dreaming is when two different dreamers share the same dream, when both are on the same reality-plane or can communicate with each other during a dream. This may sound like science-fiction, but I and other lucid dreamers really have experienced it at times. It is like telepathy but more tangible. Each dreamer keeps his/her own objective viewpoint. Whether you had a co-dream or not can be determined the next day when comparing your data to that of your co-dreamer. If you both had that dream and saw each other in that dream, you have had a Co-Dream. Thus, it can also happen with groups and is then called group-dream.

Co-Dreams do not only occur when both people are lucid, but lucid dreams make for the best co-dreams and are usually the only ones you can remember. Sometimes you know that you are dreaming while the other person does not know or vice-versa. But sometimes you can then still verify the co-dream after waking up. The lucid dreamer tells his friend who then recalls having dreamed that. The non-lucid dreamer will have a more vague memory of the event, but as you talk about what happened, that memory may become clearer. Sometimes you will dream of the other person without it having been a co-dream. A co-dream is when both of you remember certain events of the dream in detail. If I suspect I had a lucid dream with someone, I usually don't go up to him/her and say, "We shared a dream last night!" I instead ask, "What did you dream last night?" While s/he describes his/her dream, I fill in the details until s/he asks, "How do you know what I dreamed?" The dream then becomes a verified co-dream.

The first time I realized that humans actually co-dream was in my early twenties within a love-affair. Our strong feeling of being in love and thinking we were "soulmates" may have caused the paranormal event. We lived hundreds of miles apart and could not meet often, so we told each other we would maintain "telepathic contact" throughout the day. We would phone in the evenings and exchange "telepathic hunches" we had experienced throughout the day, saying what we thought the other had been doing that day.

You too will have various paranormal experiences as you experiment with these ideas, but I recommend you simply enjoy them without putting too much meaning into them. Placing too much importance will distort your perception and replace paranormal experience with imagination. You don't have to tell too many people, you don't have to become superstitious and paranoid.

The Co-Dream my girlfriend and I shared was so intense that we knew what it was while we were having it, and we knew we would tell each other the next morning. We were so excited about it that we actually tried dialing each other's phone numbers at the same time. In this case, we knew what had happened before even exchanging the details of the dream. The excitement came from the knowing that we had accessed a soul-plane where we were connected and communicating despite our distances in space. The dream was fairly mundane, but having even had it was amazing. I was standing on a mowed lawn near a beige colored hotel. There was a pink flamingo standing nearby. My girlfriend's dream-body (in both senses of the word!) approached me and said, "You walk like a flamingo." We looked at each other for awhile and then she smiled and said, "We're dreaming!" as if she wanted to remind us to stay lucid. "Yes, we are dreaming. We are dreaming," I confirmed. In this moment a very high feeling swept through me. The dream got brighter and the pink got more intense. The scene felt fluid and full of mysterious potential. I looked around and realized we were probably somewhere in Florida. At that time neither she nor I had been there, much less together. We walked around and explored the place a little, talking about how happy we were that we were sharing this dream and how we would remember it the next day. At some point the dream faded into a non-lucid dream and then deep sleep. The next day our minds were racing and competing in telling the details of the dream. She described the flamingo, I described the cars and hotel, and we filled in each other's details. We were filling in each other's stories, yet it was apparent that each of us had a unique viewpoint within the dream.. She, for example, did not notice we were in Florida or notice the cars around, but she did notice three coconuts which I had not noticed.

To experience co-dreaming it can be helpful to have friends that are also interested in lucid dreaming. In a hyper-lucid state it is also possible to pick up friends and make them lucid within their dream-world. The most amazing thing was when I got to know someone on dreamscape, which I then later met in waking life! This was as if the dream connection was a preparatory experience for our encounter in waking life. Sometimes we do share dreams with people we do not know in daily life, and sometimes we share them with people we only know peripherally. I recall actually having an affair with someone who, in waking life, meant nothing to me. She was an employee of one of my students I said "hi" too every few weeks, nothing more. But when our eyes met there was that strange recognition there that there was more going on than meets the eye. A few years ago I had a Co-Dream where the person announced that we would get to know each other in 20 years. That would be a mixture of Co-Dream and Pre-Cognitive Dream.

Another one of these was when I met one of my Course-Students weeks before the course. In my dream he said, "We will met again." I thought he was referring to the dream. But we met again in waking life as one of my students, where he told me, "I dreamed of your course and meeting you a few weeks ago." (He was apparently not aware that we had had a Co-Dream.)

Co-Dreams take place on Levels 6 and 7 of the dream-scale. Two or more people are in the same dream environment. One's own control over the dreamscape seems to be reduced since the Co-Dreamers also have some influence over the scenario. I once tried to change a dune without consent of the other dreamers. The sandy dune remained unchanged. At another time, I got the consent to change a street-sign and after my Co-Dreamer agreed, I could change it. My impression is that the dreamscape is a shared scenario and a shared responsibility, in which I can only change it if I get the others dreamer'/s' consent, or if I am more lucid than the other/s.

Seen from a higher viewpoint we always experience Co-Dreams on some level. My normal self is dreaming his normal dream while another part of myself is Co-Dreaming. According to this view, all levels of dreaming (see scale of lucid dreaming) are taking place, it simply depends which level my awareness is linked to. The levels of awareness begin with Not-I (Subconscious), then to I (Conscious), then We (Group Consciousness), and finally Planetary Consciousness (Mass-Consciousness), and then the rest of the Universe (Cosmic Consciousness), and finally Infinity (Ultimate Being). Throughout this whole process of advancement each level stays intact. That means, I can still experience individual "I" Consciousness while at the same time experiencing Universal Consciousness (me-as-Universe). This may seem like a contradiction to earthly understanding, but I've experienced the simultaneity in hyper-lucid dreaming.

Meeting friends in dreams sometimes reveals aspects that may seem unpleasant. Friends who are not lucid while you visit them can behave or look strange. Some time ago I arranged to Co-Dream with a friend of mine. We focused on our meeting while falling asleep. As I met him in dream, he did not react to me. He was in a catatonic state, as if under the influence of Drugs or Hypnosis. His eyes and head were rolling uncontrollably and he babbled nonsense as if drunk. I grabbed hold of him and said, "Hey. You are dreaming." He reacted a little. We walked around a little together. I felt a lot of compassion for him seeming to be stuck in unawareness. On our walk we met an elderly woman that addressed my friend trying to sell him something. My friend was still acting absent and strange. On the next day it turned out he did remember some parts of the dream, even though he was not lucid. He described the old lady just like I had also seen her (white curly hair, blue dress, brown suitcase), but he also perceived things that I did not experience. He said the old lady tried to attack him and how they wrestled. This is how I learned that strong emotions can distort your experience so much that you experience a different reality than others. He had experienced a nightmare, while I was only experiencing a slightly pushy old lady. Just like in waking life! Hence, the more lucid both dreamers are, the more probable it is that they will both experience a similar reality (or even have a shared dream).

I had a similar case with a girlfriend with which I had intended a Co-Dream. But apparently we should have asked her subconscious about our intention first. We met in front of a cottage in the woods. But her entire logical mind was missing. And so I learned how important the analytical part of our mind is for lucid dreaming (I had believed – through false information in books on lucid dreaming – that it was not important). She was present, but not mentally present. She could not respond to simple questions such as: "Where are we?" and: "What's your name?" Instead of creating lucidity, the questions created confusion, irrational behavior, and fear. When your Co-Dreaming Partner reacts in this way it is improbable s/he will remember the dream the next day. She was Level 1 – unaware. And experiencing that total unawareness can be a spooky experience, as if you are trying to converse with a zombie. Even if she were just half-lucid she might have been able to relate to some of the questions I was asking. I could have then made her more lucid with touch, eye contact, and loving care.

But in the state she was in there is not much I could do (something similar is shown in the movie "What Dreams May Come" starring Robin Williams – he tries to get his wife out of a lower state, but no matter what he does, she won't respond). The reason some Co-Dreamers respond like that is not because you are experiencing a nightmare but because non-lucidity usually takes you to deeper levels of the subconscious. If you meet people in a catatonic state, it's best just to move on and to leave him/her alone. If you try to force him/her out of his/her state, s/he will sometimes go violent or psychotic. Or s/he just wakes up. Interestingly, when a Co-Dreamer wakes up s/he simply disappears from your view.

Dream reality is less dependent on time and space than waking life. This becomes even more obvious in hyper-lucid states when you begin to see that you can share a dream at another time than your Co-Dreamer. I only just realized this very late in my studies. I had this wonderful dream where I was in a parallel universe version of America. This alternative-USA had experienced some change of climate which manifested as much more rain, flooding parts of the Continent. Within the reality I was in, the flooding disasters had already happened 20 years prior, and people had already adapted to what was now a beautiful but also more chaotic USA. I was driving with someone else down a freeway over rolling hills. It kept raining on and off, even during sunshine. That was one of the peculiarities of this universe – that the sun could be shining, but dark pockets of cloud produced sudden bursts of rain. The green of the land was the most glowing, full, and saturated green I had ever seen. It's the kind of green you get from all that rain. Everything had a mood of brightness and wetness. The freeway was built above the ground to avoid flooding. Nonetheless, we sometimes drove through huge puddles with great joy, as if on a ride in an amusement park. Riding on a road had never been this much fun. Once, the puddle was so deep that our car was, for a short time, completely underwater before we resurfaced. We were actually driving through the southwest which had become very green. And cars were not only on the road, some were also flying in the air. We witnessed parts of the old, sunken America and parts of the newly built America. New buildings looked extremely beautiful. They were huge, round, made of glass-like material, glistening silver and white in the landscape, and provided an all-around view from the inside. Driving through the country you could still see people living like cowboys and owning farms alongside flying cars and advanced technology.

After I woke up I shared the dream with my girlfriend, and she told me her dream. We realized we had, had the very same dream. However, she also told me she was "in a car with someone I didn't know." And I got goosebumps when she told me she had the dream a year ago. So some dreams are not recognized as co-dreams because the dreamers are experiencing them at different times. What is a year in waking life may only be a few minutes for the soul.

The places you are at when lucid dreaming are usually astral-worlds. There are lower-astral, mid-astral, and higher-astral worlds as well as even higher celestial dimensions (see my books "Levels of Energy" and "Lives of the Soul"). In fact there are so many worlds and things out there it goes beyond anything you could ever imagine. Therefore, some of the beings you meet in dreamscape are actually "spirits" and even people who have died on earth. Yes, you can meet loved ones who have died on dreamscape. You can communicate with them. I say this so that you know that not all people you meet on dreamscape are co-dreamers or even alive. Co-Dreaming is an aspect of Hyper-lucid Dreaming. The pre-stage to that is simply communicating with other beings in your dreams. The question: "How do I achieve Co-Dreams?" is like asking, "How to I speak with other people?" You already co-dream and will more consciously co-dream sooner or later.

This is not something you have to learn or achieve. In waking life you can meet a friend by inviting him or going to him. Sometimes you will come across that friend without inviting him. It really is as simple as that on dreamscape too. So this ability too is a matter of awareness which simply requires that you practice lucid dreaming.

While going to sleep simply state the intention: "I will meet _____ tonight while dreaming."

On the verge of falling asleep once more state the intention: "I will meet _____ tonight while dreaming."

While dreaming, become lucid and repeat: "I will now meet _____."

If necessary, call his/her name or fly to him/her. Once s/he shows up make sure s/he is also lucid or becomes lucid.

Make notes about what you dreamed after waking up.

Once you are lucid, all of these abilities lucid dreamers talk about become easier. If I want to contact someone, I simply intend to find that person. It can be a friend, a colleague, or even an enemy with which I want to reconcile or more deeply see on the soul level. (Yes, dreamscape is the intersection between the physical world and the soul's world, between physical and spiritual reality.) To contact a person on dreamscape you need to know what that person feels like. Feeling is the "universal transportation system" that pulls you in the individual's direction at once. Every individual soul has a unique way it feels. In order to pick up a person's signal you can't be walking around with your conception of a person, but with who that person actually is. There is your projection and then there is your friend. Your projection of a person takes place within your individual dream. The actual person (as opposed to your representation of the person) feels more vivid and exists independently of your dreamscape. You can feel whether the person is your mental creation or an actual soul. You can call a person's name and if s/he is lucid, s/he will appear. There is also something else you can do:

You can find your soulmate (see "Lives of the Soul"). You could, for example, create a door with the symbolic picture of a lovely looking person and intend that when you step through that door you will find your soulmate behind it. It's the awareness and authority with which you do these things that determine whether they work or not. Of course there are times in which people don't want to be found. In this case, you might encounter a black wall when intending to access these people. This often happens when lucid dreamers try to access the private spaces of earthly celebrities. Even on dreamscape there are protective measures, most of which were created by people's dream-selves.

Once on hyper-lucid level 6 something really strange happened to me, and it only happened this one time. I was dreaming and talking to someone in waking life. I was verbally communicating from dream-reality to waking-reality. I do not know how I did it. But the waking-life person was not conversing with me, it was another aspect of his personality that was talking to me. What does it mean? I don't know. How does it work? I don't know. The more I find out, the more I realize how little I still know. I mention this incident to show that the possibilities, in humanity's future, will be endless.

Arranging meetings with other lucid dreamers will have positive effects on your overall attitude and sense of aliveness. Being able to communicate independent of time and space is magical, you will feel like a magical person. All these people read thousands and thousands of "new age" and "metaphysical" books without even getting a crumb of real experience while you have gone way beyond telepathy. Verifying your experience the next day helps your mind integrate "paranormal" experiences. Without such factual verification, the mind easily loses interest or drifts off into imaginary worlds, or mere concepts. Once you become a hyper-lucid dreamer you will realize that there are many of us who have been doing this all along. We are already on a level where we are playing different games versus "trying to achieve lucid dreaming". What do you think the people who have already achieved everything on this earth do all day? Do you think they sit around watching TV? Think again. Some of them have gone far, far into the soul's realms. There are entire lucid-dreaming groups of people doing various projects.

Co-Dreaming is the easiest with your partner in love. The reason for this is that there is no resistance and hardness but mostly warmth. One of the best dreams I have ever had was a shared dream in which I created a dreamscape for my partner as a gift for her enjoyment. That act of appreciation elevated both her and my state to hyper-lucid level 7.

These are levels of Co-Dreaming Development as I see them:

1. Dreamer dreams other beings within his/her individual dream.

2. Dreamer meets non-lucid friends within a shared dream.

3. Dreamer meets lucid friends within a shared dream.

4. Dreamer meets people s/he arranged to meet prior to dreaming.

5. A group meets in a dream after having arranged it prior to dreaming.

6. A group is able to deliberately meet at the same place again and create a shared reality.

7. The group creates a shared network with shared projects and adventures.

8. The group finds other already existing networks,

9. From the group or several groups a new superordinate consciousness arises within which every individual remains unique but also connected to the whole.

10. The group joins an even higher level of awareness.

These are wonderful prospects, aren't they?

Precognitive Dreaming

When I was a child I once had a dream where I was running towards a cliff because I was escaping from a monster behind me. The running took a while, but I knew that I had to find some other route because there would be a cliff coming. This is your classical no-way-out nightmare situation. Having arrived at the end of the cliff I could either jump, fall and slam into the ground below, or be devoured by the monster. I jumped. I fell. Falling seemed to take place in slow-motion. Finally, I hit the ground with a painful smash and instantly woke up from the dream. It was then that I realized what had been so painful: A bookshelf which my dad had just built, had fallen off the wall, along with all of the books. The very moment the books fell on my chest and face was my moment of impact in the dream. In fact, some books were still falling as I was coming to my waking senses.

So this is very strange. My dream was leading to this event "a long time" before the event happened. How did my dream know this was going to happen? Unless of course my dream-self either has precognitive abilities or one hour in a dream is like 10 seconds in waking life. Both possible explanations point to the same thing: "Time" is not as fixed and linear as we think it is.

Sure, people have tried to come up with "reasonable" explanations for time-anomalies, but any lucid dreamer experiences dozens and hundreds of time-slips, jumps, and shifts so that there is no more doubt that the dream-self follows other rules of time.

Another similar event was a dream where I was walking towards a building of which I knew it was very loud inside. I was approaching the building with mixed feelings. I didn't want to go there because of the noise I knew I would hear when I opened the door. I did finally open it and the penetrating and screeching noise of a saw instantly woke me up. But the noise was in waking life as well. There was apparently some construction work going on and the workers had begun – not sawing – but drilling. So again I asked how my dream knew it was going towards that event? Or was time stretched, as they say in physics, so that the second the drilling began it felt like many minutes on dreamscape? (The concept of time-stretching is also explored in the movie "Inception" starring Leonardo Di Caprio.) The moment I saw the movie I remembered the accuracy of the idea.

Precognitive Dreams go even beyond the time-stretching phenomena. The term describes the ability of consciousness to dream something days, weeks, or even months and years before it happens. Our understanding of time is being revised by physics because millions of people have had precognitive experiences both in waking and dreaming. The non-physical dimension is a timeless dimension and can therefore access various "probable futures" of humanity or individuals.

An interesting point is that precognitive dreams do not necessarily predict the event but the way you will perceive the event in the future. Recently, I dreamed of a soccer match – Barcelona vs. Madrid – and that it ended 0-0. Since I had not seen the match myself but only heard from someone that it ended 0-0, that's what I had dreamed. However, the person watching it quit watching in the 70th Minute of the game, when it was still 0-0. By the end of the game it was 2-0 for Barcelona. So what I had dreamed the week before did not reflect the event but my *perception* of it.

I recall an event of waking life where I recommended someone not to go on a vacation to Japan. This was a few days after the 2011 tsunami and earthquake of Fukushima. "Why shouldn't I go there?" he asked. "I don't have a good feeling about it," I lied. Actually, I had dreamed about Japan and what would happen before it happened. That was my very first real precognition of disaster. Neither the ability nor the dreams were at all pleasant. It was as if I was accessing some problem in mass-consciousness, knowing that this problem or this energy would culminate into a disaster. That is, I did not see that it would manifest as an earthquake, tsunami, and radioactive fallout (although many people do have specific images in their precognitive dreams), I did see and sense "negative energy" in regards to northern Japan, fully knowing it was that area that would be hit.

If you don't believe that time-travel is possible, simply write down every one of your dreams in detail in a "Dream-Journal", including the date it was dreamed. Then, review your Dream-Journal many years later and notice that some of the things you had experienced during your dreams have come true. This is what I did. I wrote a dream-journal from age 22 to 26 and saw it with my own eyes. Of course a typical question that arises is: "Did your dream predict the event, or did your dream create the event?" But it is not really that important to answer that one. What's more important is to know that if you dream it, you are dreaming a probability that may or may not manifest in waking life. Whether it does or does not manifest depends on whether your energy-state remains similar or changes.

You should also know that 99% of the people reading these words, and that most likely includes you, will not remember their precognitive dreams due to lack of interest or lack of awareness. Writing a dream journal will improve these statistics. If all of you readers were to write a dream journal over the years and officially practice lucid dreaming, 99% of you will remember your precognitive dreams. Of course, you do not have to lucid dream to have precognitive dreams. It's just that a state of lucidity will help you remember them and recognize them as such. You will improve your stats by "breaks in routine". Usually when you are in unfamiliar surroundings, your dreams are more lucid.

With increased awareness of your dreams you will experience all kinds of other weirdness as well. You will experience different variations of events that happened and will happen. You will also experience symbolic events that actually mean something different in waking life. You will notice how waking life can also spill over to your dream-life (and not only dream-life to waking life). You will also start noticing that with some relaxation of the mind and concentration you can have pre-cognition in waking life too. Go to a library. Take a book into your hands. Try to get an image of something you will soon see in the book. Then, start flipping through the book. Did it work? Precognition is easier in your sleep because you don't first have to get rid of your psychological resistances and filters. Our "knowledge" of the past blocks our perception of the future. You'd have to let go of everything you know, perceive, objects, people and life prior to all the "knowledge" you have of them and simply take the "flashes" you get. That's precognition.

Sometimes it is difficult to realize you are having a precognitive dream because your dream is mixed with so many other events that have little to do with the precognition. And sometimes the precognition is not meaningful in any perceivable way. I dreamed that someone was following me through a surreal looking city. The city was a mixture of places I had been to in the last weeks. The man following me had a gun. Then there was a woman following me too, who, despite not having a gun, looked and felt even more threatening than the man with the gun. The precognitive part occurred when my dream-phone rang and a voice whispered, "There is a call from Mrs. Wenger coming in." I was told that Mrs. Wenger wanted me to pay the invoice for my gun. I tried explaining to the voice on the phone that I would not pay for the gun because it was stolen from me (this is, again, the typical non-logic of dreamscape). Throughout the dream, Mrs. Wenger or a representative of hers kept calling me. After waking up I quickly forgot about the dream. It was only until a real Mrs. Wenger called me that I remembered the dream and recognized the voice from the dream. However, the phone call was not that important and did not have anything to do with an invoice or a gun. It was just that name and the call that were tucked into the night's dream, for no apparent reason.

There have been, of course, more intense and meaningful precognitive dreams than that, but I will leave it up to you to explore those.

Out of Body Travel

Out-of-Body-Travel, how does it work? Despite countless books, projects, courses, and programs, OBE is actually as simple as this:

When the body falls asleep but part of the mind stays aware, you will experience how the energy-body (that's you) leaves the physical body at night.

That's it. That's all there is too it. Body asleep, self remains aware. You actually leave the body every night. Why? It's boring to hang-out in the bedroom all night. Why would you want to do that? So, while the body takes its regenerative break, you leave. The mind usually falls asleep too and is not aware of the travels. So you will just have to keep a small part of the mind awake in order to witness what is going on. Normally this capacity is blocked because you want to keep soul-life secret from yourself (in order to be better able to focus on earth-life), but if you practice aware sleep or deep, deep, deep relaxation (while staying aware), you will get access over time.

I know they make it sound all mysterious and esoteric, but it's not.

There are a lot of far-out journeys you can take if your soul allows. If you have been trying and can't do it, don't get discouraged. The soul has an amnesia about other realities for a good reason (see "Lives of the Soul"). I recommend you muscle test for Permission.

1. Direct the statement: "I have permission to out of body travel," at your Higher Self.

2. Then push down with your middle finger on the nail of your index finger, trying to resist; trying to keep the index finger up (if you don't know how to muscle test in this way, look it up on YouTube).

If your muscle stays strong, you have been given permission to OBE and it should lie within the compass of your abilities. If your muscle goes week, consider asking questions on how to gain permission or consider raising your overall frequency so permission comes easier. One reason most people are not permitted to OBE is for protection; for their own good. Raising your overall state of mental and physical health leads to you requiring less protection. Protection from what? From perceiving more than you planned to perceive when incarnating. Astral-Worlds can be a real distraction to your life's purpose. Once you do feel ready to take a glimpse out-of-body, it is only a matter of fully relaxing while staying awake. If you can find a way for the body to fall asleep while you stay aware and alert, you will witness your energy-body projecting out of the physical body and can join it in its travels. The more experienced you become with this, the clearer it all gets, and the more you are able to steer what goes on.

The Super-Lucid State

Once I found myself in a Super-Lucid state, floating through space in an endless expanse of huge, pulsating, and glowing stars. I felt with my whole being that I was actually there and really flying. I felt more alive than ever (more alive than in so-called "waking life" too) as the pulsation of the stars seemed to synchronize with that of my energy-body. My perception seemed 500 times intensified to "daily life". In this sparkling, twirling and fluid space and state, I realized that the more intense energy is, the more "real" the reality is. Even though I was experiencing myself as the observer of the space, I was also experiencing myself as the space and stars themselves, and also as some force outside of the observer-observed relation. The simultaneity of viewpoints was paradoxical and unique. I was in a state of rapturous amazement. Filled with limitless awareness, I was contained within all time and space but also contained it all. I experienced a level of doubtlessness my waking-life-self did not even know existed. The stars were optically closer because my local energy-body was somehow bigger. At one point while floating through space I drifted past some kind of golden temple or city that was so gigantic that its size dwarfed several stars. I recognized it as a temple or city because it had a golden door so huge that it spanned several light-years. The gold sparkled so intensely that it "almost" "hurt" "my eyes", even though I did not have physical eyes. I understood that whatever inhabited this temple hanging in open space was beyond my current comprehension, and it was OK to continue to drift away. At another point I noticed I was able to intensify my feelings. So I did. And it got almost unbearably blissful. People think pain is unbearable, but this was happiness that was unbearable. My body was not equipped to handle this much energy. It was unbearably good. Had I intensified the state more I would have exploded. During these musings on happiness I became aware that I did have a kind of energy-body that was not the unlimited super-body I was experiencing at the same time. It was this body that could not handle all the bliss. After some time the energy became so intense that something short-circuited and I lost all awareness of the dream, returning back to normal sleep. But upon awakening, I had tears of joy in my eyes. I felt high as never before for several weeks. So high in fact that all efforts of daily life, the conversations of family, friends, and neighbors seemed like a comedy to me. Everything seemed amusing and interesting. I would laugh out loud at things nobody else laughed at. Colors seemed brighter. For a few hours after awakening I could see a blue energy field around objects and plants. For hours I sat around enjoying a scenery without the need to do anything other than just sit there and smile. The high-energy state subsided after a few weeks when earthly conditioning kicked back in and people were beginning to wonder why I was laughing all the time.

Time Travel

This section will help advanced Lucid Dreamers experience verifiable time-travel. If you are skeptical about this claim, that's to be expected – it is my job to explain why and how this can work.

Awareness is the part of reality that operates outside of space and time. From its view, all pasts and futures are perceivable right now. This precious moment is the point at which all Time-lines and Dimensions intersect. Time exists *within* Consciousness. Memories of the past and fantasies about the Future exist…when? Right now. You are having these memories and fantasies right now. The evidence that Consciousness exists outside of time and space is that it can *observe* time and space instead of being *within* it. From where you are sitting you can put your attention on Millions of things which aren't even in the time and space of your surroundings. Put your attention on the Moon and that is where awareness is. How long did it take to get there? Less than a second. Consciousness or Awareness are eternal and infinite. Nothing is unknown to this core of your Being. Anything imaginable and plenty of things unimaginable can be accessed and experienced by that core-self.

In a *Super Lucid* state, time travel, remote viewing, extrasensory perception, and other "paranormal events" are not as distant as previously thought. Skepticism is then replaced by Curiosity at what else is possible. The waking life perspective is that you are a small human in a big Universe. The perspective of Awareness is just the opposite: That the Universe is within you. The "small me" perspective is only the viewpoint you have zoomed yourself into in order to live a focused life on planet Earth. You think you are so smart and learned. But to achieve great feats of Consciousness you have to go beyond your earth-learned knowledge. Your mind does not know as much as it believes. It only knows what it was told during this lifetime. To demonstrate that you actually don't know the first

thing about anything, see what your mind does with these basic questions:

Where are you?

People invest a lot of time and energy in defining *where* they are, *where* they were, and *where* they are going. But where are you? "Well, I'm at home," you might say. And where is that? "On Earth." But where is that? "In the Universe." And where is that? "I don't know." Space and Location as well as time are creations of Consciousness. They are points of orientation that can be contrasted with other points of orientation.

You can only know where you are compared to something else. But the truth is that you have no clue where you are. Maybe you are everywhere and nowhere.

And who are you?

Just WHO do you think you are? People spend a lot of time defining who they were, who they are, and who they will be. May I suggest that you don't have a clue who you are? Neither do you know where you are from, nor where you are going. You keep telling people: "My name is…" "I was born in…" But do you really know who you are? Your name is a label. Do you have memories of who you were before you were here? And before that? And before that? Maybe you are from nowhere and going nowhere. Maybe you are nobody. Who knows?

Identity is a creation of Consciousness. Who are you? Maybe a smarter question is: Who would you like to be? In an Infinite Context you cannot be anywhere or anyone in specific. You are everywhere and nowhere. This is about seeing that your "knowledge" about identity, time, and space may be limited and that maybe, just maybe time-travel is possible. Admit it: You have dreamed of being able to time-travel before, haven't you? And don't you think that longing for the ability to time-travel must have something to do with the fact that on some level, it is actually possible? Do you think you are given desires without the means to achieve them? That would be a cruel Universe if that were true.

AS WHO you approach this subject will determine what you experience. If you try learning time-travel from the viewpoint of a limited body/mind, it will be indeed difficult. Impossible even. But if you approach this from the viewpoint of the great I Am, the Alpha, and Omega, it might be an easier task.

What is so paradoxical about this is that when you practice and train to time-travel through lucid dreaming, you are training the part of yourself that cannot ever learn it. The part of yourself that already knows how it works does not need training. Nevertheless, training can remind you of that part of yourself. This is how it works: If you focus on the subject of time travel for awhile, the part that already knows how to for thousands of years, will re-awaken. The ability to time-travel is then merely the ability to concentrate. Indeed any ability and creation is the ability to concentrate.

You travel through time with Consciousness, and you use as your means of travel, Imagination. But that does not mean you close your eyes and imagine to be "in the year X". You have to project your attention in a certain way in order to perceive what is going on at a certain place "in the year X". Imagination is used to get to that place and time. Attention is used to perceive what is at that place and time. So the method is to first project Imagination, then release Imagination and replace it with Attention/Awareness.

One of the decisive factors in this is your level of certainty that you can pull this off. Here are some examples for different levels of certainty you can have regarding time-travel:

10: I am absolutely certain that I can accurately perceive a certain place at a certain time. And I am absolutely certain this is going to happen tonight in my lucid dream.

9: I am certain I can perceive a certain place at a certain time if I put my mind to it.

8: I believe it could happen tonight or another night.

7: I could imagine that it's possible to perceive other times with Consciousness. It might happen to me. I'll try.

6: I would hope that this is possible. Maybe. We'll see.

5: Maybe it will happen, maybe not. Let's wait and see

4: I don't know if this is going to happen. I have my doubts. It takes too much practice.

3: I doubt this is going to happen anytime soon.

2. I doubt this is ever going to happen. This is a waste of time.

1: This is all total nonsense. This is never going to happen for me or anyone else.

So what would have to happen or be done, thought, said, or felt in order to move up the scale to 8, 9, or 10? Which investment of time, attention, and money would be required for that? Which evidence would be required? Which exercises, rituals, plans, programs, intentions, and visualizations would be required to get you "into state"? I cannot tell you how to get into certainty. Most people can only get into certainty *after* the fact. I can get into certainty before the fact…which is why I am able to create the fact. I do this by nothing other than decision and incantation, by "getting myself into state". Some people need to read hundreds of books on something until they feel certainty (and some still don't feel it after that), for others it's enough to think the thought only once. This is connected to self-confidence. If you are a person who has experienced a lot of broken trust in childhood, it might take a little more to build up confidence…not only for this but for many more simple things.

I am asking a lot of you here. Most people can't even lucid dream yet, and I am asking you to use it as a time portal! So if this is too much for your belief-system to grasp, then at least see it as an exciting prospect for the future. And it comes easier with certainty. Of course most will say, "I will believe it when I see it," And I am saying, "Believe it first, then you'll see it!" The word "doubt" is linguistically related to the word "two" because it means your focus is not single-pointed but split between two things: The goal and something other than the goal (failure for example). As taught in my program, your focus must become single-pointed, at least during practice, for this to work.

To practice time travel first define a place and time you'd like to view in lucid dream or even in waking life (which would be time-travel by remote viewing, which is less intense than in lucidity but can still work). Space and Time arise together so you can only time-travel if you define a location to travel to and the earthly date in which you want to view that location. Let's take as an example: Times Square New York. Consciousness does know what Times Square looked like in what we call 1960. It knows what it looked like in what we call 1920. And it knows what it looked like 1830, 1600, 800, 10,000 B.C., and any other date for that matter. So you define the date in terms of what the human mind was taught to view as linear time. Let's take as an example Times Square in July, 1950. That is the location I have defined as well as the time. For certain purposes I could define the time more specifically. If for example someone tells me he was in Times Square at 8 o'clock, July 14th, 1950, and I wanted to verify if that were true, I'd define it that specifically. If I kept it more general I'd be able to view everything that was in Times Square in this our reality on July 1950. I would not be able to view things that were only there temporarily, or the things that were there temporarily would flash in and out of my awareness. There might be people walking around, but it would not be certain at which time they were there. The more specific you define space and time, the clearer your images get. The more unspecific, the more muddled things might get.

You might notice as we are talking about this, that your Imagination has already gone back to 1950 Times Square. In a sense you are already remote viewing that space and time. Some of what you see is invented by memory or imagination, some of it is true remote viewing of that place. Learning to differentiate between the two is key to all of this.

Before doing this in lucid dreaming, let's test-drive it in remote viewing. Your Imagination has already taken you to the place and location. You are seeing your imagined-version of Times Square July 1950. Imagining that it is warm in July, you probably see a sunny day. Maybe you are basing your Imagination on the memory of some movie of New York in the 1950s. Imagination here is the transportation device that will take you there. If you see a black and white image, you can be pretty sure that more than 90% of what you perceive is Imagination, basing it on black/white movies from the time. Once you are there with your Imagination, you release the Image while keeping your attention at that time and place. That is, you let go of your Imagination and see what flashes, thoughts, impressions, sensations, forms, shapes, and images come up independent of you imagining them, independent of you putting thoughts there. That's how remote viewing essentially works.

Let me give you an example of this with something more simple. Look at an object in your surroundings. Imagine and Remember all kinds of things about the object. Where you bought it, when you bought it, whether you like it or not, where it is from... And then, in an instant, let go of all of those memories and imaginings and just look at the object as-it-is. You do this same thing with your Awareness. Your Imagination takes you to Times Square July 1950. Keep your Imagination there for awhile. Imagination anchors you there. And then, just **let go of all of these images and memories while keeping your attention in the space these images previously occupied**. If you are a beginner, what might happen is that you perceive empty, blank, or black space. If that is the case, just wait for images and flashes to come up all by themselves. Whatever does come up when you are in a neutral, non-fantasizing state is most likely remote viewing that exact time and space, and in many cases can be verified as such. This is why the U.S. Military in fact had a Remote Viewing Program for many decades. They certainly would not invest Billions of Dollars into a project about something that doesn't work. The remote viewing they practiced was for what was at other places and locations.. This type of remote viewing is for what is at places in other times.

So why do I suggest combining this with lucid dreaming? Because in Hyper-lucid Dreaming the images that come up are not only vague flashes and "sensings", but very vivid, three-dimensional experiences. And that, of course, makes time travel great fun.

Once you have defined a time and location and "test-run" it in waking life, you are ready to integrate it into your lucid dreaming practice. For this I recommend you choose an anchor that symbolizes your intention. This anchor or symbol can either be a written or spoken statement, such as: "I experience Times Square in July 1950," or a real picture from a magazine, a book, or a visualized image as we've just gone through. Your anchor represents your intention for the dream. Then you fall asleep while you concentrate on this anchor. That's really all you need to do; to fall asleep with the intention. So if you have an image of Times Square in a book, you memorize that image and then fall asleep while thinking of it. If you have a statement, you think that statement over and over while falling asleep. Of course, you need to be in the flow of already lucid dreaming. Trying to time travel before having mastered lucid dreaming is possible, but much more difficult. In worst cases your dream will take you to the place, but you won't be lucid or you will hardly remember it. But if you indeed become lucid (for example by combining the anchor with the Super Lucid Technique), you will find yourself at the pre-defined time and place and will be able to walk around and explore. The dream will take on a life of its own and show you various things that are relevant to your soul's journey. You do not time-travel without any connection or context to who your soul is and what its life purpose is. So whatever you do experience at that time and place will have some special significance you would have not gotten if you had not practiced this.

I did the Times Square 1950 intention. In this particular case, I did not slip into the dream but awoke to it later. What I saw was something like this:

Interestingly, I did not have much of a conception of what Times Square looked like in 1950. Did it already have all the flashy Billboards or not? How many skyscrapers were there? I had no idea. You can imagine how pleased I was when I Googled "Times Square 1950" the next day and had my perceptions confirmed. When practicing metaphysics nothing is more important than verification. Verification builds confidence and demonstrates that one is not becoming "just another loon".

In another Session I cut out a picture of one of the Great Pyramids from a book and took it to bed. Before turning out the lights I looked at the picture for a few minutes. After turning off the lights and putting the picture aside, I continued to look at the same picture in my mind's eye. I also repeated my intention to view the Pyramid as it was in 2000 B.C., a few times. My body became heavy as I started falling asleep. I stayed aware and after about 20 minutes of half-sleep, the picture in my mind's eye begins to change by itself. I entered a very vivid and bright space, one usually associated with inner visions. I realized I was having such a vision. The image now had a moving life of its own and it was showing me precisely what the Pyramid looked like back then. It was pleasant to see that the Pyramid really was standing back then. And it's also quite amazing to see what was surrounding it. It beginning to look different than I visualized it is the indicator that perception has replaced imagination. The two feel very different. Perception feels much more tangible and stable. Interestingly enough the Pyramid already looked old in 2000 B.C. My dreaming mind knows there is controversy as to when it was built. All I can say is it already looked worn that long ago. There were additional layers to the Pyramid that are not present today. The people walking around were not the "primitives" one might imagine. They were tall and luxuriously dressed people with bronze and brown skin colors. They wore a lot of white with many touches of gold. Since I was completely lucid, indeed hyper-lucid, I intended to go further back in time to see when this Pyramid was actually erected. I did achieve that but only to some extent. The images blurred and soon lucidity was lost. I have noticed this sometimes happens with the really "big things" of human history. There seems to be so much energy involved in these events, from many different sides and forces, that it is more difficult to remain lucid when viewing them. I bet you'd like to know what I perceived? I am not going to tell you. That would only be pre-programming you. Find it out for yourself!

"He felt that his whole life was some kind of dream, and he sometimes wondered whose it was and if he was enjoying it." –Douglas Adams

The Hyper-lucid Dreaming Program

I have created a 7 week program for home study and training, available on my website realitycreation.org. This program will help you induce lucid dreams but also go beyond that to hyper-lucid dreaming and states of cosmic consciousness. The techniques mentioned on this page are enough to produce your first authentic experiences in lucidity. The hyper-lucid dream program is a journey beyond your wildest dreams.

It should be used in the exact sequence as shown here. The program is designed to last at least 7 weeks but there have been people who have expanded that time to 14 weeks or even longer. Audios should be used for at least a week or until you experience the desired effect. They should be used every day making exceptions only in unexpected time-restraints. Do not interrupt the program, even if you have to go on private or business travels, keep on going. It is preferable to save the audio files on your phone or mp3-player so that you have easy access to them every night. Do not use any of the audios in addition to the others in the first seven weeks.

Lucid Dream Intentions

This guided audio is used in the first week of the program, every day while falling asleep. It combines so-called "binaural-sounds" and hypnotic-suggestions and statements of intention especially crafted for this series and for the purpose of lucid dreaming to induce altered states, as well as improved dream-recall, and improved vividness of your dreams. "Lucid Dream Intentions" runs for 27 minutes and opens the gateway.

Hyper-lucid Visualization

This guided audio is used in the second week of the program, every day while falling asleep. Its purpose is to produce a wake-induced lucid dream by following various key-elements of lucid dreams, awareness-triggers, and unique visualization techniques. You will find yourself walking up and down winding staircases, sliding down giant slides, walking along infinite corridors, and finally awakening in a full-blown lucid dream, maybe for the first time fully experiencing your dream-self. Runtime: 30 Minutes.

Vivid Dreamer

This guided audio is used for the third week of the program, every day while falling asleep. It combines a method of circular breathing and alternating between deliberately sleeping and wakeful awareness to produce an even more vivid lucid dream experience. With this audio recording you are scheduled to move from the "Lucid" (stage 5) to the "High Lucid" (stage 6) state within only seven days. You will experience very special journeys, perceptions, and feelings, and see things you have never seen before. The audio is 21 minutes after which you are invited to continue the technique on your own until you fall asleep.

Copy Thoughts

This guided audio is used for the fourth week of the program, every day while falling asleep. It supports you in duplicating your stream of thoughts. This special method of Meditation creates a state of heightened awareness and "source-being-ness", that, combined with previously learned techniques will stabilize your ability to be awake and aware during your dreams, and thereby steer and alter reality on the dream plane as well as in waking life.

The audio goes 15 minutes after which you are invited to continue the same technique on your own. After you have learned the technique you can also apply the Meditation without using the audio for the remaining days. However, the audio does contain binaural sounds which assist in creating the altered state required for lucidity.

Open Spaces

This guided audio is used for the fifth week of the program, every day while falling asleep. With it you enter the realm of hyper-awareness after which naturally follows a state of Hyper-Lucid Dreaming, a higher level of consciousness and well-being than experienced by most people on the planet. The runtime of this audio is 26 minutes after which you allow yourself to fall asleep. The "Open Spaces" audio as well as the "Copy Thoughts" audio are recommended Meditations even outside the practice of lucid dreaming. They will heighten your well-being and awareness in general.

Ultraworld

This guided audio is used for the sixth week of the program, every day while falling asleep. It helps you repeat the experience of hyper-lucid dreaming and to possibly stabilize on a higher level of dreaming on a more regular basis. The runtime of this audio is 11 Minutes after which you are asked to continue the technique on your own while falling asleep. The technique may be used for several hours to create ever increasing levels of energy and elation.

Superlucid

This guided audio is used for the seventh week of the program every day while falling asleep. It is the most simple technique and yet the most effective when and if the previous steps and weeks were taken. This technique is sufficient to produce the state of Hyper-lucid Dreaming and can henceforth be used in place of all other techniques. The runtime is 90 Minutes but you are invited to use it for as long as it takes to produce the hyper-lucid state.

Warning: You should not purchase or use the Hyper-lucid Dreaming system if you have a history of mental illness, epilepsy, trauma, or are in ill physical health. You should not use this system as a means of escaping from or trying to avoid life. Only use the Hyper-lucid Dreaming system if you are in sound condition already and wish to expand your awareness to new realms. Just like flight is best undertaken from a stable platform, lucid dreaming is best undertaken from a healthy mind and body.

Important Notice: I will repeat it here – this program is only of use if you can upkeep the momentum of using it for seven consecutive weeks. Do not waste your time and money if you do not intend to hold that discipline. The audios are fairly easy to follow, but their magic unfolds in following them every day. Something you only do once in awhile does not make a lasting difference or impact in the quality of your life and your dreams. Something you use every day does. I want you to succeed and I want this product to have a great reputation for producing results, that's why I only want people who use it to its fullest potential to listen to it. Being willing to invest the money for the product and more especially the **time** with the product activates a psychological principle that says: "Because I have invested so much, I would really like this to work!" This attitude is instrumental in producing results.

10
Deeper Relaxation

Relaxing Into Abundance

Reality Creation teaches to live as if your true heart's desires were already true. Realize that this implies more relaxation. Why? Well, if your wishes were all already true, wouldn't you feel so mellow and relieved?

We live in a world in which success is linked to hard work and tension. I'd like to suggest that this path to success only applies to low-and-mid levels of consciousness. As we grow and mature, we realize that more is possible with less effort, that a deep sense of relaxation and well-being can in fact attract improved circumstances into our lives. Relaxation is the state we have *after* we succeed in something. You've accomplished a milestone, gotten your perfect partner, achieved financial security, regained ideal health…and then there is a sense of relief. And we also know than when you live as-if you have succeeded, your success comes to you more quickly. By this logic, relaxing = acting-as-if you are already successful = becoming more successful!

The relaxation I am referring to here is not to be mistaken with complacency, laziness, or taking stuff for granted. For example, when the ideal partner manifests in your life, I don't recommend you take them for granted and no longer invest anything into the relationship. When big money comes to you, I don't recommend you take it for granted and no longer put effort into new goals. This type of complacency is not "relaxation", but rather a pendulum-reaction to having worked too hard, and tried too hard to begin with.

The abundance-magnetic relaxation I am referring to is a peace-of-mind; it is the ease of the expert, the chilled out demeanor of the billionaire, the effortless radiance of those who know they are attractive, the inner security of those who feel comfortable within themselves.

To illustrate:

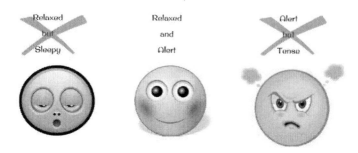

You know you are not in an ideal relaxed state when you are desperate to get something, desperately resisting something and distracting yourself with unimportant things, or when there are various health issues.

Here is a little exercise to deepen your understanding of your own relaxation and ideal state of well-being:

1. List What Relaxes You

Examples:

Swimming in the pool
Using Meditation Audios

Playing paintball
Chatting with my friend
Eating
Smoking
Reading a book slowly

I chose these examples to show that everyone has a different understanding of what relaxes them. Some of these things, such as smoking, may be harmful, but if one believes them to relaxing, one will do them nonetheless.

2. Already Feel/Imagine the Relaxation You Link to Those Things

It's good to know the things that relax you so you can do them when you need to chill. But it's even better to be able to relax without those things so you reduce dependency on them. In other words, I love going for walks and watching people, and it relaxes me greatly. Anytime I want to relax, I just take a walk. But it's not like I *have to* take a walk just to relax. Sometimes I'll skip the walk and just relax in an instant, by intention.

So simply close your eyes and imagine already doing or experiencing those things. Try to feel the same relief you would feel if you were doing those things. If you can't, it means you are addicted and should reduce the object of your dependency.

Alternatively, simply develop mental images that relax you. How does it feel to imagine…

…counting clouds passing by?

Or beautiful rolling hills? Or,

a perfect beach?

Or a heavenly realm?

I have a number of imaginary places I access that, combined with soft breathing, create instant calm. If you were already experiencing abundance in all areas of your life, how supremely tranquil would your ease be? Take a week to practice being that already. Slow down your movements. Choose your actions more considerately. Take some time to just sit and observe the world. The time you take is the time you give yourself. It means you value yourself. When you value yourself, you become more valued.

Peace of Mind

People tend to think that "relaxation" refers mainly to *physical* relaxation. So when I say, "It's so important to relax," they think of hanging around in sun-chairs and getting massages all day. But when I use the word "relaxation" I am not only referring to physical release, but **relaxation of the mind**. You can be physically relaxed, prior to falling asleep for example, but your mind could still be racing. Relaxation of mind leads to true **peace of mind**. Sometimes physical methods support the resting of mind, but that's normally not enough. Indeed resting the body sometimes causes *tension* of mind, as in: "Am I not supposed to be doing work in the office instead of lying here all day?"

Resting of mind is achieved by having no unfinished Business. No incomplete communication. No lack of integrity or contradictory intentions, thoughts, words, and deeds. It can also be achieved by focusing the mind on one object. As you focus, energy is accumulated and one-pointed, allowing all distraction and pressure to disappear. Other ways toward peace of mind: Through continuity of life and actions, through thought-releasing (just letting go of whatever comes to mind), by sitting and observing the present moment, by gentle and committed study or reading, by contemplation and reflection, by mindful and slow movements, by having attention-on-attention or awareness-of-awareness, in sports and physical activity, while being in love or very appreciative of something (noticeable by dilated pupils…the pupils of the eyes expand 45% while looking at someone or something you love), and by not labeling interruption and distraction as such, but "integrating" and "acknowledging" such as part of the whole.

Is Suffering Really Necessary?

If there is one thing I have learned in my 25 years as a reality-creation-coach, it's that every human being goes through the whole "human package" of ups and downs…**no exceptions**! I've worked with the rich and poor, the young and old, the smart and dumb, they have **all** suffered to some extent. Along the way they have all experienced loss and achievement, grief and ecstasy, good and bad fortune, frustration and joy. I think it's safe to say that every soul on earth goes through the whole scale.

But is Suffering really necessary? And if so, to what extent? There seems to be a belief-system common to planet earth that suffering is somehow needed. Researchers of human motivation and psychology say that it is in moments of suffering that we reveal who we really are. For example, you cannot practice Courage if you never face any challenge and you cannot grow if there are no problems. I agree with this. Adversity helps us rise to the challenge. Without trials and tests, problems and blocks, there is no growth of personal will, choice and strength. We don't really want less burden, we secretly dream of having broader shoulders to carry the burden. That's what most stories and movies of humanity are about.

But this idea can also be taken too far. Buddha taught "life is suffering", so you see some Lamas in Tibet prostrating themselves on the hard desert floor in the hot sun for days, until their knees bleed. Suffering is associated with "balancing bad karma".

Some Christians believe that being poor and sacrificing one's well-being or flogging oneself until bleeding, to "bear the cross," is saintly and good. If I prefer cruising down the beach in my BMW Convertible, does that make me a sinner in their eyes? I know a "football coach" who believes that inflicting maximum pain, sweat, and tears in his trainings is the only path to success. He believes that violently humiliating his players is a "path to their enlightenment". But I've been following the path of this football-coach for a decade now, and his methods never succeed long-term. They work for about one Season, then he is off to coach the next team, leaving his old team burned out. From what I can tell, a little bit of suffering awakens you and keeps you **alert** and on your toes. Too much suffering burns you out. You can and should stretch yourself, but if you overstretch, injury will follow.

It's also a matter of consciousness-level. Above a certain point of maturity, extreme pain and suffering is neither desirable nor necessary. Instead suffering becomes an indicator of wrong thinking and doing, whereas relief and success becomes an indicator of right thinking and doing. If you are perpetually ill, for example, then that does not mean you are "virtuous", but rather that there is something in your belief-system that is not compatible with how life works. If you are perpetually without money, it's because you have some mistaken belief-system about money, not because you are "a more pure person".

So is suffering necessary? If you're a human being, you probably won't be able to avoid it entirely. But if you live consciously, you will be able to reduce suffering to a minimum. The path of less suffering is twofold:

1. Cease to pull suffering into your life.

2. Cease to push suffering away.

You neither draw suffering to you by calling it a "virtue" nor do you try to get rid of it as in denial.

Peace of Mind Is Not Conditional

Here are some things people think will "make" them happy, which actually don't. They may be nice, but they are not the final determinants of "Happiness":

"If I get a new job, I will be happy."

"If I have less work to do, I will be happy."

"If I find a partner, I will be happy."

"If others change their ways, I will be happy."

"If things change, I will be happy."

"If things don't change, I will be happy."

"If I always get what I want, I will be happy."

When you quit your job, stay in your job, or get a new job it will make some difference in your life, but that's not the final determinant of happiness. Whether you stay solo, have a relationship, or go into a new relationship makes some difference, but not a deep and lasting difference because you essentially stay the same person, even if the circumstances slightly shift. Such changes are like **changing the movie you are watching…but the watcher remains the same.** Fundamental change comes from shifting the watcher, not the movie.

Your experience of Life is maybe about 20% circumstance and 80% your experience of it. So it is more fundamental to change the Experiencer (the 80%) rather than the Circumstance (the 20%).

All of the statements above have one commonality. They are conditional "If…..then" statements. "If X is achieved, I can feel better." That takes you out of the here-now, your only moment of power, into some hypothetical future. But the only time **peace of mind** can really be experienced is now, not in the future (this is why the the Bliss Course asks you to let go of the idea that something external or in the future will bring you joy).

Happiness is a heightened state. It's bringing higher states that are not all too common in this dense realm, down to planet earth. It's experiencing "a piece of heaven". There are not many who experience genuine happiness regularly. People in love with their partners, children, and pets will experience it here and there. But a more permanent state of happiness can be gained by allowing the mind to relax and unstack thoughts and emotions, and by allowing the less superficial parts of yourself…the subconscious, your core beliefs, your core identity, and consciousness itself to shift.

Another key to Happiness and peace of mind is to stop looking for it. It is painfully obvious that the people who never began searching for happiness in the first place are overall happier. That's because the role of being a "Searcher" implies that there is a lack; something missing. But what if nothing is missing? What if you already are and have everything you need to experience joy, today, by your mere inner intent and decision?

Successful sailing and surfing in high winds, waves, and wild waters is best achieved in a peaceful state. Not always a relaxed body but in fact, a relaxed mind.

Stress Is Subjective

With the exception of traumatic incidents, stress is mostly subjective. In normal daily life there is no such thing as stress.

If that weren't true you could point to stress and say, "That is stress," just like you could point to a tree and say, "That's a tree," or to a car and say, "That's a car." Can you show me stress? You can't because it's not an objective reality. You might mention what causes you to emotionally and physically react and label that "stress". Several phones ringing, someone shouting at you, someone criticizing you, a schedule-planner full of important appointments, or the screaming of a baby, but nobody is forcing you to react to any of these things, much less to react with stress. A screaming baby is just a screaming baby and a schedule-planner is just a schedule-planner. Some people react strongly, some don't. What you actually mean by "stress" is an inner resistance and contraction of body muscles, which creates a certain tension. This conditioned response to noise and upheaval can deliberately be reversed.

In my experience, illness and self-created stress go hand in hand. Scientific research has tried to correlate everything from cancer to Alzheimer's to stress because so many of the patients themselves testify to stress being the cause. The reason science has not been able to find conclusive proof for what most people already know is because most test-study-groups are done with the presupposition that stress is caused by objective external factors. The researchers will then typically test people who have been in difficult external circumstances. However, not all people react the same to circumstances, therefore many of these studies are somewhat skewed.

There is a small percentage of conditions that objectively create tension and psycho-spiritual wounds. A few examples of such conditions would be losing a loved one, being involved in a war, having a car accident, being betrayed or cheated on, being violently assaulted, etc. In such instances it will take some time for the wounds to heal, and you are not expected to be grinning and happy on the very next day (that would in fact be a sign of suppression/denial of the event). But all of the other daily life cases we call stress can be released in an instant – the overwhelm of having "too much to do", time-pressure, worries about money, concerns about the future, regrets about the past, high expectations from others, public speaking, being criticized, being in a traffic jam, having a messy desk, etc. And you can do so without suppressing your feelings. If you suppress stress rather than release it, you eventually become flat and emotionless. If you release stress, you become calm and free.

So how to do this? You do it in the very moment your conditioned reaction to external pressures arises. You stop whatever you are doing, and you simply observe and witness your reaction to whatever is happening. In that very second you are no longer the react-er but rather the observer of the conditioned reaction. In that space you have more of a choice of whether to continue reacting or not. In my seminars I usually do a 30-minute exercise where I deliberately put people into stressful and overwhelming conditions, while coaching them to calm down, reduce reaction, and "become the witness" rather than the one resisting the event. This is such a radical shift from the normal human conditioning that it feels genuinely liberating, and makes one's whole life a brand new experience. I tell people to "become the eye of the cyclone". A cyclone is one of the most aggressive, chaotic, and overwhelming storms there is, but in the center of a cyclone, in its very "eye", there is total peace and stillness. It is important to note that this deliberate reduction of one's reaction is not a suppressing or flattening of the physical and emotional responses. One lets the responses pass through without doing anything with them. So when someone disapproves of you there might be a slight hurt in the solar-plexus for example. You do not try to get rid of this hurt or do anything with it. Neither do you go on a spree of action trying to "fix it" (that would be reactive and only create more conundrum). Neither do you take pills or eat foods to suppress it. Instead, you simply witness it, witness the automatic responses, witness what is going on. The more you witness and become aware of what is happening, the more it releases over time.

"Reducing Reaction" is one way to release stress. Another way to do it is by embracing whatever seems to be causing stress, thus becoming bigger than the stress. Whatever you can embrace, you are bigger-than. Instead of projecting a "no" attitude, you begin projecting a "yes" attitude, as if you could easily take on 10 more errands, 10 more phone calls; 10 more inconveniences. This shift requires a radical change in your definition of life. If you define life as having to cater to your whims, and if it doesn't, its bothersome, you will have difficulty with this. If, on the other hand, you view everything as belonging to life, as happening to you for a good reason, this will be rather easy and stress will be a thing of the past, at least most of the time. Thus, you are able to increase your "threshold of overwhelm" (the point where you get overwhelmed and begin losing energy and getting emotional) to a fairly high level.

In other words, performing in front of a large group of people can be a joy, it does not have to be a stress. Getting hundreds of customers a day can be a joy, it doesn't have to be a stress. If you believe: "They expect too much of me," exchange that with the belief: "They just want to have fun." Cleaning the household can be a joy, it does not have to be a stress. If you have the belief that "Cleaning up is boring," exchange that with the belief that "Cleaning up is meditation if done consciously. It will empower me beyond belief." If you believe that travelling is stressful, exchange that with the belief that "Travelling is fascinating because so many new things are seen and learned." If you believe that a traffic jam is stressful, exchange that with the belief that "Traffic jams are a great opportunity to think about some important things."

Deeper Relaxation

Have you ever become so lost in a book or a piece of music that you jumped up startled when someone spoke? That trance-like state is relaxation.

Does it sometimes feel as if you won't allow yourself to relax because you worry that you will lose focus? That's not true.

Do you suspect that you avoid deep and thorough relaxation because you don't want to become so aware and sensitized that you realize what a miserable life you are leading? Well, that's nonsense.

If you never take the time to slow down, life will pass you by and you won't feel it. Nor will you have creative input that will make your work better. Always working is not smart working. The better and more deeply you can relax – intentionally and consciously – the more energy you have for later activity. Both tension (focus) and relaxation (release of focus) have their time and place.

Top 10 Ways to Relax Deeply

Relaxation, Well-Being, and being able to concentrate and learn arise together. Where one is practiced the others are too. *Deep* Relaxation means that you can stay awake and aware, not fall asleep. Sleep is a form of Relaxation, but being able to deeply relax while staying awake provides an even deeper experience of well-being. Choose any one of these for an experience of rest and regeneration.

1. Tense and Relax

Tense the right foot and toes for a few seconds. Relax them. Tense the left foot and toes for a few seconds. Relax them. Proceed in the same way for each and every part of your body, including your face. You can do the same with thoughts: Grip a thought tight (think it more intensely), and relax it (let go of it). Do one of both of these for 5-15 Minutes. Now that's relaxation!

2. Breathe and Relax

Take a soft, gentle, and deep breath in. Hold your breath for 5-20 seconds (as long as feels comfortable). Breathe out softly and slowly. Do this for 3-5 Minutes. Feeling smooth yet?

3. Fall and Relax

Close your eyes and imagine/feel a sense of falling, letting go, and sinking, releasing everything. But stay awake.

4. Float and Relax

If your local area has a Floatation Tank, go visit it. Sensory Deprivation combined with zero muscle resistance as you float on saltwater is the best way to relax and mediate. If you are already accustomed to floating, take one of my Audio-Meditations with you to accelerate your inner work.

5. Massage and Relax

Sign up for a massage. Try all the massages they have in their catalogue. Also be sure to try out a 4-hand Hawaiian Lomi Lomi Massage by a certified practitioner.

6. Stop and Relax

Lie down in bed and cease to move. Do not move your body (except for breathing and perhaps some scratching) for 15 minutes or more, eyes closed.

And stay awake.

7. Release and Relax

Lie down and give up all resistance to everything. Un-know everything. Forget everything. Breathe out any tension. Loosen all muscles. Relax deeply and profoundly.

8. Body-Scan and Relax

Put your attention to your left toe. Feel it. Be with it. Relax it. Proceed this way through every part of your body. This takes 10 to 20 Minutes.

9. Observe and Relax

Sit somewhere eyes open. There can be a lot of people there or none, it doesn't matter. Just sit and observe. Release your reactions, intentions, impatience, and analysis and just sit there and observe what you observe until you feel a deep and profound peace.

10. Visualize and Relax

Sit or lie down with the intention of daydreaming.

Close your eyes and daydream yourself to a nice place. Do not do this with the intention of creating something for a later date, but with experiencing beauty right now. A general recommendation is to stay awake while slipping into slight trance. Depth of Trance and ability to stay awake will vary at different times of the day. "Normal Life" is either getting Tired when relaxing or getting Tense when fully awake. The state of wakefulness combined with Relaxation is the perfect Union.

Relaxing Down into Delta State

Some measure progressive states of relaxation by the frequency of brainwaves. Traditionally, the scale goes from Beta to Delta. This is how we at Reality Creation Coaching see the states:

High Beta
Panic, Tension, Fear, Racing Mind, Short Breathe, Defensive, Contracted

Beta
Normal Waking Life, Awake, Alert, Attention Extroverted, Lots of Thinking, Working, Talking.

High Alpha
Normal Waking Life but Relaxed, Calm, At Ease, Content, Observing, Aware, More Open, At Ease

Alpha
Relaxed, Dozing, Meditating, Attention Introverted, Dozing, Drowsy, Creative Thinking

In this state you are normally on the verge of falling asleep. If you manage to stay awake and aware, interesting things start happening. Stay awake here and you become more perceptive and lucid, your intelligence increases, and you can think both more clearly and deeply. Learning Languages is more easy in this state, among many other things.

Theta
For most people this is just sleep. If you manage to stay a little awake and aware here, lucid dreaming becomes possible. If you stay fully alert despite your body being fully at rest, extrasensory perception, high intuition, reprogramming your mind and its beliefs, spontaneous healings, and other altered states are possible. Experienced Meditators have no problem staying awake in Theta.

Delta
This is near-death which is why out-of-body-experiences, paranormal perception, time-jumps, and the miraculous are more likely to happen. Dimensional Travel and access to Parallel Universes are also somewhat easier from here.

Just in case you were wondering why me and other teachers in the new-age/spirituality/reality-creation field harp on and on about Relaxation, Meditation, and Releasing, this is why: All the special abilities are found in inner Silence and Deep

Calm.

Feeling At Ease at Important Meetings

Got a Job Interview coming up? Or an important phone call? A blind date? And are you apprehensive, nervous, and/or concerned about succeeding or failing?

And wouldn't you rather be completely at ease?

What would your life be like if you were always **completely at ease**?

Mental Relaxation equals power, health, prosperity, and happiness. There is no value in feeling unwell. There is some value in excitement and tension, but if you go overboard on that it turns into fear and inhibition, which blocks progress. You are unlikely to get that job or impress that date or convince that customer when you are in Fear.

The cause of fear or discomfort before or during Important Meetings, is one or many of the following:

- Starving for success but seeing success as something outside of yourself and difficult to get.
- Starving for approval but seeing approval as coming from others and difficult to get.

You can clean-up and clear worry about a meeting within a few minutes. This is how:

Just sit down. Focus on the worry and try to find out where it comes from. What images are you showing yourself, what story are you telling yourself for your energy to feel that way? Ask yourself: "What must I be thinking to feel this way?" Once you find out what nonsense it is you are telling yourself (and all low-emotion is based on nonsense, that's why low emotion comes up, to tell you, you are involved in nonsense), you naturally release it.

Then, shower yourself with appreciation and respect for a few minutes. You'll be feeling much better. And then mentally and emotionally shower the person you will be meeting with appreciation and respect for a few minutes. You'll be feeling even better.

Most importantly, reverse of the flow of energy. Quit wanting approval, instead give approval. Your whole vibe in that Important Meeting will go up. Oh, and one more thing: Quit calling it Important. That will relax you.

The Art of Calm

Yesterday I took a bike ride into the unknown. There

was no specific goal or intention but to ride. Having no A-to-B path can make the linear mind restless. So, I rode the bike until that success-oriented part of me was at rest. After 3 hours of riding, I came upon a most tranquil and beautiful lake. It being a workday, I had almost the whole lake to myself. Green rolling hills, huge shady trees, and quaint wooden houses surrounded the waters. It was as if I had stepped into another Dimension because a few minutes prior I had been riding in fields and through housing areas, and there was no sight of any lake or rolling hills. The lake was hidden behind a lot of green.

After 15 minutes of sitting there, I again noticed the success-oriented-self wanting to get up and "move on". This was recognized as the part of myself that won't calm down, and I am sure many other people out there have a similar nagging voice within themselves: "Alright, you have rested, now it's time to move on!" While I appreciate my success-self, (there is a time for that self), there is also a time for the tranquil-self and this was his time. So I released the success-self for the time being, in order to relax more deeply into the present moment. I sat there until the urge to leave was gone and until there was no urge to distract myself with my iPhone.

Tranquility became deeper. The Art of Calm had been cultivated. Later that day when I returned to work and into the rush of Downtown, my breathing was calmer, my movements smoother, and my thinking clearer.

Your ship best reaches its many destinations on calm seas. Calm is extremely beneficial for your health. Calm will heighten your perception and intelligence. Calm is a gateway to the observer-self (your soul) that is always tranquil and untroubled by the wild winds of life. Release of tension is the ideal springboard to create deliberate tension for the purpose of some achievement. The benefits of calm are countless, therefore the deliberate practice of calm is one of the best things you can do to improve.

Breathe-Walking

Taking a walk in the fresh air or sitting down to observe your breathing would be enough for most people to rest back into that natural state of calm. But both combined, make for a deeper regenerative rest. I will share two techniques of breathe-walking. These techniques not only produce calm, they fill your bloodstream and brain with oxygen, improve your circulation, and increase your energy-state for better concentration. The first method is to:

1. Take a deep breath while walking a few paces.

2. Hold your breath while walking 10 to 20 paces.

3. Breathe out slowly while walking a few paces.

These steps are repeated continually without a break. The exercise should be done for at least 10 minutes, but probably for not more than 30 minutes without a proper break.

The second technique, which some might prefer is as follows:

Take one step and breathe in, another step and breathe out. Take two steps and breathe in, take two steps and breathe out. Take three steps and breathe in, take four steps and breathe out. Count this way until you have reached 10 (some may choose to go further), and then count yourself back to one in this manner. With each step the volume of breathing will increase and then, when you count back, decrease. This can be done for ten to thirty minutes.

I trust you will enjoy the natural high.

Calm Is Not Laziness

So how tranquil can things get? There is no limit to the amount of calm that can flow through you. Some people mistake calm with laziness, tiredness, or inertia. The opposite is true. It is from deep relaxation that you can become the most dynamic, fast, and strong. Good tension is the basis of good relaxation, good relaxation is the basis of good tension. People who get tired when they relax don't get tired because of the relaxing, they get tired because of the various resistances that have built up throughout the day. Sleep then, is a method to clear those resistances and push "reset". In time, deep calm will not make you less active, it will make you super-active. Laziness is a consequence of overwhelm…of not having gotten enough relaxation and regeneration. The body then goes into "depletion mode" and does nothing at all.

The Face Dive

I add this method for those of you who have found this section looking for a method to alleviate stronger surges such as panic, rage, and anxiety. If there is an urgent need for calm, you can achieve it by dipping your face into cold water. For this you would fill a sink/wash basin with very cold water, and then dip your face into it for 30 to 60 seconds. Upon removing your head from the sink your fear or anxiety will take another 60 to 120 seconds to melt away.

If you do not want to get your face wet, another way to do this would be to fill a plastic bag with ice and hold it to your face for 30 to 60 seconds. The ice-pack should be held from the scalp to the lips.

Any performance anxiety or bout of anger you had will swiftly disappear. This is "cooling down" in is truest sense. The effect lasts for up to one hour after which you can reapply the face dive. However, since most attacks of anxiety are only temporary, the likelihood of having to reapply it is low. If you keep having anxiety attacks, then there is a deeper seated issue that needs to be addressed. I'd say that anything that is not calm, joy, or love requires addressing and releasing.

Sweet-Relief

When the mind is running rampant with all sorts of concerns, errands, and importances its time to once again introduce the art of calm. Do not let your life be run by tension. If you are the master of your life, you can sit down and become poised before making your move. The Art of Calm is more often not about doing various things but not doing anything. For instance, breathing happens all by itself. If you were to obsess about breathing instead of just leaving it alone, your breathing would become erratic. In this case it is **your interference** that is causing a tension. Many things such as breathing are not meant to be managed, tampered with, controlled, or altered. Some are, but many are not. Calm comes from letting go of trying to manipulate that-which-is-as-it-is. If you try to manipulate your sleeping time, for example, telling yourself that you "must" sleep longer or "must" sleep shorter, you are setting yourself up for all kinds of unnatural tensions. The best path is to sleep when you are tired and not to sleep when you are not tired. You release your preoccupation with whatever it is that is bothering you, and what was bothering you disappears.

Inner tension creates intolerance of others, irritability, irrational thought and behavior, a low tolerance of noise, pessimism, fear, and boredom. Inner tension may be caused by "deadlines" (what a negative word), guilt (or trying to hide something), vanity (inauthenticity), Over-ambition (trying to do too much; overstraining your capacities), anxiety and fear (worries about the future), frustration (for instance you have a very important message to give to someone but cannot call them because you are stuck in a traffic jam in an area without phone reception), greed, and lust. In short, desire and resistance cause inner tension. Learning the art of calm is learning to release that tension into sweet relief.

Retreat to the Comfort-Zone

To succeed in any endeavor, it is necessary to leave your comfort-zone many times. But if things "get too much" and your nerves are wracked, you should retreat back into your comfort-zone to regenerate. The characteristics of a comfortable zone in which you can relax are:

- **Silence**

This is a place there are no harsh or shrill noises. You close the door behind you and enter into a blissful quietness, where nobody demands your attention and nobody hoists a bunch of expectations upon you. Temples, Churches, and Spas are ideal for this kind of silence.

- **Lack of Stimuli**

Neither is there "noise" in the form of shape or color. There are no running TV or computer screens, no ads, no pop-ups, no aggressive neon-lights, and no foul smells. Instead, the setting is modest or minimal and there is not too much to do. Think Zen-monastery or lakeside for example. "Lack of stimuli" also includes fresh air as well as orderly surroundings. The garbage heap may lack stimuli, but its disorderliness will increase rather than reduce stress.

- **Safety, Comfort, and Privacy**

Your comfort-zone is safe and private. There is nobody and nothing threatening, unpleasant, or unfinished. You are dressed comfortably, the chair, sofa, or bed are cozy, the temperature is pleasant (65 to 78 degrees Fahrenheit or 17 to 26 degrees Celsius would be ideal to Northern Europeans and North Americans, whereas more southern countries would require higher temperatures to feel completely comfortable).

If you do have such a zone to retreat to, to collect your thoughts, gain perspective or calm down, you are well advanced in the art of calm.

The Focusing Technique

A rapid way to calm the mind and emotions is to simply...focus. On what? On anything. Deliberately focus on some object, item, or thing, and keep your focus there until you calm down. I have had people solve anything from dizziness and nausea, to exam-stress and worry, to heartbreak with this simple suggestion.

It works because all tension/worry is mind/ego created. And when you focus on something or do **any** deliberate action the mind slows down. You can't really force the mind to slow down, but you can occupy your field of attention by focusing. If you are very shaken, mixed up, or upset, it may take some time until you even *can* focus. One of the characteristics of being upset is the seeming inability to focus on anything. But as you attempt to zoom in on something and examine it, the mind gradually calms down and your emotions cool down.

You can use this technique in any situation of upheaval. If someone is shouting at you, for example, instead of preparing for what you are going to shout back, see if you can focus on his/her heart-chakra and send him/her well-wishes. Or perhaps you can focus on the beautiful landscape outside of the window while s/he is ranting? Well, of course you can.

Focusing produces a state of rest and regeneration that does not require any drug or stimuli. Here is yet another method of alleviating nervousness, fear-of-spotlights, and chaotic inner chatter:

The Touching Texture Technique

A school teacher who tells a kid to stop playing with objects (such as pens) while listening, is in error. Playing with the object puts the child in a calm state of mind where he can actually process what the teacher is saying.

Sit or walk around your home and touch various textures. You take an object into your hands, play with it a little, examine it, touch it, and get a good sense of its texture. Then you put it aside and look for another texture to explore. Ignore the urge to go away and do something else, ignore the impulse that this would be a boring task, and move on with it in a childlike manner until you feel deeply connected to the physical universe. "Touching Texture" is also focusing, albeit with your hands.

You might be wondering why and how "touching texture" works. It's simple: States of unease and tension are mind-created. They indicate that you have been "living in the mind", have been preoccupied with worries of past and future. By touching various textures you reconnect to the **present moment,** as well as leave the mind, and experience the sense-input of the **physical**. The mind is never that present and relaxed, it considers all these textures and objects boring. But the innocent aspect of you thinks these textures as well as sense-experience is highly interesting. The problem of our mind-dominated modern times is that most of us escape into screen-reality (Computer, Internet, TV) to relax. While that may work to some extent, it is also exclusively mind-based and will not generate the calm that touch and connection to the physical can.

Of course the **best version of this technique is to touch and be touched by other human beings.** Just putting your hand on someone's shoulder can immediately give him/her calm and slow his/her breathing. (Unless s/he is hiding something, in which case s/he will resist touch. Why? Because touch transfers information from one human to the next and makes it more difficult to hide things.) So if you are a generally tense person, then check whether you have been single for too long.

When you are in a state of disarray and confusion, you might want to try to walk around and start touching, feeling, and handling things. In fact, **doing a household clean-up in this conscious manner**

can be tremendously relaxing.

The bottom line is to focus outside of the mind-sphere, thus letting go of all mind-created concerns.

Now, Now, Now, Now, and Now

Watching the clock tick, waiting for something, yearning for another time to come along are all states of un-calm. These states of non-fulfillment are the default states of the ego/mind. The Art of **deep and tranquil calm and bliss** is a gateway to the real you; your soul, because the unfulfilled world-self/ego-self is thereby replaced with here-and-now presence. You can sink into this state by deciding to stop looking for another time or a better time, and becoming **interested in what is happening right now** instead of thinking…

"When he leaves, I can finally…"

"As soon as money comes, I will…"

"I'm waiting for things to get better so that I can…"

"In a few hours I can finally go home."

"I'm waiting for the weekend, so that…"

"Once I have to travel less, I can finally…"

"Once I'm able to travel more, I can finally…"

"As soon as I get out of the cold, things will be much better…"

"Once I get some supplies, all will be well."

The formula of inner tension is always the same:

Before X (relief), there must be Y (something to "get").

The formula for calm is also always the same:

For X (relief), let go of thinking there must be Y (something to "get").

You see, **you always only have the present moment; there is no escape from that.** The minute you embrace the present and give up trying to "get somewhere better", things do get better. Instead of trying to get away from a person, project, place, or thing, try embracing it and seeing what happens. See where the stream takes you when you stop swimming against it.

Inner tranquility is derived from the belief that you are **always** provided and taken care of by that life force that creates all things. For those unfamiliar with spiritual thought, this may be an abstract idea at first, but as it is practiced, it becomes a reality. I know nothing else that provides the sort of permanent inner calm than the ultimate creative source which I remember, reflect on, and call on in any instance of turbulence. Too much dependence on external things is contrary to calm. Calm is only available here, now, internally.

Calm comes from not getting too caught up in the content of life and remaining aware of its overall context. **The ego/mind sees only consequences, not causes.** The eye does not see itself, that's why the ultimate cause of all things is often missed. The divine energy-field called Consciousness is cause.

Nothing earthly or worldly can possibly be cause. Your body, for example, is not causing anything. Cause lies one context higher, in the realm of thoughts. Thoughts on the other hand, do not cause themselves. Their cause lies one context higher in the realm of Awareness. But awareness in and of itself does not cause itself. Its cause lies one context higher.

The inner calm that comes about through **spirituality** is never affected by external turbulence. It is like the silent eye of a cyclone while a wild storm rages around it. It is not prone to falling for media-hype, doomsday-warnings, threats from people, popular hysteria, and attacks by negative people. Why? Because it's the aspect of you that is not from or of the earth, but of a spiritual dimension that remains forever unaffected by the world. This is the witness, the part of you that is accessed during Meditation.

Tense and Relax

In deep calm you **receive** new ideas, deeper than the surface-chatter that normally occupies the mind. One interesting way to relax is by deliberately creating tension and then releasing it. In a method called "progressive muscle relaxation" you create tension in each muscle and then let it go, all through the body. The resulting condition is one of mellow warmth.

In the same category, **a good method to release stage-fright is by exaggerating that anxiety in turn with a normal state.** So if you are about to hold a speech, a song, a show or a performance, I'd have you act out the tension and then relax, over and over again, until the fear loses charge and your body is loose. I also recommend you **do facial grimaces before being filmed** or photographed because it loosens your face muscles. giving you a calmer expression. Those who do sports are generally more relaxed because they deliberately build tension. That tension naturally releases after they are finished with their workout, their bike ride, or their swim. Not to mention all the other health benefits sports provide.

The "tense and relax" principle also applies to mental releasing. As taught in the Bliss Course, as you hold on to a thought and let go of it, and repeat the hold-release pattern several times, your mind becomes tranquil and flexible, and it becomes easier to let go of rigid and old patterns of thought and mental habit. Tension and Relaxation, Focus and Release, Contraction and Expansion, Effort and Effortlessness are two sides of the basic duality of life. This duality should be experienced in balance because you cannot have one without the other.

Pseudo-Relaxation

Pseudo-Relaxation is when people do something "to relax" that is not actually and fundamentally relaxing. Examples of such are:

- Watching Movies
- Eating
- Going to the Beauty Parlor
- Crowded Beach Vacations
- Taking Pharmaceuticals or Drugs

I am not bad-talking any of this, just pointing out that these are not real methods of calm and tranquility in the deepest sense. Most movies are really rapid-fire imagery that brings the mind into turbulence and excitement rather than calming it down. The only calming-benefit of movies is that your attention extroverts. While attention is extroverted it goes away from inner mental and emotional chatter. So if there is really no other way you are able to calm down, then movies are the next best thing. Eating, going for a beauty session, taking drugs including alcohol and tobacco...these create a temporary externally-induced calm. They won't suffice to produce that deep and tranquil home most people secretly miss so much. And needless to say, many so-called "vacations" do not really provide the context in which to regenerate and receive creative new ideas. A beach is a wonderful place of calm...unless it's overcrowded and noisy. Such "vacations" are only an option if it is your intention to party and drink till you drop

.To summarize, each of these are **options** with which you can **relax within a minute** or a very short time. Remember that you have the **option** to calm down and thus improve your overall state. You are already familiar with these means of relaxation; the trick is in remembering that you have the option to consciously use them at any time.

1. Deliberate slow motion (walking, sitting down, doing something slowly)

2. Slow and deep breathing

3. Stretching body parts

4. Focusing on one object

5. Thinking of someone you love, while knocking three times at the Thymus, and saying, "Ha, Ha, Ha."

6. Taking in an upright body posture

7. Closing your eyes and watching the phosphenes

8. Taking care of a small item you have been postponing

9. Holding one negative thought (confronting), while releasing resistance

10. Holding one positive thought (imaging).

If you enjoyed this book, check out other books, audios, and videos at www.realitycreation.org

Printed in Germany
by Amazon Distribution
GmbH, Leipzig